DEAN CAREY has been a Director of The Actors Centre in Sydney for the past ten years. He was Head of Acting at the Western Australian Academy of Performing Arts (WAAPA) 1990-93, Associate Head of Acting at NIDA and a tutor there for eleven years.

He has directed *The Rover, Dark of the Moon, The Golden Age, Peer Gynt, Così, A Month in the Country, A Touch of Silk, The Kid, Flora the Red Menace, The Bride of Gospel Place, Late Arrivals, Children of the Sun, Sunrise, Tales from the Vienna Woods* and *Savage Love.*

He is author of *The Actor's Audition Manual* and *Masterclass,* consisting of two volumes, one for men and one for women, both of which are sold in the USA and UK. He also contributes to *Cinema Papers,* through his column, 'Peak Performance—the Director's Edge'.

He has taught for Sydney Theatre Company, Belvoir Street Theatre, New South Wales Conservatorium of Music, Australian Film, Television and Radio School, QUT, Victorian College of the Arts and conducted guest workshops at Yale University in New York State, the University of California in San Diego, CalArts and the University of Southern California in Los Angeles, the American Conservatory Theatre in San Francisco, Ensemble Theatre Company in Florida, the Los Angeles High School of Performing Arts, and the Shchukin Theatre School in Moscow.

He is currently preparing two new books: *Creative Renovation: A Handbook for the Actor and Director,* the new actor's process, for both actors and directors; and the other on screentesting.

THE ACTOR'S
Audition
Manual

VOLUME I

DEAN CAREY

Currency Press • Sydney

First published 1985
Currency Press Ltd,
PO Box 2287, Strawberry Hills,
NSW, 2012, Australia.
Revised edition 1998.

NATIONAL LIBRARY OF AUSTRALIA CIP DATA

Carey, Dean.
    The actor's audition manual. Vol. 1.

    Rev. ed.
    ISBN 0 86819 516 2.

    1. Acting—Auditions. I. Title.
792.028

Typeset by Dean Nottle

Printed by Southwood Press, Marrickville, NSW

Cover design Anaconda Graphic Design

Foreword

Dean Carey is a remarkably talented theatre professional. Beyond his formal training at the National Institute of Dramatic Art, he was able to pursue two equally successful careers as an actor/director and as a teacher of acting. He has participated in the growth and development of a remarkable group of young Australian actors with whom he worked as a teacher at the Western Australian Academy of Performing Arts and The Actors Centre in Sydney.

Dean is also an incredible optimist about the Australian entertainment industry and has an absolute belief that trained, talented individuals will survive and find success as performers, both in Australia and overseas.

During his tenure with WAAPA, I was fortunate to witness Dean's enthusiasm for the audition process and to see how much he valued the decision-making that takes place at that time to determine whether those who present themselves as likely candidates for a professional career will be able to succeed. His enthusiasm for the audition and his realisation of its importance in winning an actor a place in a top training institution or subsequently with a major employer is contained within this book. The 150 individual scenes that comprise this valuable tool for both the new actor and the accomplished performer have all been tested *in situ*.

Dean Carey has a remarkable eye in spotting talent. He is equally as astute in identifying text which will showcase the many facets of an actor's ability. On top of identifying appropriate material, Dean skilfully gives appropriate advice as to how to prepare the scene and enable the character therein to be real. Important too is the advice about the selection of material which must be related to the actor's own age, energy and physicality. In film and television, performers are rarely asked to play a character much outside their own age group or physical type. Finding the right material and the appropriate connections between yourself and the text is an essential part of the actor's preparation.

Finally, he asks young actors to remember their obligation to words and language. It is no good feeling the piece if your imagination and preparation is hampered by a lack of skill in getting behind the dialogue and honestly communicating the intentions of the language.

After twenty years of leading the growth and development of the Western Australian Academy of Performing Arts I am still excited to read a text of this calibre which reaffirms my faith in, and commitment to, the Australian entertainment industry.

Dr Geoffrey Gibbs,
Director,
Western Australian Academy of Performing Arts

Contents

Introduction

Welcome to the totally reworked edition of *The Actor's Audition Manual Volume 1*. This first volume deals with the initial preparation and approach to your audition, and also gives a step-by-step investigation of the rehearsal process. Volume 2 in the series, *Masterclass*, picks up the journey continuing into bolder and more advanced territory. It offers dozens of rehearsal room exercises and outlines techniques designed to unlock and engage your authentic, creative self.

There have been many books written about acting. Once you have the part, almost every aspect of the journey from rehearsals to performance has been covered to some degree. But *getting* the part is often the most daunting task of all. 'Where do I start? What should I choose? What do they want to see me do? Why aren't I getting the parts? Why don't I feel effective in the audition room? Why does it work at home, but not when it counts?'

The Actor's Audition Manual aims to de-mystify the audition process through offering:

- A detailed approach to finding the right audition speech for you
- A practical step-by-step guide to rehearsing your piece
- Ways of discovering the possibilities and range your speech contains
- A comprehensive investigation of the essential elements for a successful audition
- Over 150 contemporary and compelling Australian audition speeches—all rich in range and impact for your audition.

Acting in an audition is quite different from acting in a play or shooting a film sequence. Quite simply, you're there for different reasons. You must show as much of your talent and as many of your capabilities as you can in the short time you have available. Therefore the speech you present must contain contrasts, depth and a good emotional range. It needs to be engaging and allow you the scope to present and develop what you have to offer. You must forget that you are doing a 'speech', and remember that it is actually a collection of moments from a character's life. Your task is to recapture and relive those initial utterances, and to add all the richness, depth and unpredictability of the human condition. Nowhere is this more import-ant than in those fifteen minutes spent with your potential employers.

Acting should be an exciting experience, based on energy, an outward search for contact and communication, and an appetite for knowledge about the world and the way people survive in it. These and countless other reasons explain why many actors have chosen to pursue the career path they love. But the thought of auditioning for a panel of unknown faces, to show your 'wares' in the hope that someone thinks you're worth something, takes many of us hurtling straight back to Primary School—standing awkwardly against the wire fence, waiting to be chosen (or not) for the sports team. Or collecting your English essay after you've put your heart and soul into it, only to find a scribbled mark on the front: 4/10. *Someone is judging us*, as to whether we're good enough, right or wrong, success-ful or unsuccessful—valid or invalid.

Let's tackle this dilemma and find the ways through. Many actors I know have found a moment in their careers when they have managed to turn the audition situation around and *embrace* it as an opportunity to do what they love—act. This is possible for all actors, given the right approach.

In this book we will deal with these issues by focusing primarily on the life of your audition piece and exploring ways you can create this reality in order to rocket yourself into a new, totally involving experience which is both unique and secure. *The Actor's Audition Manual Volume 1* will, I trust, bring you closer to achieving this, and help you to realise, in powerful ways, your full auditioning potential.

Enjoy the process!

Dean Carey
Sydney, 1998

1. Make or Break!

Approach and Attitude

Many actors go to an audition with one major focus—*to get the job.*
That is one reason for being there, and a good one. However, when
that is your sole purpose, unwanted attitudes can easily slip into the
room with you. To alleviate the stress and fear caused by that single
blinding thought, 'I've got to get this job!' and to counter the
desperation and futility that is a familiar companion for many actors,
you need to think of other reasons for walking into the audition
room. If you *host* your own audition, rather than being at the mercy
of it, you can use your audition to achieve the following:

- practise your craft
- extend your skills
- meet and become known to directors, casting agents
  and producers
- become more familiar with new scripts and current
  writing
- add a new piece to your audition repertoire
- gain confidence and acquire a relaxed, open and
  receptive manner
- learn what makes an effective audition *for you.*

Once you have shifted your focus to these broader, more active reasons for being there, you will emanate a quality which can be engaging and highly employable—a positive outlook. Employers are not only looking at your abilities and talent, but also what you will be like as a fellow *worker*. After all, they are going to be stuck in a rehearsal room with you for eight hours a day or on set for maybe ten. If they pick up any hint of desperation, negativity, hopelessness or unworthiness, then they'll think twice about hiring you no matter how talented you are.

Instead of only thinking about the desperate struggle for that elusive job, host your own audition and the thought of, 'Oh well, here goes nothing!', will be the furthest thing from your mind. This concept of hosting your own audition can be very powerful and very effective. Try it when you next audition and remember—it's *your* time, it's *your* skill, they have *chosen* to see you, they *want* to see you, they *want* you to do well. If you respect yourself and the work you have done in preparation for the audition, then every moment counts—take full control and empower yourself by becoming the host of the event. Don't just feel you *deserve* to be there, but *demand* to be there—present, focused, alert, charged.

Is there existence beyond employment?

We too easily fall into the trap of equating *employment* with *validity*. If we have a job, or at least one coming up, we can relax: 'I'm O.K.—someone out there thinks I can do it. And what's more they're going to *pay* me for it!' When we're out of work, the opposite applies: 'I'm not wanted, therefore I mustn't be worth it.' This self-assessment can be a tough nut to crack. With so much unemployment around, the time between jobs can be long and barren. The creative child inside, who simply wants to come out and play, doesn't get invited to many parties any more. And when the child turns up to a casting only to be told: 'Thank you, but go home', it doesn't take long before the child gets sullen and angry.

As a result, auditioners see endless numbers of faces wishing they were somewhere else. It is essential for actors to break this spiral and *choose* to be there, *with* those people, *doing* that audition.

Speaking practically, how many parts would you be offered from ten auditions? One? Perhaps two? Jobs are scarce. So, rather than letting yourself in for nine rejections out of ten possibilities, think of them all in terms of the guidelines set out above. Of course you *want* the job, but you should want these other objectives just as much. Keeping this in mind will help to make the audition process a more positive, fruitful and progressive experience. If, after all of this, you actually get the job, terrific—all the better—what a bonus! So leave the make or break philosophy by simply reminding yourself: go along to *do* the job, not to *get* the job.

There is one sure-fire way to prevent yourself from achieving a positive attitude, and that is to listen to those actors who sit in the waiting area dealing out inside information on the particular ins and outs of this audition: 'They are looking for... type of audition piece.' (Fill in whichever type of speech you did *not* bring.) Or, 'They want singers.' Or, the biggest soul-destroyer of all: 'They want a name.'

Forget all that and get back to hosting your own audition by allowing all of your energy to rest purely and simply on *preparing to present your character's emotional life.* That is what you came for, that is what you rehearsed, and the opportunity is at hand to use your craft and to put it all into practice.

If fear does grab you as you wait for your name to be called, remember that if you have invested your thoughts, your feelings, your truth into the piece, and then added your own positive energy into being there, you will present something which is unique. Then you can begin to *play* again and your child will realise that this audition *is* the invitation—you are *already there*, discussing, exploring and doing what you love. Yes it does get hard, yes it can be impersonal, yes you may at times get angry. There is nothing to be done—we have to audition—we need to be seen in the flesh, doing our stuff. But the more you put the above into practice, I can assure you, the less impersonal and difficult it will become.

Once you have completed the audition, keep this positive and forward-thinking approach and do not judge your success by the auditioner's reaction (or lack thereof), but by how many of your personal objectives you have achieved, and how truthfully and accurately you have portrayed the life of your character. This, after all, is your ultimate goal.

Points to remember

- Become the host of your own audition
- Set practical, positive personal objectives
- Go along to *do* the job, not to *get* the job.

2. The Actor's Wish List

Essentials

Following are all the elements to making your audition effective and compelling. Once outlined, you will, in the chapters ahead, discover how to achieve these essential elements in your speech.

Think of a recent film or piece of theatre you have seen which greatly affected you. Upon reflection, you will probably find it contained most of the following elements: conflict, importance, discoveries, events, love, humour and opposites. If all of these are apparent, you can be assured of a compelling and unpredictable experience—something which makes you sit up and take notice.

In *Audition*, Michael Shurtleff has included these basic elements of drama amongst his twelve guideposts, showing them at work in various scenes. Your audition speech should also contain these elements.

Conflict

In all audition speeches there is a character objective—the thing you want and/or need and which drives you through the scene. There are, however, obstacles to achieving that objective. Sometimes the obstacle may be external, for example time is running out, your enemy is within earshot, the character you are talking to does not wish to listen. Sometimes, however, the obstacles are inner ones, for example you want to tell her the truth but your own sense of guilt gets in the way, or you want to plead for forgiveness but pride gets in the way. The dynamic set-up between the objective and the obstacle produces the dramatic conflict of the scene. The greater the obstacle to achieving your objective, the greater the conflict and the greater the interest for an audience. Drama feeds on conflict. Find as much of this in your speech as you can.

Conflict does not necessarily mean aggression. In Henry V's proposal speech, 'Marry, if you would put me to verses or to dance for your sake, Kate, why you undid me', Henry's obstacles are his lack of command of the situation, his inability to woo Kate in ways he thinks she will understand, and his embarrassment at showing his true feelings for her. And, of course, the most obvious and humorous obstacle of all is that she does not speak English! The more these obstacles manifest themselves, the more conflict there will be as Henry tries to effectively pursue his objective, which is to gain Kate's agreement to his proposal of marriage. This conflict, whilst neither aggressive nor confrontational, still feeds the scene with the dynamic necessary for its dramatic structure.

There is a wonderful documentary produced by Melvyn Bragg on Dame Judi Dench and her career in the theatre. In it she sings 'Send in the Clowns' from *A Little Night Music*. In a remarkable interpretation, Dench discovers *irony* to be the basis of conflict in the song. What could be a gentle and reflective final comment on a failed relationship, becomes a deep need to know why everything has fallen apart when all seemed to be in place: 'Me here at last on the ground, you in… mid-air…' The struggle to come to terms with the absurdity, the irony and the savage and cruel twists of fate which Dench uncovers, creates enormous conflict between her character and the situation in which she finds herself. The words and music become an inevitable part of her journey to understand, resolve and perhaps undo this present conflict. The effect is bittersweet, unpitying and devastating.

Importance

Importance goes hand-in-hand with the comments on conflict. The more consequences there are to every idea or thought you utter, the better. The more important your objective, the greater the emotional journey will be when the obstacles appear. Therefore, be prepared to invest emotionally in all the issues and needs in your speech.

So often actors discuss the content of their speech in terms of: 'It's *just* a holiday. It was *just* a vase. He was *just* an acquaintance. I *just* touched her. It's *just* a fight. It was *just* a marriage proposal. It's *just* a small problem. We were *just* getting to the important bit.' 'Just' is a de-energising word which drains intent and diminishes importance. You must make everything in a scene mean as much to you as possible if you are to find the drama. Otherwise, you will be just another auditionee, just another actor, in just another scene.

Discoveries

Discover as much as possible throughout the course of your audition speech, because audiences love to watch people change, adapt, regroup and respond. Life is made up of moments such as these. Chapter Four's section on 'Thought Springboards' will help. You should discover the ideas in the piece out there on the floor, during the actual audition. Viola does not know she will say: '*I am the man*'; Richard III does not know he will say: '*Was ever woman in this humour wooed?*'; Hamlet does not know he will say: '*Bloody bawdy villain! Remorseless, treacherous, kindless villain!*' The point is, you must not ignore these discoveries through pre-empting what is about to happen or you will close doors on the very life of the piece.

Discover the words as you discover the ideas, out there, in the moment. Discover the size of the thoughts, the weight of thoughts, sensory connections more deeply felt than you previously imagined, more painful, more pleasurable. Discover new and unexpected associations or implications to the ideas. Remember, nothing ever goes strictly to plan. No moment in life is ever exactly as you had imagined it. No moment in life is ever the same again. There is always something new to be found. Discoveries promote spontaneity which, in turn, creates momentum.

There is nothing worse than an actor introducing his or her audition speech, describing its content, and then outlining what happens in the end! Imagine you are the auditioner. An actor walks in and says: 'I'm doing a speech from *Little Murders* where Patsy tells the story of how depressing her day is in an effort to try to buck up Alfred but it doesn't work and he walks out'. How can this actor now take herself and the auditioner on the journey of the speech?

The most interesting moments in drama are moments of change. For this to happen you must discover something and let it affect you accordingly. The more discovery, the more potential for change, for the journey to develop, and for the audience to be engaged. As we have said before, the best response you can create in your audience members is the expectation of 'What will happen next?' This will occur if they go with you on your journey of discovery.

Events

Few things are less exciting or less memorable than watching an audition monologue where nothing actually *happens*. The words and emotion flow, there is movement, energy, the actor has good focus and a certain grasp on the situation and character, they create a reality and even perhaps an atmosphere. But, nothing actually happens, there is no notable occurrence, there are no *events*.

Something must happen in your speech. If this moment in the character's life is worth our full and undivided attention, if the character feels that it is imperative to speak uninterrupted for *three minutes*, you can bet there will be many moments of deep significance which imply personal consequences. These moments charge your audition with intent and invest it with meaning. Without them, the focus often remains on you the actor, and how well you are doing at the job of acting. But once we begin to witness the character experiencing and attempting to deal with major events, we relinquish our role as judges or objective observers, and we become attached to and involved in the character's circumstances. Our focus falls on what we think the consequences of these events may be: 'What will they do *now*? How will they find their way through? How will they cope and what will they say in response? What would *I* do if that happened to *me*?' This is how you connect an audience's *imagination* to the world you are presenting. If you can connect your audition panel on this level, then you will be creating a vibrant, involving reality.

The Journey students' end of year performance *Dying to Love*, directed by Tanya Gerstle and Chrissie Koltai at The Actors Centre (Photo: Peter Holderness)

Events can be moments of conflict between:

- you and some part of yourself you wish to change
- you and another character
- you and the situation and circumstances you are facing

Events have many faces. Each one could be a moment of: conflict, discovery, an ordeal, an achievement, an adventure, an admission, encounter, hazard, stunt, incident, exploit, milestone, eventuality, episode, risk, peril, feat, trick, deed, contest, accomplishment. All of these show potential moments where we see you *deal with* something significant and, by so doing, they become *events.*

Many student actors seem to ignore or lessen the impact of events which are clearly huge turning points in the text. For example, the following lines are all moments of great change:

VIOLA:	I am the man!
HAMLET:	O, vengeance!
RICHARD III:	I'll have her, but I will not keep her long. What!?
BEROWNE:	Then fools you were these women to forswear.
HELENA:	Come night, end day! For with the dark, poor thief, I'll steal away.
VOLUMNIA:	Down, Ladies. Let us shame him with our knees.
OPHELIA:	O, what a noble mind is here o'er thrown!
PHILIP:	Why rail I on this commodity? For it hath not wooed me yet.
LADY PERCY:	O yet, for God's sake, go not to these wars!
JOAN LA PUCELLE:	See, they forsake me. Now the time is come that France must vail her lofty-plumed crest and let her head fall into England's lap.
QUEEN MARGARET:	Off with the crown, and with the crown his head, and whilst we breathe, take time to do him dead.

| HELENA: | I will go tell him of fair Hermia's flight. |
| LADY ANNE: | O, gentlemen, see, see! dead Henry's wounds ope their congealed mouths and bleed afresh! |

You can also create an event by investing a moment with greater importance than perhaps the text suggests. A major discovery can become an event. An idea hitting you like a thunderclap can become an event. A moment charged with a deep sensory connection can become an event. You can plot in another character attempting to interrupt, or preparing to defy you, or have them begin to walk out, any of these could provoke an event.

Events are the results of major discoveries which have significant implications for you. Therefore they become your major signposts along the journey, yours and ours.

Love

The need to give love, to share love or to receive love is one of the prime motivations of life. Find the love, or loss of love, or lack of love, in your speech. It is so important in our moment-by-moment existence. To do this will require a deep vulnerability and a strong sense of intimacy between you and the idea you are expressing. In your rehearsal, dig deep for these connections. They are powerful and arresting.

Humour

'You've got to laugh!' How often have you heard this said in a serious or tense moment? We try to find the humour in every sticky situation. Otherwise, we would never survive. We would run the risk of overloading our emotions, we might short circuit and blow a fuse. This is not to say that we make jokes, but our attitude can be laced with a buoyancy or apparent lightheartedness. It is a way of releasing tension, becoming centred, relieving anxiety and of *breathing* again. Humour can also be found in sarcasm and particularly in irony. It can make moments of strong drama *more* cutting, or pertinent, or savage, or dangerous. It will increase the range of choices and the dramatic landscape you cover which will, in turn, tell us more about the character you are creating and engage us on a deeper level.

No matter what speech you are preparing, uncover moments of humour. By increasing the range of the speech in this way, you can produce startling results.

Playing the opposite

You can turn the audience's expectation of how a line will be delivered on its head if you play the line in exactly the opposite way.

Many young actors make the choice which appropriately displays the emotion the character is feeling—anger, sadness, desire. If the character is sad, and you show us sadness, we tend to think that you have fully shown the depth of the sadness felt. But if the character appears controlled, detached, almost reflective, and we *know* this is not the case, our imagination will go into overdrive. We endow the character with a cavernous pool of despair or rage that is so strong, we fear that if you gave into it, it would be all consuming. Through making an opposite choice, you have actually engaged us on a far deeper level than you could have by playing a more obvious choice.

Look at Tom Junior's speech on page 54, beginning with the line: 'You remember that time you came home broke?' Instead of playing this threateningly, as is the more usual interpretation, try playing the opposite. Imagine if Tom Junior found this to be a humorous recollection and one without any potential conflict. Continue playing the opposite until you find you have to start letting your *real* feelings out, possibly on: 'And sometime, during that time, you got something besides your gigolo fee from Minnie, and passed it on to my sister, my little sister.' The audience feels the tension rise, that you are trying to quell your real feelings, and that you are struggling in fear of what might happen if they escape. As the actor, you have successfully engaged the audience more fully than you would otherwise have done, and you have done so with one of the most powerful tools in acting—simplicity.

Opposites surround us every day. Watch someone trip in the street. The outward appearance immediately afterwards is one of instant composure, a casual glance over the shoulder shows that, although the trip has occurred, it has had no effect. The inward embarrassment that we imagine is being felt will be in direct proportion to the effort made to cover up that embarrassment by adopting an opposite response. Check this for yourself the next time you go to pull the door marked *push* and then push the door marked *pull*, then try both only to discover a large sign which reads: 'Please use other doors'. Notice how you play the opposite in order to hide your inner feelings.

When someone faints, in the moments preceding the fall they are searching for the extreme opposite. They try to rise above the impending collapse—they physically build themselves up, breath in, widen their eyes—they seem to be *increasing* in height, strength, calm and control. But then their legs collapse from underneath. Even on the way down the person often remains looking up and striving for the opposite.

On hearing that a person has attempted suicide, close friends often remark: 'But he or she always seemed so happy.' Many of us are conditioned throughout our lives to hide our true feelings. We are taught to avoid conflict, to skirt around crises or unpleasant situations, to avoid *making a scene*. Hence, our ingenious (yet often regretful) use of opposites.

Playing the opposite, then, can shed light on the human condition and compound the emotional content and dynamic of the scene. It also provides that other essential acting component—unpredictability.

Play the extremes

Finding the extremes in your speech can double the choices your speech presents. By focusing on the A to Z journey of your speech, and making these two points as far apart as possible, you will be more likely to find everything else in between.

For example, whatever the main thrust of your speech, its opposite extreme should also be there. Look at Viola's ring speech. This piece is full of confusion as Viola tries to sort out her bizarre dilemma and solve the puzzle. What is the opposite of this confusion? Quiet, calm reasoning. The speech must not be driven by confusion all the way through. Within that confusion, find the clarity. Within the frustration find the revelation. Within anxiety, find ease.

Equally, whatever passionate objective your character wants in a scene, try and find a moment or moments where *the opposite extreme* is wanted just as passionately. If I am trying desperately to convince the other character of something, I should find a moment where I seem to have given up—where convincing and trying to change her or his will no longer interests me. I may then seem aloof, offhand, even resigned to the fact that my words will have no effect at all. Then, when my original objective reactivates itself, it will resurge with double the power, velocity and vigour, enhancing the journey yet again.

Finding the opposites in your piece means you are more likely to find everything else in between, opening the range, creating events and adding depth.

Your jumping-off point

For many actors, this is one of the most important moments of all— the moment when you take your position, shuffle your feet, look intriguingly at the floor, clear your throat, uncrick your neck, try and clear your head, try *not* to think: 'Well, here goes nothing', take a deep and sharp intake of breath and then initiate 'speaking' whilst hoping to validate and justify your presence. Your body is so aware that something feels wrong, alien, manufactured, that you begin to force and flood your work. This is no way to host your own audition.

Why does this happen? Simple—most times it is the *actor* preparing to make a speech, instead of the *character* reacting to a given situation. This creates a lie—the actor breathes but the character speaks.

To begin securely, the character needs to *react, breathe*, then *speak*. The moment of reaction needs to be created, by you, in rehearsal—something has had to have happened to produce the need for you to speak. You need to create the world which exists directly before your speech begins. It must be full of detail and potent enough to make it *inevitable* that your character now has no alternative but to react in such a way as to cause her or him to speak uninterrupted for the length of the text.

Think of a musical. The scenes and songs should not feel like separate entities, which can often happen if each is rehearsed separately and by different people. The audience is in the midst of a play, when suddenly the music rises and we have switched to a musical. The music finishes and we are plunged back into the play—jolted from genre to genre. For a musical to work seemlessly, each song in each scene must become an inevitable part of the journey for the characters involved. In other words, the scene prior to the song builds to a level of such intensity, that words are no longer sufficient for each character to communicate and release their feelings. They choose a higher form of communication, where rhythm, pitch, concentrated imagery and music now join forces to help communicate the character's needs and feelings.

The moment before your speech begins should also be a startling enough stimulus to you that you inevitably *leap* to a higher form where it takes forty lines of dialogue to deal with what has just occurred. For no speech just *begins*—it comes from something dynamic which has gone before. Make this moment as strong and involving for *yourself* as you can. Your reaction might necessitate a physical move. This physical response can make for a very good starting point as it can engage your body in a real and releasing way. This can achieve a most satisfying dynamic for the actor, where you are catapulted from the exposing reality of the actor into the adventure world of the character.

In an audition, there is no curtain to raise or spotlight to hit you. A strong physical moment can create focus and cause impact. Use the space, make an entrance, face upstage for the first line and then turn sharply. Go to exit and then be stopped by your chosen stimulus. Be lost in another world entirely, and then be surprised by a question or demand, before slowly coming to your feet. Whatever decision you make it should suit your text and not be a gimmick added for its own sake. Remember that there is immense strength in simplicity.

Every speech will require a different jumping-off point, and that is exactly what it should be. Your beginning moment should transport and propel you into the scene whilst giving you the impetus and motivation you need to go on. For example, in Launce's speech from *Two Gentlemen of Verona*, Launce simply enters, closely followed by his dog, Crab. This works well in a performance with the entire play preceding it, but for an audition you may wish to translate this into a more engaging entrance. You could, for example, set the speech in the market-place in Verona outside the servant's entrance at the rear of the Palace. After you have introduced your speech to the auditioners you exit from the room. They then hear shouts, bangs and thuds from outside. All of a sudden, the door flies open and you enter in mid-air and land in a heap face down centre stage. You regain consciousness, begin to drag yourself to your feet, and then discover us—watching. You realise that the entire market-place has come to a standstill—everyone is staring at you in silence, startled and accusing. You see your trusty dog Crab wander innocently from the havoc he just caused at the Queen's table, and plop down before you, panting attentively. Full of anger and a deep sense of humiliation, you have no alternative but to justify yourself and tell us in no uncertain terms where the true blame lies: 'When a man's servant shall play the cur with him, look you, it goes hard!' You now have an imaginative and engaging beginning which will propel you, and us, out of an audition into a new and involving reality.

Of course, the beginning moment does not have to be as explosive as this. Take, for instance, Phillip the Bastard's speech from *King John*. Before the first line: 'Mad world! Mad kings! Mad composition!', use what has just happened as your beginning moment. Begin from the moment King John and his entourage depart. Stand there drawn in amazement at the sight of what has just occurred. Allow your disbelief and astonishment to prompt the first thought: 'Mad world!' Obviously, the more you endow the imagined exit with meaning, and the more important you make the quandary in which you have been left, the stronger your beginning moment will be. This will also give your scene a pre-life because we learn where you are coming from and what you are reacting to, and this makes for a more specific onstage reality. If you can draw the auditioners in with the impact and detail of the first few lines, you are more likely to have their full attention for the entire speech.

Points to remember

- The greater the conflict, the greater the interest for the audience

- Make the issues and needs as important as you can
- Discoveries promote spontaneity which creates momentum
- Find the major events; make sure something happens in the piece
- Find the love
- Find the humour
- Play opposites if possible
- Play the extremes
- Make sure you create a strong, engaging beginning moment to propel you into the scene.

3. The Perfect Piece

Choosing Your Audition Material

There are two types of auditions—the *general* and the *specific*. The general classification covers those auditions aimed at getting a place in a drama school or theatre company. For this type of audition you may be asked to present up to three contrasting speeches to show your range and versatility. They will be looking at who you are as an actor and what you have to offer as an ensemble or company member.

In the specific audition, you will be trying out for a particular role. Here you will probably be asked to prepare a scene from the script, or to present a speech which will show similar qualities to the type of character for which you are auditioning. When auditioning for a specific role, you have a focus and function: to show you can conceivably be cast in that role and that you can play it effectively and believably. This will determine what piece you choose, how you dress, and exactly what aspect of yourself you wish to portray. Your choices are made much easier. You may also be asked to sight read from the text, so if possible study the play or film script beforehand.

But choosing a piece for the *general* audition can be one of the hardest tasks of all. It is a highly personal search, fraught with doubts: 'What do they want to see? Is this an over-used selection? Does it suit me anyway? Maybe there's something better out there? Where's that perfect piece?!' There seem to be so many questions to answer that you forget to ask the most important ones of all:

Do I *like* this piece?
Do *I feel* an attachment to it?
Would I *enjoy* performing it?

This is an excellent guide. Quite simply, the auditioners want to *see* what you want to *do*. If you *like* a piece, your instinct or inner hunch is telling you that you have a connection with it. If you *feel* an attachment to it, then its emotional life triggers something within you. If you literally *enjoy* performing the piece, then a quality ensues which is natural, confident and assured. When an actor stands in front of me and begins a speech, I can tell almost immediately whether s/he is enjoying the sheer process of saying the words, contacting the ideas and presenting the issues. When you enjoy a piece your personal investment is stamped upon every line, thought and action. Even if the speech doesn't have a tremendous range or exactly suit you, your abilities and talents will still be in strong evidence.

Once you have answered 'Yes' to these three questions, a number of other considerations will also need to be addressed to make the most dynamic impact possible:

Would I be cast in this role?

It is important to present a scene in which you could conceivably be cast. Many actors choose characters a long way from their own age, experience or physical appearance. Although you may think this a challenge and a chance to show how *extreme* you can be, remember that in the general audition the auditioners want to see who you are. They need to see you relating and communicating the thoughts and feelings of someone close to your own age and of your own sex and general appearance. If you are an eighteen-year-old girl, do not perform Lady Macbeth or Juliet's Nurse. Think about Portia, Juliet, Viola, or Helena. The same rule applies to the male roles: if you are twenty-two, forget about Shylock or King Lear and instead think about Prince Hal, Berowne or Henry V. Think along these same lines when dealing with contemporary pieces as well. Of course there is no need to typecast yourself or to do only those speeches that relate to your own experiences, but think about roles which you could conceivably play. The auditioners can then see your potential *now,* rather than where you might be cast in twenty years from now.

At the same time, remember that there are some speeches which are written for characters much older than yourself, but which can be easily performed by a younger person. This is because the content of these speeches does not reflect age and the story or issues are universal. Therefore don't let age range be your sole guide. But be aware when choosing.

Is it too long?

To launch The Actors Centre in 1987, we invited the New York casting director and author of *Audition,* Michael Shurtleff, to Sydney. One of the participants asked him when does an audition speech become too long. His reply was that every audition speech he had ever *seen* had been too long! In the audition situation an enormous amount of information can be gained in an extremely short space of time. As actors, we so often forget that when we begin our speech, all the energy of the people out front—that is the energy normally channelled into living, eating, travelling, achieving, etc—is now focused on us. The auditioners cannot go anywhere or do anything else—they are waiting for something to happen. With that kind of commitment, their perception is heightened and they 'read' more into what we do and say. Stage or screen time becomes distilled and highly concentrated. You don't need a lot of it to achieve an effect. So keep your audition short and to the point.

Also remember that auditioners are looking for a certain quality whether it be vocal, physical, personal or a combination of all three. As soon as you begin your piece they can usually tell whether you can act, and after ten lines they may have decided whether you have what they are after. Why then plunge on with another hundred lines of monologue? The last thing they need at this stage is proof that you can remember lines. One-and-a-half to three minutes is a good length for an audition. Any longer, and you will suffer from diminishing returns.

Don't forget that the director may ask you to do something totally different and often unexpected with the speech—to alter your listener, or set the speech in a different environment, to expand different character or situational dynamics. This is all part of the audition process. If the piece you have selected is short you may get the chance to try it several different ways, which will allow the director to see you take and incorporate suggestions, and show different sides to your work. A short speech is manageable and adaptable—an advantage both to you and to the auditioner.

Is it a self-sufficient speech?

A speech which stands on its own is far more powerful than one which needs a detailed explanation of its context before it makes sense. The self-sufficient speech runs on its own energy—it has a distinct *beginning, middle* and *end.* It needs next to no explanation and the listener, as a result, is far more satisfied. It is also more memorable because it is often motivated by one major idea—it sets this idea up, expands upon it, considers its consequences, and then uncovers the conclusion which, in turn, moves the character to a resolution.

This is the journey which every good audition speech should make. If you do it well, the auditioners may down their pens and go on the journey with you. Because so many speeches ramble on without seeming to arrive at any specific point, when one does, the auditioners will recall it clearly and therefore remember you.

What will the impact of the content be?

Beware the depressing speech. If it is not written and performed extremely well, it will not do you justice. When an actor walks slowly out to centre stage looking solemn and preoccupied, pauses for eight seconds, then breathes deeply and begins: 'He was... always a happy kid... until that day in May', the panel know they are in for a real downer. These speeches are difficult to pull off successfully. Unless you can find a way to drive through the thick emotion and actively find the character's fight and struggle through the subject matter, don't do it.

Some speeches contain a contrary emotion which makes playing against the depressing nature of the content far easier. Jan from Barry O'Keefe's *Barbarians* is a good example. Although he is talking about a moment of horrific consequence following his mother's tragic suicide, he is also remembering his great love for his mother, the people who admired her and the Saturday nights spent together singing in the pub. This speech has two emotional extremes written into it—a great sense of love, *and* the savage loss. But if your speech lacks this and you cannot find a way to make it buoyant, it is safer not to attempt it.

What about comic speeches? To watch someone enjoying performing and to be highly entertained at the same time is always a very positive experience. But your choice depends on the role for which you are auditioning. If it is Puck in *A Midsummer Night's Dream*, then obviously Jan's speech, mentioned earlier, is inappropriate. Suit your choice to the role that is being cast. For a general audition it is essential that one of your choices is comic.

Be prepared!

We all know that suiting your speech to the audition is only commonsense. But it is incredible how many actors offer the most inappropriate speeches because they only have one or two prepared. After twelve years of training actors at the major drama schools around Australia, I am still amazed at how many of them graduate without *any* speech they feel is appropriate or which they actually enjoy performing! This is a ludicrous situation. Always make sure you have at least two speeches, rehearsed and ready, from each of the following categories: strong dramatic (direct/gutsy/powerful), light comical (sensitive/lyrical/ humorous) and classical (comic and serious). At least three of these should be contemporary Australian pieces and two or three of them should also be suitable for screen tests. This means you need a minimum of seven monologues to be ready for *any audition opportunity.*

There are countless actors I know who have completed their screen test or audition and been asked if they have another selection to show. There are a number of reasons why this might happen. Perhaps you do not look like the photo your agent sent in and are not suitable for the character. Or the casting director has found the perfect person for the role that morning, but luckily you look perfect for *another* role in the film or play. The director then offers you the chance—your chance to keep hosting your own audition. Don't miss the opportunity because you are not prepared. Feel confident by offering them three to four other selections. You might even find yourself being considered for a bigger or better role. Never miss the opportunity to show exactly what you can do, at exactly the moment they need to see it.

What makes this moment so special?

'What makes each moment in my speech important for the character and different from all the other moments in the play? Is this thought/ idea/situation of vital significance and a first for my character?' The answers to these questions show how important a speech is, and the more important the better. The speeches I have chosen for this book change the action of the play. They are speeches which propel the character forward or those which significantly affect other characters. Because they are the attention-getting speeches, they work wonderfully in auditions.

If you think the speech you have selected is not important enough, and there are many speeches that work well in the context of the play but are lightweight in isolation, then you have two alternatives. Either find another piece or change the given circumstances of the one you have and *make* it important. You can change the *where,* the *when* or *who* you are saying it to—or change all three. As you are using the speech as an audition tool you have the liberty to do this if it will add to its impact and effect.

In David Hare's *Slag,* Joanne's speech about feminism and isolation takes place whilst she is watching a cricket match. Two other teachers have just played a joke on her by setting her up in a collapsible deck chair. In the play this works well, but for an audition it can be clumsy and awkward to stage. Instead, you could try setting the speech in the office of someone who has power in the school. Start the scene after the deck chair incident, with Joanne, humiliated and upset, but more determined than ever, exploding into the office. Set a chair or another actor downstage facing you, stride in, approach the hard-nosed official and begin: 'Let me make myself clear. I didn't come here to be liked. I came for different reasons and it wasn't to entertain you or to fart arse on your behalf.' This makes for a cleaner, less cluttered scene, and one which holds more weight and importance in the context of the audition.

Another example is a speech by Glenda from the play *US*, which was developed by Peter Brook with the Royal Shakespeare Company, on the subject of war and its brutality. In the play Glenda talks to the audience, to make it effective in your audition be precise about *who* she is addressing. Perhaps she is at a peace rally or, better still, an RSL function. (You would have to justify why she had been invited there to speak.) These changes will affect the way every syllable of the speech is delivered. By making your audience necessary and specific you will have contacted everyone present at the audition more directly. You will have added importance to the words and created a gutsier, more confronting speech, where every word is purpose-built.

If you do make changes, only do so if those changes are viable to, and justified by, your speech. Sometimes the most important adjustment is simply to care more about the issues and ideas with which you are dealing. I observed an audition at England's Royal Academy of Dramatic Art (RADA) where a character related a story involving his best friend. The speech was only thirty lines or so, not at all important and not particularly funny. But the actor endowed the ideas with such life and vibrancy that it became both comical *and* important. The more he remembered the incident and his friend's mishandling of it, the more we were entertained. We saw the strength of their friendship through how much he cared about the ideas and his absolute need to tell us about them. Through his inventiveness and involvement this actor made something quite simple into something special.

Points to remember

- Do I like this piece?
- Do I feel an attachment to it?
- Would I enjoy performing it?
- Would I be cast in this role?
- Is it too long?
- Is it self-sufficient?
- Have I thought about the content?
- Is it important enough?
- Am I ready to offer other selections if required?

4. Working Alone

Preparation and Rehearsal

You have chosen your speech and are preparing to rehearse it. *Wait...*

Read the play! Yes, discover the landscape from which your speech springs to life. Many actors come to work with me *without* having read the play and wonder why they encounter so many surprises and shocks. I am forced to explain to them the actual situation, relationships, content and meaning of the thoughts and images in the context of the play—a waste of time for both of us. Read the play so that you can make informed and intelligent choices. If you cannot find the play or anyone who knows it, then you will have to simply do your best—find the theatre program, read the reviews, anything. This is your responsibility.

The power of ideas

Too many young actors, or would-be actors, seem to have little regard for the rigour involved in the art of acting. They want quick-fix solutions, instant acting. They strike out with force and abandon, displaying emotions with full energy and attack. They strike postures and gestures with confidence and with the full pyrotechnics of their personality. It can seem and sound impressive. Yet most of these actors haven't read the play and can't articulate the *ideas* driving the speech. Energy without intention doesn't leave the audience with much. Emotion without ideas leaves even less. As we watch theatre we want to *understand* why people do what they do. We look for insight. We want to be taken behind the scenes and glimpse what it is that drives a character. It is neither sufficient nor satisfying to simply see Richard III's anger. We want to come face to face with a man who believes he *deserves more* and who will allow nothing to stand in his way. In the 1992 film *Deep Cover*, Jeff Goldblum's character sits staring ahead in the dead of night with his drug empire on the verge of ruin. Quietly and with immense power, he discloses, 'I want my cake… and I want to eat it too.' He expresses not merely fury, but the idea of ultimate control through domination.

Emotion doesn't tell a story, it merely tells us how you feel. When actors begin asking 'what is this moment *about*', then they start to penetrate the character's psychology. This approach requires rigour on behalf of the actor—a searching mind, a detailed investigation of the play, a deep curiosity about the events that take place and the character's reactions to them—and results in informed choices. Aim to be the type of actor who passes this wealth of insight on to an audience. There are no short cuts.

Read the play for sense, imagery and an understanding of the events and their significance. Jot down your first impressions of your character and of your speech in particular. It is very important to record these impressions at this point, since this is the only time that you will respond to the piece as a member of the audience— ready to be surprised, thrilled, outraged. From here on you will enter the play's world and the character's existence. Your task as the actor is to recreate all of these moments and to allow them to live anew each time you rehearse the scene or present it. Your first instinctive responses to the text are very important. If you later lose your grip on the scene it is of great value to be able to refer back to them. Whether or not you have stuck to your original interpretation is immaterial. It is equally valid to remember why you changed or discarded something as it is to recall why you stayed with it.

Find the facts

- Write down every fact you can extract from the text about your character
- Write down the things your character *does* during the play

The Journey students' end of year performance *Dying to Love*, directed by Tanya Gerstle and Chrissie Koltai at The Actors Centre
(Photo: Peter Holderness)

Dean Carey at The Actors Centre (Photo: Stuart Campbell)

- Write down everything your character says about the other characters in the play
- Write down everything the *other* characters say about *your* character.

This process is a good starting point. Eventually you will have to supplement this information with your own imagination, but first begin directly with the facts from the text. All of these facts become *leads* as we begin our detective work to uncover *what* is happening and *why*. At The Actors Centre, one component of my acting course is called *Script Sleuth*. It involves a detailed investigation of the gifts that the playwright presents to you on the page, waiting for you to see their purpose and use them dramatically to create detailed action.

These gifts include word usage, imagery, the length of any thought and how it develops or changes, punctuation, stage directions, pauses, silences, questions, exclamations. Also look at what other characters do as a result of your own character's words or actions, the telling words they use because of how they have been affected by what you have just said or done. Acknowledge these, commit to them, and see where they lead you. When followed, this path takes you to the essential truth of the speech.

Sensory connections

Your preparation time should not be spent intellectualising. You need to understand and empathise with the character on a *sensory* level. In *Respect for Acting*, Uta Hagen says:

> Everything you do in preparation for the performance of a play [speech] should eventually lead you to real walking, talking, seeing, hearing, smelling, tasting, touching and feeling.

Jot down anything about the speech which means something to you: use colours, fabrics, words, images, music references, sensations, anything and everything which impacts upon your senses: 'This moment *sounds* like shattering glass, the screeching of tyres, a soft breeze bending wheat in a field... this moment would *taste* like metal, choking on foam, a poisonous gas, sipping an exotic cool drink... this moment would *feel* jagged, prickly, cold as ice, as light as silk.' Think how the camera would capture the moment. A high aerial shot speeding down towards the subject? An extreme close up? A fast tracking shot? A hand held running shot? A point of view shot of the killer seeing his or her feet stepping over logs, pushing through the swamp and approaching a small misty clearing to view the muddied half-buried arm twisted amongst the undergrowth?

Eventually you will have to walk, talk and breathe your character's thoughts, whatever they be. Collect all you can on a developing *sensory* level in order to propel yourself into the next stage. Never mistake the power when your senses and imagination combine.

Muscle over mind

When I was teaching in Moscow we had many late night 'conferences' about teaching practices. When I explained how and what I taught, I was asked a bizarre question—when teaching, how did I change the actor's *muscles*? This question stumped me. What did it mean? It is not enough, I was told, to tell an actor something or even to explain it. There's no point describing it, theorising about it, philosophising upon it. If the notion doesn't penetrate an actor's *muscles*, then it has little relevance and won't inform his or her acting on a level which will last and be profound. This notion changed my teaching from that moment on.

Through your sensory connections, the world of the play will open up to you and the character's beliefs and needs will begin to surge through your veins. The second book in this series, *Masterclass*, has many dynamic exercises to initiate this process and help you achieve significant and lasting connections with the senses which will inform your acting and create compelling work.

Placing yourself in the picture

An actor came to me and explained that she was having difficulty with a scene in a film in which, after killing her brother, she was burying him in a forest. The director had strong and specific images as to how he wanted it performed. The scene was to be full of opposing emotions: remorse, satisfaction, horror, guilt, searing pain and yet deep relief. The actor couldn't connect—the words weren't real to her. She understood the scene, but couldn't seem to act it. In the film, the scene of the actual death did not exist. Yet before you are able to act or react to the aftermath of an event of this magnitude, the event itself must be absolutely real to you, detailed and particular, and it must have an impact upon your senses *as if* you had experienced it moment by moment.

Many of us have been so influenced by the power and immediacy of film that our imaginations now contain an entire cast, crew, every exotic location conceivable, every required weather condition and special effect, and a state of the art and instant post production facility. All we have to do is to announce 'Roll tape' and the curtains will glide back to reveal wrap-around footage and sensurround sound. So why not use it. I suggested the actor experience the following exercise.

Lie on the floor, with appropriate music playing as an underscore. See yourself as the character in the room. See exactly what you are doing and the exact look on your face: preoccupied, bored, plotting, heavy. See your brother. What are his feet doing? What impression are they making in the carpet? What can you smell from him? How is his hair stuck to his forehead, because it's hot in the room— almost stifling. See everything in close-up. Slowly track, or zoom, or pan, or crane—travel to each and every detail until it fills the screen in your head and consumes your senses with reality.

As the seconds tick deafeningly by, see the look on his face that represents the one reason to you... that he must die. Catch it in stop-start slow motion grabs as you zoom in closer. Now see yourself from an aerial shot—inactive, yet staring. Intersperse cuts of the iron cooling down on the ironing board. Cut back to a twisting aerial shot as it descends closer to you. Suddenly something snaps—almost without warning—without sound—without struggle. In your mind's film you see a shot of the roof of the room: the iron is thrust upwards, its cord dangling, then thumps down and out of shot. And again. And again. And again. Somehow we know the woman now has strength and purpose, nothing confuses her, almost robotically and without effort or strain she commits to this action—over and over. Until she simply stops—hardly breathing yet not out of breath.

We realise there has been silence during the incident—like the micro-second after detonation before the explosion is heard. But as the camera cranes ominously upwards, the noise of her new terrifying world slowly emerges—the noise of her kneeling on the carpet, the sound of the button on her blouse tapping her belt buckle as it flaps in the breeze, the whirr and knocking of the fan as it struggles to correct its direction, the scraping sound of metal against metal as the iron drags across her brother's throat catching his chain and cross, her tongue as it attempts to unlock itself from its imprisoned state, a bead of bloodied sweat as it drops and splashes on her open hand, the rattle of the fridge as it stabilises its temperature, the sound of a cockroach scratching for its release from a trap. As the camera reaches its zenith, her new world is now in full view. As her head falls back, her mouth prizes itself open and the camera drops toward her and is engulfed by her silent terrifying scream.

Gruesome, yes. Detailed, yes. Over the top? Who cares! This is not the finished product, and we have endless stock of film so we are shooting everything and anything that grabs our attention. At least now when the actor comes to the burial scene she has an enormous stockpile of sensory connections from which to draw. Why do you think so many novels become superb films? Casts and production teams have an absolute wealth of rich and finely drawn material which details history, relationships, atmosphere, landscape, sounds, smells—everything which transports them by sensory means to being in that time, with those people, experiencing their situation. One quarter inch of the novel might only produce one short scene for the film—but the depth and potency and impact of that scene will *feel* like forty pages of information.

Try this filmic approach of placing yourself *in the picture*—literally—of your scene. Include either what has happened just before, or what you refer to during your speech. Use it to explore fantasy as well—what your character *wants* to happen—their ideal outcome. This initial exploration work centres you, it places your feet in the scene, it allows the power of your scene to slip under your skin. Many actors make the mistake of trying to get the piece *on its feet* as soon as possible, adding performance energy and attack and trying to find the form and flow before this real groundwork has been done. Going too far too fast makes for a very shallow and generalised result, where the sound of the words becomes more important than the impact of the ideas.

The life of the play

Your speech, if it is an important one, will probably have come from a climactic section of the play. Make sure you know why it is a high point or pressure point. Know what has gone beforehand and what is forcing the character to say these things. Know also what happens after the scene. Know how your speech affects the rest of the play as this will help you to ascertain just how important it is. Every moment in a play should be a movement *into the future*—developing the themes, challenging us with ideas and concepts, and exposing its psychology. Know how your speech contributes to this journey. In fact think of your speech as a domino in a line of dominoes. The momentum that has gone before impacts upon it and your speech creates the momentum which drives the play ahead.

Don't think 'how' think 'why?'

When you have chosen your speech it is often very hard not to be seduced by the trappings of how you might perform it. 'How might I say it? How will I move it? How have I seen it done? How do I imagine it being done? Would I fall to my knees here? Is this where I'd get loud and my voice goes up?' It's rather like trying to predict the ride ahead before saddling the horse. Beware of such unproductive questions. They will not get you to the foundation of the experience but will contaminate every step of the process.

Instead, ask 'Why?' and connect the answers to your own experience or to a similar situation you yourself have encountered. Doing this will help you to claim the thoughts and feelings for yourself:

> *Why is this moment so special?*
> Because he has never before had the courage to tell her how he really feels and now, at this exact moment, he is about to. (When have *you* felt a similar moment of destiny?)
>
> *Why has he not told her before?*
> Because the time has never been right. His fear of rejection, looking stupid or appearing vulnerable always got in his way. (When have *you* experienced this frustration and apprehension?)

Why is he saying these things to her?
Because she embodies all he loves and respects in a woman. (When have *you* felt the same deep connection and recognition in another?)

Why is he saying these things now?
Because tomorrow will be too late. History is in the making. She is leaving and he knows he will never have this opportunity again. (When have *you* experienced a similar urgency and pressing need?)

What obstacles are in his way?
Time, because it is fast running out. His shyness, because he finds incredible difficulty putting words to his feelings, and perhaps the fact that her husband-to-be is in the next room! (When have *you* experienced such enormous obstacles and faced stakes as seemingly insurmountable as these?!)

With questions like these you should begin to experience the sensory connections we spoke of earlier, now charged with your own feelings and associations. This is the beginning of the empathy, or personalisation process—claiming the situation and all it contains as your own. You now begin to enter into someone else's experience. And once you take the *next* step of claiming how *they* deal with the situation and what *they* do and say, you will begin to characterise from a basis of truth, and from the best raw material you can work with—yourself.

Ros Gentle, a Sydney-based actor and teacher, offers a workshop at The Actors Centre called 'Creating a Real Response'. She often reminds actors that they will never create a character more unique and real than the one they already are. This simple comment contains a wonderful gift for many actors. We are often scrambling to find the answers elsewhere, to adopt reactions or qualities we think might fit the situation in order to create a belief in ourselves. There are no answers—no stick-on solutions—merely a journey which enables us to open ourselves to the experiences of the character and to allow deep and significant associations to occur.

Remember: being true to your imagination means working honestly and truthfully from what you think and feel, not from what you have seen or done before.

To experience, or not to experience

The process outlined above should help you steer clear of the most common auditioning fault—*demonstrating*. This is where you 'show off' or represent the emotions, by showing what it might be like *if* you were feeling these things. The result is a generalised and manufactured style of acting where emotions are forced, moves and reactions exaggerated and the sense of the piece stilted. In other words, rather than *responding* to the actual experiences, you *exhibit* the character's attitude towards them. Rather than *penetrating* the character's thinking, you *parade* his or her feelings.

This can easily happen if you do not trust your rehearsal work, or if you have not approached your speech on a sensory level. If you have, you can trust that when you truly *experience* the emotions and thoughts in your piece, your voice and body *will* respond and they *will* convey all that is needed for the audience to understand and empathise. You won't need to squeeze and manufacture emotion in the hope your work will carry. This is why your approach to rehearsal needs to be solid and grounded—it must give you a firm foundation on which to build.

If you think this sounds simplistic, consider this example: You are talking to someone who is stating his ideas or opinion to you. You listen intently, nod at the right times, say 'Yes', and follow his train of thought. Suddenly he breaks off and says, 'You don't believe me, do you?' Before you have had a chance to realise that he has read your mind, he is giving you yet another example to back his claim. How did he know? You were giving all the right signs of listening and you were not visibly objecting violently. In your mind, it was just a niggling thought which occurred to you. Yet your friend saw it and heard it as clearly as if you had jumped up and shouted, 'I disagree entirely!' It is very difficult for the body to conceal what you are truly feeling. Trust that if you truly experience the sensory connections of your *character*, they will show and carry to an audience without the need to telegraph them.

Often though, under the stress of nervousness and tension, an actor will throw away this trust. For example, actors spend five weeks rehearsing their play. It feels good, truthful, they seem to have served the function of the play, and the director is pleased at its depth and precision. But at the preview the director witnesses the actors pushing the emotions and straining the sense. This situation stems from the fact that the actors have momentarily (one hopes) lost faith in what they had found to be true. With the introduction into their safe environment of a group of potential critics and judges, the actors suddenly doubt their work and grapple to support it through over-emphasis. They push and force moments which end up flooding the work and muddying the clarity they have found in rehearsal. Of course opening night arrives and, hopefully, all is back in place. But in your audition, there are no previews and no second chances.

By using personal ownership through sensory connections as your foundation, aim to become not the demonstrational actor but the *experiential* actor—one who presents not what it *would be like* but what it *is* like to experience the character's situation, motivations and thought processes. Your work will be simpler and more credible, and all the more involving for the audience. The demonstrational actor shows us a world, but the experiential actor invites us into theirs. The latter is far more desirable as it has truth at its base and you as its creative interpreter. Trust, connect and surrender—reality and atmosphere soon follow.

Avoiding the pitfalls of characterisation

Trying too hard to *be* someone else takes a lot of unnecessary energy and, if not approached in the right way, can greatly diminish the experiential side of the work. I refer once again to the notion of trusting that we already *possess* the personal dynamics on which to develop the character. We do not have to search outside ourselves in order to be believable. If we develop *our* connection to power, honour, love, ambition, betrayal, redemption, loss, sacrifice or whatever issue the character is facing, then we will be well on the way to *doing* what the character *does*. Rather than developing a character, think of it as *revealing* a character.

An inroad to begin this work is to realise that we all play dozens of different characters every day without realising it: the friend, the lover, the confidant, the student, the workmate, the child, the clown, the lonely soul. Each has its own accompanying moods, rhythms, attitudes and responses. It is not that we are lying or being false when playing these roles, the circumstances around us alter and we make these role adjustments accordingly. We adapt in order to become effective within our given situation. This is why at your own birthday celebration you can often end the night exhausted. Each knock at the door requires you to walk down the hallway unsure of which relationship (and therefore role) you are about to enter. Opening the door and seeing who is there will depend on what role and reaction you adopt—a joyous welcome, a cold withheld welcome, a sensual inviting welcome, an all too familiar 'Oh, it's you again' playful welcome, or the controlled, orderly, responsible welcome when confronted by the police because the party has raged on to the wee small hours.

Your character experiences this same instinctive role-playing in the world of the play. If you can place yourself in the circumstances of the play, you will begin to adopt these roles and your character development begins. By putting yourself in someone else's shoes and feeling and responding accordingly, you will find *in yourself* the leader/king, the knowing philosopher/court jester, the seducer/destroyer/devil, the eternal searcher/lover, the ultimate saviour/hero.

Think of all the roles that Hamlet adopts which could be your starting point. For example:

Abandoned son:	'O that this too too sullied flesh would melt.'
Vengeful son:	'Remember thee—aye poor ghost, whilst my body still has breath.'
Personal tormentor:	'O what a rogue and peasant slave am I.'
Self critic:	'Am I a coward? Who calls me villain?'
Spiritual philosopher:	'To be or not to be, that is the question.'
Bully:	'You are my mother, my father's brother's wife! And would it were not so you are my Mother.'
Spurned lover:	'I did love you once.'
Derailer:	'He dines with the worms—not where he is eating but where he is eaten.'

| Betrayed Son: | 'Let me not think on't—frailty thy name is woman.' |

Don't ask yourself what Hamlet might be feeling, but see what insights are revealed to you when you forget displays of emotion and adopt the actual role the character is playing. This leads to revealing the psychological state of the character—decidedly more interesting than merely showing us how they feel.

Sometimes you may encounter a character that demands specific physical and vocal adjustments that are very different from your own. For example Richard III or Laura from *The Glass Menagerie*. Beware—extreme physical adjustments of this type can be very off-putting to watch unless they are researched and rehearsed accurately. Instead, aim to find the inner justification for these external changes. For example, what makes up the character of Richard III? A clubfoot? A hunchback and deformed spine? That is only the surface. Beneath, the life and outlook of the man is crippled, twisted and deformed as he pillages and destroys in his search for retribution, control, and ultimately divine power. You must find the reasons and justifications for his inner life before attempting to portray the external characterisation. Always begin internally and extend into major physical and vocal changes only if they are necessary. The internal workings are your blueprint to creating character.

Form and shape

The rehearsal is a time for exploration, to see how far you can take an idea, to capture, through the imagery of the language, every nuance and subtle shading of each thought and to eventually reveal the experience of the piece in an exciting and imaginative way. So often, however, actors use the rehearsal process to impose a form and a shape on their speech. Their early aim is to make it look and sound 'right', appropriate, the way they imagine it should be. This leads to quick-fix solutions which can deny truth.

I was on the audition panel for NIDA where one of the suggested pieces was from *Twelfth Night* where Viola begins: 'I left no ring with her.' Each actor articulated very well, painstakingly examined the ring and made the speech sound very proper and very 'Shakespearean'. A voice from the panel then suggested: 'Drop the accent, forget the ring, disregard your set moves and just tell us about your dilemma. What's happening to her? What is she trying to work through? How does it affect her?' After each actor recovered from the shock of having their well-rehearsed moves, highs and lows and 'performance element' taken out, they presented a speech in which we, the auditioners, began to actually *understand* and share in Viola's embarrassing dilemma. We began to see through the veil of performance, of shape and form, and the 'correct way' syndrome. Suddenly we felt what Viola was feeling, for the actor had simply begun to tell us the story—revealing her situation and thereby engaging us in her journey and its consequences. Do not demonstrate—experience. Do not *show* us a world, *invite us into* the world—*your* world, backed up by *your* empathy, *your* truth, *your* feelings and therefore *your* reality.

When you begin to tell us the story, the form and shape of your piece will emerge by *itself.* It will reveal itself once you forge personal connections with the experience the story describes. If you use this as the basis for your rehearsal process, you will begin to discover moves and accompanying action. While you will discard some of them, you will keep others because they serve to make the text clear and help bring the situation to life. You will discover moments and events and responses which will, when combined, communicate the *life* of the piece truthfully, creatively and coherently.

Don't think of rehearsal as the dictionary suggests: 'to repeat out loud, to recreate, to recite, to recapitulate' or your audition will reflect this external and barren approach. Instead redefine rehearsal as to experience anew, to delve more deeply than before, to clarify each thought more fully, to investigate and discover once again. This is the true rehearsal, and indeed the actor's process.

> Discovery consists in seeing what everybody else has seen, and thinking what no one else has thought.
>
> Albert Szent-Gyorgyi

Points to remember

- Read the play
- Find the facts
- Record your first impressions
- Uncover the ideas
- Don't mistake energy for intention
- Look for the gifts from the playwright
- Forge sensory connections with your character and the text
- Place yourself in the picture
- Ask why is this moment a high point or pressure point
- Don't think *how?*, think *why?*
- Experience, don't demonstrate
- Trust, connect, surrender
- Rehearsal is discovery.

5. The Dramatic Terrain Ahead

The Journey

After the first ten lines or so of your speech, the auditioners will have probably summed you up to a certain extent. Scary, but true.

They will have noted:

- your physical and vocal strengths and weaknesses
- your personality and watchability
- your energy and dynamic
- your sense of release and communication
- your ability to create atmosphere
- your clarity of intention
- your ability to craft images and bring them to life
- your use of language
- your emotional life and presence
- your 'impact' within the room.

When I mention this in my audition classes, many students believe that perhaps I am exaggerating in order to put more pressure on them to 'act better sooner'. But I am not. It is extremely important that you understand this if your audition is to be striking and effective. To demonstrate the point, I ask students to monitor themselves as they watch someone else's speech. After the first ten to twenty seconds we stop. They realise that they have already asked the two fundamental questions any auditioner (or indeed audience member) asks:

Do I want to continue watching?

Do I want to continue listening?

If the answer is 'No', something isn't working and obviously this needs to be addressed for a successful audition. If the answer is 'Yes', then the audience will ask, 'What is going to happen *next?*' Every moment on stage should be a movement into the future. We want our audience to be curious about where it is travelling. Over what terrain? What is the significance of the journey? What will be encountered? Where will it lead? What will we learn? Therefore the journey of your speech is the major focus of this chapter.

Development and progression

Given that your auditioners will have made certain decisions about your acting by the time you have said your first ten lines, you need to think about what follows. What different aspects can you show of your work? What unusual choices have you in store? What surprises can you offer? How will you *develop* the piece so that it is interesting and compelling?

Most auditioners are likely to know the speech you have chosen word for word. How are you going to engage, excite and surprise them? It sounds like a lot of pressure. But while we want to avoid the feeling of having to prove ourselves, we do want to produce imaginative and memorable work. But how do we achieve this *without* focusing on it?—through a detailed approach where significance *increases* as your speech progresses. The journey of your speech is all important.

No speech is static. It begins somewhere and ends somewhere else. Every line should reveal more of the needs and motives of the character, his or her dramatic situation and their sensory experiences. By taking the audience on this journey you will reveal the hidden ideas in the piece, breathe life into every thought, and develop the action. Through your creative powers you will deliver an *experience* of the speech that will not be complete or satisfying to the listener until the very last syllable of the last word has been uttered.

Think of your speech as a large blank canvas. Connect to the reason why you utter the first thought and then dot, dab, splash or scratch colour on your canvas. The journey has begun, a mark has been made, it is specific, particular. The audience sees this first mark on the page like a join-the-dots puzzle. We do not know what image will be revealed, but we have witnessed something particular. Thus begins a journey which will eventually reveal an exact image. Thought by thought, image by image, the main ideas and issues fuelling your speech begin to give the canvas shape. Every new thought *adds* something new; every image adds depth and texture; every stroke is a movement into the future, compelling and inescapable. Finally, the last line completes the canvas and we step back to view the complete 'experience' created before us.

When your speech becomes a journey, no two thoughts are the same, no two moments are repeated. It *becomes* dynamic, compelling, revealing, unique and, consequently, so do you.

The emotional wash

The emotional wash is the most frequent obstacle to this journey.

As early as five lines into your audition speech a listener can usually tell if you have decided: 'This is my sad or happy or angry or sincere or retrospective speech.' If you take such a superficial approach then every thought and line will be saturated with the same emotion, and the listener will no longer hear the individual thoughts, ideas and sense of the piece.

If you have ever heard a politician, priest or public speaker drone on without change, think how frustrating it is. If your speech is sad, or cheery, or defiant all the way through, you too will hit only one note and lose your audience. A speech is a collection of moments from a character's life, full of richness and depth, varied and unpredictable. Why strangle the very life out of it by bringing it down to one common emotional denominator? If you categorise and pigeon-hole your speech, it closes doors, spoiling the dynamic journey you want to take us on.

I want the speech to work for me

The emotional wash can also intrude if you search for a speech with a particular end in mind. You may want a strong, direct, gutsy piece for a specific audition. You find a speech which has elements of these qualities and, unconsciously, you twist the rest of it until it fits your specific wants. By so doing, however, you neglect the depth and development of the speech. If you are to interpret the ideas of the speech truthfully, then the speech must dictate to *you* what is required. Ask yourself, not what can this speech do for me, but what can I do for the speech? It's fine to search for a speech which shows a certain aspect of your abilities—strong dramatic, light comical, sensitive and lyrical. But be careful not to let your rehearsal approach be confined to revealing only these qualities. Approach your speech openly otherwise you will limit your options.

I'm feeling it, therefore it must be working

Another example of when the emotional wash gets in the way is if you try to act the character's emotional state. You cannot act *frustration* for example. This emotion is a by-product of two things: your objective (your want), and your obstacle (what gets in your way). In *An Actor Prepares*, Stanislavski describes an improvisation class in which Maria, a young actor, must find a brooch which has been hidden in the fold of a curtain. Maria searches frantically, frenetically, she is full of suffering and drama and tears fall from her eyes. She exits holding her head and beating her chest. Maria has forgotten the purpose of her search and even what she was looking for because she has been too busy acting an emotional state. Because she has fallen into this acting trap, she forces the audience to view her state and to sit in judgment. This cannot be stressed enough. If you show us feelings, we focus on them and spend our time deciding how real they seem. For you have made us aware of the actor *acting*, as opposed to the character *dealing with* a situation. We do not want to see the actor *proving*, we want to become involved with the character *responding and relating*. What the character says and does should be more important than how they feel. To avoid playing the state of 'frustration', Maria should have set her sights on exactly what she was searching for, why she needed it and what it meant to her. Then when she was unable to find it, the truthful emotions would have produced *themselves*. The same applies when dealing with your audition speech.

You may have noticed that I have avoided as often as possible the term *emotion,* preferring to use *sensory connection.* Maria demonstrated her emotional state to her class. If, on the other hand, she had made a sensory connection in her search for the brooch, her sensory experience may have *included* frustration, but it probably would also have included moments of clarity, control, fury, desperation, anger, reflection, calm, humour, irony, passion, pain or disinterest. Because the actor *predetermined* her emotional state, however, she reduced the experience to one dynamic—predictable and unreal—and forced us to judge her acting instead of becoming involved in her situation. Many actors approach their audition speeches in the same way, trying to *make* it become something, rather than trusting the situation to reveal itself.

> The false acting of passions, or of types, or the mere use of conventional gestures, these are all frequent faults in our profession. But you must keep away from these unrealities. You must not copy passions or copy types. You must live in the passions and in the types. Your acting of them must grow out of your living in them.
>
>   Constantine Stanislavski, *An Actor Prepares*

Tell us the story—by doing what the character does and saying what the character says. The feelings will look after themselves.

There are words, and there are ideas

Another cause of the emotional wash, and probably the hardest to detect, is when an actor makes the mistake of learning the *words.* Gale Edwards, the Australian-born international director, often reminds actors not to learn the words, but to learn the *ideas.* Words are merely the result of ideas and every idea is as different in rhythm, mood and feeling as the one that has gone before.

What is an idea? I mentioned earlier how contemporary student actors regard emotions as the be-all and end-all of acting and, when asked what idea is *driving* and *producing* their emotions, they blink vacantly.

The Journey students' end of year performance *Dying to Love*,
directed by Tanya Gerstle and Chrissie Koltai at The Actors Centre
(Photo: Peter Holderness)

The dictionary states an idea is a 'concept, conception, hunch, image, impression, notion, view, perception'. The words characters utter attempt to make a particular concept clear to themselves or to someone else. The idea might be, for example, selfishness, honour, loneliness, pride, vanity, revenge, love, passion, forgiveness, abuse, neglect, independence, submission, mutiny, responsibility or respect. There are countless thousands more. How the character *feels* when explaining, arguing or defending this idea is second to the idea itself. Hence, as with our canvas analogy, the essential idea or ideas of the piece are revealed and developed as the speech progresses. This development creates detail, involves consequences, and takes the audience on a journey of discovery. It makes exciting and compelling viewing. Much of my teaching is directed towards allowing actors the opportunity to feel how much easier and simpler it is when their focus changes from the display of emotions to the adventure of exploring ideas. Suddenly each actor feels the pressure lift, the expectation to make it 'real' vanish, the crippling search to make it 'right' disappear. Many feel, some for the first time, that the speech is leading *them* and they merely follow. Remember—every word is purpose-built—commit to the words themselves and they will reveal the ideas moment by moment. Surprise yourself with this simple discovery process.

An actor at the Berliner Ensemble once ran to her director after four months of rehearsal crying, 'I'm sorry, I know it!' What she meant was that she felt a deadening, pre-determined knowledge not only of what she was about to say, but how she would say it. She had lost the discovery of the moment-by-moment thought progression which springs from the ideas. The way to avoid this is to claim the ideas behind the words from the very *start*. You can always find something new in an idea, but it is nearly impossible to breathe new life into a pre-learnt collection of vowels and consonants.

If I asked you to 'Act anger', you would have a certain image of how anger should look or how you would do it—a set expression on your face, your voice at a certain pitch. Compare your reaction if I said to you: 'Deal with the idea of *betrayal*.' This opens a whole new world that is driven not by emotional results, but by dozens of thoughts that will lead you along dozens of paths such as:

Why did they do this to me?
How could I have fallen for it?
How will I pay them back?
How will I defend myself?
How will I conceal I have foiled their plan?
What are my options and what strategies will I employ?
Who can I ask to be my ally?
Who might be in league with the enemy?
What do I foresee as my ultimate revenge?

These thoughts rocket you into the pressure cooker situation the character is in by opening up layers and dimensions, probing implication and consequence. Much more interesting to live this adventure than merely acting the state of anger! Therefore leave the emotion behind, connect to and deal with 'ideas' and a much more particular and potent journey takes place. It will, of course, be *full* of emotion, but because it surfaces naturally, it will be highly particular and full of meaning.

You must understand what creates and motivates the words, discover the drive behind them—discover the *ideas*. This will help you avoid the emotional wash by keeping your piece dynamic and spontaneous for countless auditions.

The objective

To discover the spine of your journey, you should start with an intense curiosity about the reason your character is in the scene. What is the character's driving need? What does the character want to achieve through the scene? What is the character's *objective*? You may alter your choice, or perhaps become more specific about it as you rehearse the scene, but you must ensure that your initial decision is not passive or negative. For example don't think: 'I never want to talk to him again,' or 'I want to get out of the room.' This gives you very little, if any motivation to propel yourself into the scene. If you do not want to talk to him, stop. If you want to leave the room, simply go! The important question for the actor here is: '*Why* are you there? What stops you from leaving?' Once you have found this reason you will have discovered your objective. The words will *inevitable* as each syllable begins to lead you closer to what it is you want. Once the words have become inevitable—you feel they *must* be uttered, now and in this order—then you know you are connected to the organic drive of the speech.

Find the reason that prohibits you from leaving the scene. Use it as a clue to finding your objective. For example:

> Before I go I want her to realise how she has destroyed my life through her selfishness and petty-mindedness—I want satisfaction!

Now you are finding a more specific and much more playable reason for being in the scene. Your objective is now charged with need and intent:

> I want him to leave because his presence forces me to face my failure and I cannot deal with what I have done—I need repentance!

Always make your objective active and positive. Find a reason for being in the scene and know what you are fighting for. Once you hinge your scene upon your objective, you will have found a purpose and a focus, something to drive towards. If you then inject energy and intention and discover the multitude of ways you can go about *achieving* your objective, you will be well on the road to establishing a new and involving reality.

Fuel for the future

Remember, your objective must be something which creates a *muscular drive* within you. Low-key objectives produce low-key acting. Dry, rational objectives produce dry, rational acting. Neat, logical objectives produce neat, logical acting. Objectives which have little meaning or relevance to you will produce hollow, superficial acting. What is fed in must come out. Fuel yourself with the most potent, juicy, athletic want, then sit back and watch what will happen when you don't get it! This is where acting becomes an adventure for the actor.

Most actors (if their instinct is strong) *thrive* on struggle and feel *charged* when faced with adversity. This hunger and forward thrust drives top athletes as well. They have their eyes fixed steadfastly on their goal, but the obstacles they encounter on the way create a spectacle millions of people around the world find enthralling. As the *physical* endurance of these athletes is stretched and tested to the maximum, so too are the *mental* and *psychic* muscles of actors. The hallmark of good acting is a palpable and focused energy which *charges* the atmosphere and *creates reality*. If you choose well, your objective trips the trigger and allows all this to happen.

Some speeches do not seem to have easily defined objectives when you first read them. Think about the Shakespearean soliloquies where the characters talk their thoughts aloud. They have not entered to play a specific objective on another character. Hamlet, for instance, is fighting to find a way through a shocking and devastating dilemma; Macbeth is attempting to rid his mind of plaguing and damning thoughts; Juliet is trying to come to terms with her overwhelming sense of frustration and deep desire; Richard III is taking stock of his immense power and plotting future treasons.

If your objective does not seem immensely engaging, then the *reasons* propelling you towards it should be greater. In other words, the less important the objective seems to be, the more compelling must be your reasons for wanting it.

Stanislaviski says your objective must 'carry in itself the germs of action':

> An objective is live bait pursued by our creative will. The bait must be tasty, have substance and the power to charm. Unless it has these qualities it will never attract our attention. The will is ineffectual until it is inspired by some passionate desire. The inspiration for it lies in a fascinating objective. This is a powerful driving force, a strong magnet for our creative will.
>
> *An Actor Prepares*

The path we travel along to attain our objective is, of course, our journey.

The key line

As you start to work on your chosen speech, seek out *the most important line*—the line which comes closest to obtaining or revealing your objective. This will be of enormous help in defining your journey. It is this idea/revelation/admission/denial/accusation towards which you have been driving to from the very start. This moment actually reveals the essence of the speech. Of course the character does not know what she or he will say next as each thought is occurring spontaneously, but the *actor* must know where s/he is driving the speech.

Let's look at Jay's speech from Daniel Keene's play *Low*:

I'm talkin' about years ago, right? My old man used to take me. He used to take me everywhere. He would've taken me around the fuckin' world if he'd had, you know, the necessary. He's gone now... a long time ago. But yeah, he took me there, more than once. It's all changed now, right? I haven't been there since I was a kid. I remember the Ghost Train... that fuckin' Ghost Train, it scared the shit out of me. I got off. No, listen, talk about dark. The old man wasn't with me. He had this... thing about, you know, bein' confined... somethin' in the war, he never said. So I got off, right... and I don't know where the fuck I am. The train's been jerkin' around in the dark. I was sick almost. I'd already been on the Roller Coaster, and the Scenic Railway... all those rides. I'm about to lose my lunch... and all this shit I'd eaten, so I dive off the thing. Stumblin' around, you know, scared shitless. It just went on and on... and I could hear all the other kids screamin', like in the distance, you know? I'm walkin' into all this shit, all this stuff they got hangin' down... spider webs, rubber hands... bones and skulls... and I go crazy, right, I'm tearin' the place up... I'm tryin' to get out... and then I hear these footsteps behind me, right, someone's runnin' towards me... and I freak... it's pitch dark and there's someone runnin' at me down this long black tunnel... so I brace myself, and I'm waitin' and I hear this breathin', this panting... and it's gettin' closer... then it brushes past me and I'm kickin' at it and screamin' and it's tryin' to hold me down, it's got hold of me and I'm thrashin' around... and I start gettin' dragged. I'm bein' dragged along the tracks... so fuckin' dark I couldn't see my hand in front of my face. So with me fightin' all the way, we get to the end of the tunnel, out into the light... and it's my old man's got a hold of me... he's white as a sheet... fuckin' terrified. So terrified he couldn't speak... and there's blood streamin' down his face where I'd kicked at him in the dark. He'd raced in when he saw I wasn't on the train when it come out... he'd raced into the tunnel... scared shitless like he was of the dark, 'cause of the war or somethin' like that... he never fuckin' told me... and he's rescued me, right? I could feel him tremblin' you know... tremblin' like a... like a bird or somethin'. [*Beat.*] Who's buyin' the next round?

The moment when Jay discloses that his father saved him, 'He's rescued me, right?', reveals the enormous impact on Jay of his father's act of selflessness. This is the moment when the *central idea* or *theme* of the scene is revealed. It is the moment that spins every other thought in the speech into a gravitational orbit. Without this moment, the speech would lose substance and purpose and would be without an outcome. Substance, purpose and outcome *create* the journey for the audience. Deny them, and you deny the speech its meaning. And meaning is the ultimate goal of any theatrical moment.

The meaning or implication of this moment of Jay's can vary depending on your interpretation. It could reveal that he has felt guilty all these years about his father's spontaneous act of great love because he feels he didn't return it when given the chance. It could imply that this was the first time Jay came face to face with his father's dedication and love towards him. It could suggest the first time in Jay's life when he felt he was actually *worth* something. Whatever meaning you attach to this key line, this moment of revelation must propel the moment for it to have its full impact.

Let's look at the journey possible with this speech. It may begin lightly as a reminiscence of Jay's youth. This evokes 'adventure' memories of being a kid and the significance of Luna Park. This sense of fun and seeming normality is shattered when fear strikes Jay deep inside the ghost train. He realises that not only is he lost and alone in a nightmare world, but that someone is *hunting* him! Now as the prey, Jay desperately tries to elude his predator, but comes face to face with his adversary. A struggle erupts. At the pinnacle of the fight, both crash through the tin doors of the ghost train, are blinded by daylight, and it is only then that Jay sees the bloodied face of his father. Knowing his father's abject terror of the dark because of his wartime experiences, Jay realises his father must have made a superhuman effort in order to save his son. Hence our key line—'he, he's rescued me, right? Shakin', shakin' like a bird or somethin'. Every single moment adds the right colour, texture, energy and dynamic in order for this outcome to achieve maximum effectiveness.

This speech has been performed for me a number of times by actors who have no clear knowledge of what it actually means. There is no key line, no moment when the speech's main idea is articulated, and therefore no moment when the audience is brought face to face with its *meaning*. Consequently, I feel excluded. Why am I spending three minutes watching and listening to a collection of words and displayed emotion? It is your responsibility to create purpose and meaning—the speech cannot do it alone. The key line becomes your guide.

Only by knowing what you are driving towards from the very start, can you expect to build your scene in a progressive and sustained way. This will not only help you avoid the emotional wash, but create and propel the journey as well—both for yourself and your audience.

Discovering individual thoughts

Now, return to the beginning of your speech, read it through slowly, and discover how and why each line aids and strengthens the journey toward the key line. How does each and every thought build the total picture? Imagine the speech as a tapestry—every line weaves something new and different into it in order to create the finished image; a thread of silk, barbed wire, hessian, steel wool, satin—each new thought adds new colour, a different image or perspective, a certain sensory connection vital to the piece, a new dynamic, an increase of energy, tension, pressure.

Look at Tom Junior's speech to Chance Wayne from Tennessee Williams' *Sweet Bird of Youth*:

Excuse yourself from the lady and come on down here. Don't be scared to. I just want to talk to you quietly. Just talk. Quiet talk.

You mean to say my sister was had by somebody else— diseased by somebody else the last time you were in St Cloud? I know, it's possible, it's barely possible that you didn't know what you done to my little sister the last time you come to St Cloud. You remember that time you came home broke? My sister had to pick up your tabs in restaurants and bars, and had to cover bad cheques you wrote on banks where you had no accounts. Until you met this rich bitch, Minnie, the Texas one with the yacht, and coming back Mondays with money from Minnie to go on with my sister. I mean, you'd sleep with Minnie, that slept with any goddam gigolo bastard she could pick up on Bourbon Street or the docks, and then you would go on sleeping again with my sister. And sometime, during that time, you got something besides your gigolo fee from Minnie and passed it onto my sister that had hardly even heard of a thing like that, and didn't know what is was till it had gone on too long.

My little sister, Heavenly, didn't know about the diseases and operations of whores, till she had to be cleaned and cured—I mean spayed like a dawg by Dr George Scudder's knife. That's right—by the knife!

The character paints the picture delicately, yet dangerously, syllable by syllable, until the end of the speech:

And tonight—if you stay here tonight, if you're here after this rally, you're gonna get the knife, too. You know? The knife?

Chance Wayne is left with a frightening picture of what is to come.

With every image in that speech you can feel the picture on the canvas taking shape, building and coming to life; images of St Cloud, Heavenly, Minnie, late nights, Bourbon Street, sex, diseases, Dr George Scudder, the knife. You, the actor, should aim to have a different attitude to each image; different in rhythm, weight, degree and delivery—in other words, each image will have its own *implication*. Remember, this is something which cannot be outwardly manipulated. It must come from your rehearsal of the piece and your personalisation of it. To do this, remember that each image should produce a different and specific sensory connection within you.

But how does one achieve this delineation of thought, and encourage various sensory connections to be aroused by the images within the speech? There are three points to consider:

- Where the thought originated
- The length of the thought
- The springboard into the next thought.

On-line connections

Keep in mind that *every full stop marks the end of a thought*. This means that within that line of dialogue there is a specific thought—a point which must be made and an image set firmly in our minds. The *length of the thought* therefore, becomes a direct reflection of the character's state of consciousness. It portrays how fast the character's mind is spinning, how ordered and controlled the character is, how chaotic and helter skelter, what momentum has built up, what intensity is created, how accurate or haphazard the character's ability to deal with the situation is.

Consider the following short excerpt from Sam Shepard's *Curse of the Starving Class* where the abused son Wesley describes waiting in his room for his drunken and violent father to return. I have set the speech out line by line to help demonstrate the importance of the exercise. As you read, take note of the length of each thought—don't think ahead—imagine each single thought to be the entire speech. As you do this, place your entire focus on its length and let this lend weight to each thought as you read:

> I was lying there on my back.
> I could smell the avocado blossoms.
> I could hear the coyotes.
> I could hear stock cars squealing down the street.
> I could feel myself in my bed in my room in this house in
>   this town in this state in this country.

> I could feel this country close like it was part of my bones.
> I could feel the presence of all the people outside, at night,
> in the dark.
> Even sleeping people I could feel.
> Even all the sleeping animals.
> Dogs.
> Peacocks.
> Bulls.
> Even tractors sitting in the wetness, waiting for the sun to
> come up.

What you can see, and probably feel, from reading this excerpt is that every thought has a life of its own and a reason to exist. Obviously all thoughts do not demand or justify equal weight and importance, but they each serve a purpose, and the length of each thought tells us a lot about the character.

Wesley begins to paint the scene by describing how alert each of his senses were: 'I was lying... I could smell... I could hear'. The short lines reflect how acutely aware he is of his world whilst he waits for the inevitable fear to descend. His next thought spins away from his attempt to box or control his fear, as he is almost catapulted to an out-of-body experience: 'I could feel myself in my bed in my room in this house in this town in this state in this country'. Note there are no commas to order or contain this thought—he is literally taken over by it as he was when he first experienced the sensation—that of extreme isolation and enormous vulnerability—one small, frightened boy, an insignificant speck amidst an unforgiving landscape. Then there are three single words—three single thoughts—'Dogs. Peacocks. Bulls'. Three totally different species to capture—the domestic, the exotic and the trapped—implying how tuned he was to each and every dynamic surrounding the farm house, every other living, vulnerable creature. Whatever decision you make about the implication of each moment, know that the length of the line represents the character's state of being. Claim how they deliver it, and begin to claim how the character thinks and feels as well.

Breathe as the character, not as the actor

Before commencing a speech, many student actors take a large breath as if the character knows she or he is about to launch into a speech. Most characters do not. All they know is that they are reacting to a situation. Their reaction takes the form of dialogue—a single thought is uttered. At this precise moment, the speech (which so far is all of one line) could stop. It could be interrupted by another character. But this is *not* always the case. Hamlet does not say, 'To be or not to be that is the question', and then stroll pensively off stage—something drives the character forward, something is incomplete. Further resolution or understanding can only take place if this initial thought is expanded and developed. The character lives in every moment—for the moment—until driven forward. Once you begin to deal with your scene in this way, two vital things occur which are essential to engaging drama. First of all, you begin to work specifically; secondly, because you are living and breathing moment-by-moment, you create spontaneity—it looks like the character is facing this situation *for the first time.* Your audience now becomes fully connected to your evolving reality.

To begin creating this moment-by-moment life on stage, find which word, image or idea in the line propels you to the next one. By dealing with each separate thought in this way, and reasoning why the speech does not end there, you begin to discover what makes it inevitable for you to continue, what drives you forward into the next thought. Find the *springboard* from line to line, and you are on the road to discovering everything that lies within the speech. It will place you not just in the picture, but in each and every moment.

I've said my line, why go on?

Let's examine this process in more detail by applying it to an example. Read aloud these lines from *Travelling Light* by Leonard Kingston:

> I'm going to find a guru. A religious teacher. Yes. I can't stand England any longer. I've simply got to get away. This is a terrible country! Oh, I don't mean England especially, I mean the whole of the western world. It's so gross and solid. So materialistic. It smothers me! Quite seriously.

Did you read that short excerpt for sense and meaning, or merely to make it sound 'natural'? If the latter, you probably washed over the thoughts with one single emotion and significantly reduced the potential and range of the speech. Remember, there is no such thing as instant acting when dealing with a text. You must start with the *content* in mind, not the *form*. Form is what you are left with after the truth of the content has dictated to you what is required. So let us consider the content.

Think about why the character goes on to say: 'A religious teacher'. What image from the previous line propels him onward? He is obviously specifying what he means by guru, but why does he feel the need to do this? Does the word *guru* suggest to him that he will achieve religious teaching and inner calm? If so, then *this* becomes your trigger—being lifted to a higher plane of consciousness. Or perhaps he detects some cynicism in the listener and wants to clarify his apparently radical statement. (This is an example of where the springboard might come from an external source rather than the previous line.)

Why does he then say, 'Yes'? Is he still responding to the hint of cynicism he felt in his opening line by convincing his listener that to seek a religious teacher is totally rational? Or perhaps the word *religious* conjures up a mystical communion with nature and his 'yes' becomes an affirmation of the enlightenment ahead. If so, then perhaps this image of what he wants might stand in stark contrast to his life at present, and how ridiculous it is. This trigger propels him forward: 'I can't stand England any longer.'

What forces him to say next: 'I've simply got to get away'? Has the thought of putting up with England and his life as it is, forced him to justify his radical decision to escape? (Why does he use the word 'simply'? That is worth thinking about.)

Why does he say: 'This is a terrible country'? (Perhaps the clue to finding out why he uses 'terrible' lies in the reason why he uses 'simply' in the previous line.) By specifying the word 'country', perhaps he feels he has limited the problems he has encountered to only one location, so he expands his theory: 'Oh, I don't mean England especially, I mean the whole of the western world.'

How does he feel about the last two words—'western world'? Something behind them suggests progress, machinery, technology and he is forced on: 'It's so gross and solid'. His images expand, get heavier and more specific as he views the house which surrounds him with distaste. He thinks of the money market, corporate takeovers, greed, the fight for power and control and the whole western capitalist system: 'So materialistic'.

Now it all gets too much, he has lost his view of a peaceful Utopian India and the simple life, and this trigger overloads him with images of the twentieth century: 'It smothers me'. He realises this may sound strange, being smothered by what people call 'normal living', so he points out that he is not joking, and that it does all mean something profound to him: 'Quite seriously'. And so it goes on.

Return now to the beginning of the speech and connect to each individual thought and its possible meaning. You should now be reading it for sense and meaning, as well as becoming intrigued by the myriad of possibilities in the piece as you hit the triggers that create the lines ahead.

This process of seeking out the thought progression via springboards is a good way of finding the journey. You will realise quite quickly that no two thoughts are the same. Each one builds the scenic picture of plot, character and situation. It also forces you to think about how you feel towards each element within the speech—*a guru, the western world,* the words *solid, materialistic, smothers, seriously.* You begin to view the speech as dozens of tiny thoughts, all with their own attached imagery, and all with the potential to make you feel differently towards them. You are beginning to work in detail through specifics, leaving the emotional wash behind.

Choices

It is up to the actor to uncover the exact idea driving each individual thought. What is the character really saying? Or what is the significance and consequence of the thought? Take nothing for granted—question everything and discover the variety of possible choices on any one line which will craft meaning for your audience. This is where the actor's empathy, imagination and skill can be realised.

In one of my scene-study classes, we were working on scenes from Sam Shepard's *Fool for Love*. At one point in the text Eddie, May's lover and half-brother, rises from the table and exits with the line, 'I'll go'. I asked the actor rehearsing the scene what Eddie means by this, for it was unclear what choice he had made. The actor replied, 'Just... I'll go... I guess'. I suggested that the actor contemplate the following possibilities:

I'll go and you will be the loser.

I'll go but tell me to stay.

I'll go but *don't* ask me to stay.

I'll go, I won't cause any more trouble.

I'll go and within two hours you will be on your knees begging me to come back!

I'll go and you've really blown it this time, May.

I'll go and I wouldn't stay if you pleaded with me.

I'll go, but tell me why it should end this way?

These are very different interpretations of the same line, motivated by different ideas. You should find the choice that works best for the dramatic function of the moment. To help discover which choice serves the moment most effectively, ask the following questions:

Which choice drives the drama forward?

Which choice adds significance to the moment?

Which choice develops the idea or theme present at this moment of the play?

Which choice deepens May and Eddie's relationship?

Which choice alerts us to crucial and impending consequences?

It should be clear from this example that 'I'll go' are merely words. If you don't think about the choices that can be made which create meaning, you will end up with a limited and unspecific interpretation and you will starve the text of its true potential.

Preparation is your responsibility

Too many actors arrive for an audition tutorial with me and don't allow me to work *reactively*. By this I mean that when they begin their scene, their energy and emotional output is indiscriminate or without purpose. They have not made the necessary choices, as outlined above, and their scene is without meaning—'sound and fury signifying nothing'. Therefore I end up working *actively*— explaining, prompting, illuminating, motivating. This is not my job nor that of the director. We are there to help you edit your choices, to help you find the strongest dramatic sequence for your choices, to sharpen the significance of your choices. That is our function—to work reactively and in collaboration with you, not to push, prod and invent meaning for you.

Lindy Davies "Impulse Workshop" as part of The Actors Centre Professional Series
(Photo: Stuart Campbell)

This is why we have a policy at The Actors Centre not to work with a student preparing for an audition for more than three sessions. If we did, a student might book a staff member for, say, six to eight sessions and expect the teacher to work towards an effective presentation for the student. This sounds reasonable enough, but it leads the teacher to inject his or her own ideas, taste and choices into the student's work. The teacher ends up *directing* the speech. This is not what auditioners want to see as it does not accurately reflect the student's current abilities or instinct. It is also unfair to students because the panel may ask them to try the speech another way and actors who have not made their own choices in the first place will find this very difficult to do. Because they do not own the speech, they stumble and become lost. You should only get private work on your pieces to help you clear away any approach you may have taken that may do you a disservice or cloud your work.

Remember, it is your responsibility to explore all the possible choices in a line, for this is how you craft meaning for your audience members. Once meaning is present, it implies consequences, and these consequences lock an audience into what they expect may happen next. Engage this, and you have engaged their imaginations. Engage them imaginatively and they will begin to pour their energy, focus, and importance into your scene. What more would you want from an audition?

Origin of the thought

Let us consider now the source of a particular thought. Is it an emotional or intellectual thought? Is it born of the mind, body or heart? Does it rocket up from your centre as gut instinct? Is it driven by sexual desire, manipulation, greed or love? These are all possibilities in the furnace in which each thought has been forged.

Sometimes actors make the mistake of thinking that all the thoughts in a speech come from the same source. A common example of this happens with the speech from *Rosencrantz and Guildenstern are Dead* beginning: 'Have you ever thought of yourself as actually dead? Lying in a box with the lid on it?' This piece is often played as though each thought is born of the intellect. Every line begins to sound like an intellectual exercise pontificating on the abstract concept of death. But there are other thoughts in this piece that are born of fear and an obsession with the very idea of being stuck in a box dead! It can also sound as though Rosencrantz has thought it through before, but it is much more humorous if his thoughts hit him like thunderclaps, twisting him into knots, propelling his obsession and developing the idea of eternity and its many serious and dire consequences.

You need to think not only about the thoughts which propel you forward, but also how they arrive in your mind. Do they spring on you? Creep up on you? Are they subtle, niggling thoughts in the back of your mind? Are they like a thunderclap? Do they explode in your psyche or do you think the thought through aloud, arriving at the main point only at the conclusion of the sentence?

Have no idea what will happen next

A very interesting exercise is to experiment by beginning each line *not knowing* what you will say at the end of the line. 'Have you ever thought of yourself as actually... dead? Lying in a box... with the lid on it!' When this is appropriate, it can produce a great sense of spontaneity. The character's energy is released as it sets forth to discover the words suited to the idea that needs to be expressed.

Also think about whether or not the character actually wants to give in to those particular thoughts. In the example above, the more Rosencrantz tries to ignore his thoughts and to deflect his uncertainties, the funnier the speech becomes. There is a similar example in Tom Junior's speech referred to earlier in this chapter (page 54). The more he tries to stay calm and rational when he comes to the highly emotional lines dealing with his sister Heavenly and what he blames Chance for doing to her, the more potentially uncontrollable and violent he becomes. (*See also,* Playing Opposites in Chapter Six.)

Thought transitions

If the origin is where the thought comes from, and the springboard is what forces you into the next thought, then *articulating* the springboard can create more detail.

An exercise which I find very useful as a rehearsal technique is to say the first line of your speech and to stay with that initial thought until the next thought springs from it. For example, think of Eddie's speech from *Fool for Love* where he describes his father's strange obsession and distraction. Detailing each springboard might go something like this:

> *This went on for years.* (It was incredible. I just watched in amazement.) *He kept disappearing and reappearing.* (Not just for a while, but for as long as I can remember.) *For years that went on.* (I thought it would never ever end, until that one particular day in June.) *Then, suddenly, one day it stopped.* (I couldn't believe it. Dad was back. But he wasn't the same.) *Just stayed in the house.* (Day in and day out. He sat there.) *Never went outside.* (I wanted to go and ask him if I could help, but I knew he wouldn't or couldn't talk to me.) *Just sat in his chair.* (He rocked back and forth.) *Starin'...*

This exercise will not only help you to claim each individual thought but also to find the transitions between them. It is this depth and clarity which the actor must probe, and which auditioners look for.

So remember, your speech contains dozens of thoughts. A full stop usually means a thought transition. Find the reason to go on and you have found the journey. Enter into every moment of that journey, and you have entered into another person's thought process and their current state of being.

Now, ask how?

At this point in the rehearsal process, having explored your objective for the speech, and having done exploratory work on the text, it is time to ask, 'How?' Once you set in motion your feelings and responses to the *why* questions you asked in Chapter Three, the *how* will begin to emerge: 'How will I achieve my burning want or need?' Through pleading? demanding? confronting? humouring? cajoling? seducing? reprimanding?

These are *actions*, they are *doing* words. They describe what we *do* to each other in order to get what we want. In real life we play actions automatically and in rapid succession. When one looks like failing, we switch to another. The same is true in your audition speech. Hopefully, your *how* will be full of these actions and dozens more to make the speech as rich, as human and as full of range as possible. The golden rule to follow when dealing with the 'how' is:

> Whenever your character is not getting what they want, try another way.
>
> Whenever they *are* getting what they want, want *more*.

If you do this it will promote the drama of the scene as it will develop its ideas and raise the stakes.

There is no need, however, to predetermine the actions you intend to play in your speech. You must discover them in rehearsal according to how you affect the person to whom you are talking, how you face the obstacles put in your way, and how you pursue your objective through to the end. This idea will be explored more fully in the next chapter. We will also look at what to do when the person to whom you are talking is not physically there.

This chapter has been designed to help you present a scene with a clear structure, thought delineation, progression and development based on detail and your truth. No matter how many times the auditioners have heard the speech before, if you commit to a personal investigation of your piece, you will present it with your stamp upon it—your ideas, your emotions, and a personal insight which will make them think: 'What will happen next? It sounds different. I haven't heard so many new ideas in it before. What unusual choices. It's as if I'm hearing this piece for the first time!'

If you can initiate this kind of internal dialogue in your auditioner, you are on the way to presenting a highly successful and effective audition.

Points to remember

- Every moment on stage is a movement into the future
- Beware the emotional wash
- What the character says and does should be more important than how the character feels
- Learn ideas, not words

- Every full stop marks the end of a thought. Why go on?
- Find your objective and drive towards it
- The less important the objective seems to be, the more compelling must be your reasons for wanting it
- Find your key line
- Discover the individual thoughts
- Discover the springboards
- Think about the choices on a line
- Think about the origin of the thoughts
- Significance should increase as your speech progresses
- Whenever you don't get what you want, try another tack
- Whenever you *do* get what you want, want more!

6. Safety in Numbers

Your Onstage Relationships

The exposing world of the actor

One of the most common obstacles to an effective audition is that 'implosive' feeling many actors experience. As you begin your speech you feel as though you are *predicting* every word you utter, any gesture seems only to diminish your size, and as you stumble through the piece missing all the moments you had found and glossing over every thought, you discover yourself observing what you are doing from the outside and criticising every sound and move as you make it.

When this happens the focus of the audition event is totally within you and there is no outward flow of energy, no command or control of the situation. You have become *self-conscious*—something every creative artist dreads. You have become your own chief judge and censor. The audition panel have become the jury, weighing heavily and with great portent your innocence or guilt, and you stand before them seeking, often begging, their approval. This is obviously no way to achieve creative release and personal satisfaction.

How do you reverse this process, grow with every line and feel bigger than your oft times ominous surroundings? The solution to counteract this crippling situation is to do what we do whenever we are effective in life: *create a strong relationship* with the person to whom we are speaking, and then *play to affect* them. Your focus and energy will then move from yourself and will rest firmly on the task at hand. Once you have created this interaction, your self-consciousness will vanish.

Stop acting, start relating

If I handed you a telephone and told you to tell the person on the other end of the line your deepest, darkest secret, the first question you would probably ask is: 'Who the hell is it?!' Your every word, image and action would alter depending on whether it was your oldest dearest friend, your fierce adversary, your soul mate, your mother, talk back radio or the Pope! We craft our communication for maximum effect. The person we are addressing will not only determine every single syllable we utter, but how we utter it. For every word is purpose-built, based upon who we are talking to and what effect we wish to have on them.

To *act* does not simply mean to *be*, but to *do*. Instead of just surviving your audition and hoping to muddle through it as best you can, the art is to know what you want to *do* through your speech and then to go out there and *do it*! Once you have created this solid, potent relationship—one that has real meaning and purpose for you—you now have something to *do*, and this will focus your energy, direct your concentration and give you an aim for every moment on stage. Relationships become the reason driving everything you say:

- It is his *neglect* which makes you want to shake some *sense* into him.
- It is her *arrogance* which drives you to *topple* her from her position of *power*.
- It is his *fear* which creates the need for you to *affirm*, *encourage* and *inspire*.
- It is her *pain* and *guilt* which sets you on a path of *healing* and *renewal*.
- It is his admission of *love* which sees you diving for *cover*.

Create the appropriate relationship, and watch the words you say become inevitable. Use your words to create change within them, and vanquish your self-consciousness forever.

Creating strong relationships

When you stand on a stage and commence King Henry's speech, 'Once more unto the breach, dear friends, once more', it is impossible to look out into an empty auditorium and galvanise dead space into action. If you try, you will end up feeling that your audition is forced and unreal, that you are working in a vacuum, for you have failed to create a strong and intimate relationship with the characters to whom you are talking, and you have forgotten that every word you utter lives solely for their benefit. Try the exercise outlined earlier. Lie on the floor and 'roll tape' to transport you filmically to the battlegrounds as your army prepares to re-storm the castle—passion, fury, exhaustion, chaos, fear, pain and allegiance all reside in the eyes of your soldiers. Create this relationship and the communication becomes two-way—give and take, cause and effect. Your words at last have purpose.

Michael Shurtleff says that *communication is duplication*. When we communicate with someone, we want 100 per cent agreement. We want them not only to understand and empathise with our point of view, but we also want their total belief and commitment. That is our aim. If they try to raise an objection, we raise our voice and press the point harder. If they shake their heads in disagreement, we introduce new information to change their minds. If our actions do not seem to be working, we change our tactics. If they begin to appear to be slightly affected by what we are saying, we use a lower tone of voice and move closer as we feel the moment of duplication within grasp. We charm them, woo them, attack them, confront them, inspire them, in order to get the desired reaction—the duplication of *our* own point of view in order to change *their* point of view. This is where, in my acting teaching, I have moved the emphasis from discussing solely what the character wants, to focusing the actor's energies onto trying to change the other person's *will*. For this, in essence, is what an objective is—one person's journey towards altering someone else's path of action.

Acting is reacting—simple, but elusive

There is an exercise called 'Do you want a date?' It's a simple and
effective way of allowing student actors to feel the difference
between having the focus on themselves or on someone else. It also
shows the potential folly of focusing too heavily on one's own
objective.

Person A sits on a chair. Person B exits the room. B's objective is
to come through the door and ask A on a date. The only dialogue
uttered is the first and last line of the scene—'Do you want a date?'
If convinced, A agrees and they both exit. However, if not convinced
or if unaffected by B, A will say nothing. B now stands there
waiting—hanging in the balance. Vulnerable, alone, and without any
other dialogue in the scene, B can only retreat and exit the room.

Each actor is allowed five entrances—five opportunities. What
mostly happens is that B literally launches into the room either fired
with enthusiasm, dripping sensuality, imbued with charm and
confidence, begging like a needy forlorn child, or worse still, doing
all of the above. B often encounters five non-responses, for A has
remained totally unaffected and uninvolved. Too often, as happens
in the lonely audition process, B is only concerned by his or her own
wants. Self-aware, self-possessed and self-conscious, B pushes,
forces, squeezes, strains and becomes entangled with the effort.

To allow the actors to see and feel the difference between acting
and reacting, without B knowing, we change the set up. Whilst B is
out of the room, we secretly alter the position of A. Let me describe
a typical example of what happens next. Brian, as B, storms in as
usual towards Anna, playing A, whom he thinks is sitting in the
chair. Striding across the floor, staring at the floor and pumping his
bravado, Brian comes to a screeching halt in front of the chair, looks
up ready for the *big line,* only to find Anna leaning against the
window ledge twenty-five feet away, preoccupied and lost in her
own distracted world.

Brian's dramatic trajectory is now off course. What he had
intended to do is irrelevant because it bears no *relationship* to
Anna's *will* now that Anna is not sitting patiently in the chair
awaiting his arrival. Brian stops, takes in this new information, and

now begins to *react*: he walks slowly towards Anna, hesitates a moment or two, then steps cautiously into her line of vision. He waits, she shifts her weight, he holds his breath and allows his weight to fall forward so as to lean near to her. Anna traces a path with her fingers through a thin layer of dust on the ledge. Brian's fingers tentatively arch toward hers, he looks to see her response, then as she begins tracing a new circle, his finger falls into position and traces it with her. She stops, looks down and he follows her gaze. She smiles, so does he. She breathes in as if to say: 'Look, I know you're trying to help, but...' Brian seizes this most delicate of moments and offers, caringly but also with a touch of humour, a chance for her to begin again: 'Do you... want... a date...?' After his line, Anna takes a sharp intake of breath, then straightens up. Brian mirrors her actions, but she turns away and moves swiftly towards the door and exits, leaving him as distracted and unfulfilled as herself.

Brian has experienced the flow, release and ease that comes from:

- committing to a relationship on stage
- acknowledging another person's will
- working with that will in order to change it

Once you can do this, most other acting concerns fall into place. For you are now relating, not acting—responding, not inventing. Not alone in the space trying desperately to justify your presence, but finding yourself finally and absolutely naturally, in *reaction* to someone else.

The more specific you are about this person, the greater the probability that you will lose your self-concern and become focused on the effect you are having on them second by second. Once this has been achieved through the rehearsal of your speech, you really do begin to experience the difference between going along to *do* the job, rather than hoping to *get* the job.

Projecting images through your energy

How do you cope in an audition when the very person to whom you are saying all these things is not there?

You must create this person—or people—strongly and in full

detail in your *imagination* during your rehearsal period. As King Henry you will have already made a sensory connection with the members of your army—the looks in their eyes, the glint from their weapons, the mist from their horses' nostrils. You will have heard their breathing and nervous shuffling in the dirt, seen the armour, the leather, the steel and the sweat. This lives now in your imagination and will help to create the other, more important half of the duplication process. Of course, when you stand on a stage and commence your speech you will see hundreds of empty seats, the exit signs, the bottom of the dress circle, the light reflecting off the table onto the auditioners' faces. If you audition in a room, you may be staring at a blank black wall. Do not waste time and concentration trying not to see these things. King Henry's army will exist in your imagination as you will have already formed solid and specific associations with each image. These associations now live in your outflow of energy and this will create the other half of the duplication process during your speech and will activate your energy towards them, hence creating a life-like reality.

Find their reactions then play to affect

Next you must find the other character's reactions to what you are saying. As with our 'Do you want a date' exercise, focusing on the other character(s) can release your energy and actually craft its intent. By plotting the other character's reactions into your speech, you are actually plotting in whatever you need to spur you on to the next line. In other words, *the other character* becomes your springboard and triggers your next line.

King Henry says: 'I see you stand like greyhounds in the slips'. What makes him break from what he was saying to make this observation? Does he see his closest friend in the ranks shift in his place, lift up his chest, stiffen his grip on his sword and look towards him with passion in his eyes? What propels him into the next line: 'The game's afoot...?' Does he see, high on the hill behind the troops, a lone horseman galloping towards the camp with flag upraised? Whatever the images you choose to use, make them *real*, *detailed* and *inspiring*, so that you can draw from them the power and momentum that allow the lines ahead to become inevitable. For this is when acting can become exhilarating—when you feel all you say and do is *inevitable* and the adventure of the situation surrounds and propels you.

There are dozens of moments in every speech where you can plot in the reaction of the character to whom you are talking. Make them, in your mind's eye, *do* something—react, walk away or begin to say something. Let this propel you on to your next thought. When you have established the reality of the other character(s), *play to affect* them. Work at duplicating your own thoughts and feelings in them as you attempt to change their will. Get the focus off yourself and onto what you are doing to them. The more you do this, the less self-concerned, and the more purposeful and believable your audition will become. For this is what we do in life.

If, after a while, your audition piece begins to feel a little stale, try changing the responses you have imagined from the other character. Imagine that you are being looked at differently. If you are low in energy for a particular audition, decide whoever you are talking to is more resistant than ever before to what you are saying. This will make you work harder to be more convincing. It is up to you to create the other half of your reality, to complete the two-way contact in the speech and to add the missing life.

How am I doing so far?

I was working with an actor on a screen test for a role in a television series which required a high dramatic tension and in which he had to play a very forceful, dominant character. The actor was constantly concerned with how he was coming across, how he could look more like the role, how he could seem more powerful. After every line I could almost hear him asking: 'How am I doing?' This, of course, led to forced, unreal and self-conscious acting. I suggested he forget about acting *the gun* and start to aim for *the target*. In other words, he needed to stop trying to play the end result and start *relating* to the other person, who would make him into the character in the scene and impel him to say his dialogue. *She* was his major obstacle —her stubbornness and implacable attitude. With this new focus in mind he became freer and more dynamic almost instantly. Choices began to emerge as he was no longer concerned with looking the part, but with affecting change within the other person. As a by-product of this interaction, he began to *pressure* the other person more, to *bully*, *interrogate* and *defy* her. Without worrying about it he *became* a powerful figure and the scene found its bite. The same is true when trying to play the *boss*—forget about trying to play the end result. Begin by making those around you feel like *employees* and you will automatically *become* the boss. Creating strong and specific relationships *makes you who you are*. Once again, acting is reacting, borne out of relationships—your character 'in relation' to another.

Don't forget that, as suggested in Chapter Two, you can, if need be, alter the given circumstances—the *who* in this case. You can choose exactly which character you would like to address. Usually you will want to use the character specified in the text but, if not, choose another character who will give you something different to play against. For example, you may choose someone who is totally unsympathetic to your character's view so that you have to work harder to convince them. Or play to your best friend, whose presence is a comfort to you and therefore allows you to disclose your innermost thoughts. Choose someone who gives you emotional mileage by making them important and vital.

The main point to remember is that you should never play to a general mass of people or an unspecified individual, ie. not just your 'brother', but the person who received most of the love, affirmation and unconditional support from your parents. Not just your 'ex-lover', but the person you found cheating on you at the exact moment you thought the love you shared was destiny. Be particular about who you are addressing, create the inner conditions to make them real in your imagination and integral to your scene, and then play to affect them. This will give your scene focus, direction and purpose—you will have a reason for being there and this relationship will *create* energy for you and become your ally in the audition.

If you are on stage alone, the same approach applies and will be detailed in the coming chapter.

Points to remember

- Create a strong relationship with the character you are addressing
- Create the inner conditions to make that character real in your imagination
- Play to *affect* that character
- The other character creates the role you play and makes your dialogue inevitable.

7. Trust, Connect, Surrender

Essential Thoughts

Your introduction to your piece

The introduction to your scene can be almost as important as the speech itself. It is the first time the auditioners see you not only as the actor, but as *yourself,* the person they may employ. Your auditioners want an actor, and also a worker; someone who is reliable, consistent, positive, dependable. If your introduction is confused, soft, smug, arrogant, unspecific, rambling, apologetic or non-committal, this will tell them a lot about you. Whether this is the truth about you or not is immaterial—the impression you have just made is all they have on which to form an opinion. You must know precisely how you are coming across, and make it the best possible *version* of yourself. This first impression is very important to the auditioners' open-mindedness when you begin your speech. If you alienate them during your introduction, however unwittingly, you may have a battle during the first minute of your speech to win them back.

Usually you state your name clearly and then give the title of the play and the name of the playwright. When giving the character's name, you may prefer to say: 'I am... (and give the character's name)' rather than 'I'm playing the part of...' It can make the beginning more immediate, command more authority, and propel you into the reality of the piece more easily. It also gets the focus off you so that you can begin the outward flow of communication so necessary to the successful audition as you draw upon the character's energy and confidence. This decision depends entirely on the speech and the character you are playing.

You may then briefly outline any essential information that directly concerns the piece you have selected. But don't let this become a laborious delay to your start! Make it as short, to the point and as engaging as possible. For example, your introduction to Launce's speech might go something like this:

> I'm Launce. My master, Proteus, is madly in love with Sylvia but she wants no part of it. He has therefore instructed me to deliver her a present in the shape of a dog. Unfortunately, on the way to the palace, the hangman's boys stole the dog and left me empty handed. So I have decided to give her my dog, Crab, who is ten times bigger, and therefore ten times the greater gift. This is the market-place, and that is the rear door to the palace where we have paid a visit to the Duke. (Then you exit to begin the scene.)

Anything longer is too much, and if you can shorten it, do so. Most auditioners will know the speech anyway, in which case an outline is unnecessary. The important thing is to *set the scene* efficiently and effectively to allow the auditioners direct access to your scene the moment you begin.

Your audition, your time, your moment

Whatever you decide to say in your introduction, know that this moment can be instrumental in your effectiveness or lack thereof once your speech begins. For you may begin your speech nervously, unsure of yourself, distracted or preoccupied by what *may* happen (based on what happened at your *last audition*). Perhaps the speech went well in your final rehearsal but now you feel you won't be able to repeat it in front of an audience. Renegade thoughts such as these will translate into physical responses which have nothing to do with the situation or state of your character. Therefore you must use your introduction time to achieve the following three goals:

The Actors Centre, Sydney, established in June 1987 (Photo: Peter Holderness)

1. To claim the space. You may have been sitting watching others audition for an hour, or just chatting to the auditioners in the auditorium. But the shock of walking from carpet to floorboard, darkness to light, safety to isolation, can be very off-putting. Therefore, use your introduction time to claim the stage, hit centre and feel you *own* it. Walk up there as if it is yours and give yourself the right to be there. Physically *host* your introduction so your body feels connected to the space and your presence there is legitimate. These few seconds of physical command and assurance can play a significant part once you begin your speech.

2. Make direct eye contact with all present. Despite your nerves, challenge yourself to look at everyone engagingly and openly. If you can involve and invite them in now, you will find it much easier when you begin your speech. Use this time to form a relationship with your audience, to claim that they are *important* and *integral* to your audition. For *acting* is a public event, it was conceived as a means of sharing. Begin to share through your introduction.

3. Collect your thoughts and begin to communicate them across the space. This will help to combat that feeling of implosion we discussed in Chapter Five, and will open up the channels of communication you will require when beginning your speech. The character communicates, he or she uses energy to craft thoughts and ideas, to channel their power, so you too must do this through your introduction. Centre, focus, harness, and begin to relate.

What we are aiming for is a seamless segue from preparation through to presentation. The introduction is a valuable time for the actor. Learn to use it to your advantage, for when properly engaged it can have extraordinarily positive and compelling results.

Playing to an empty chair

If you can use another actor as your listener in your audition, set them facing you downstage (between you and the audition panel) to your left or right, and play in order to affect them. It often helps to have a real person listening, rather than an empty chair. Although they won't be familiar with the reactions you have plotted in for them, nevertheless *imagine* them to be thinking and reacting in the way you have rehearsed. If you are very clear in your reactions to *them,* you may just find they tune into the situation and involve themselves accordingly.

It is possible, however, that this person can put you off. There is nothing worse than picking a stranger, beginning your speech, and then becoming aware that this unknown face is watching you. You may find yourself confused, and your energy will go into rearranging what you had rehearsed in order to adapt to this new person, rather than concentrating on what you should be saying and doing. Or worse still, the listener may begin to *act* as well, giving you totally inappropriate reactions. If you have a choice, choose someone who looks or feels the way you had imagined the character. If you get time before the audition, meet them however briefly, make contact and clearly set the scene for them. This will make it easier and even comforting when your turn comes to do your speech.

Focus

Remember not to focus your entire speech on this person at the expense of your audience and the auditioners. Remember acting is a public event. This involvement is sometimes called *playing out front.* The awkwardness of this term can make it sound as if it's a theatrical device and artificial. But we actually *play out* in real life constantly. We seldom stare relentlessly at the person to whom we are speaking. We turn away to gather our thoughts, find new motivations, paint images of the subject matter, then turn back, fired with more energy and purpose. In your audition, all you are doing is slightly redirecting this natural occurrence towards the auditorium. You know you wish to share what you are saying and feeling with both your fellow actor and the audience, so let this sharing help you involve all those present, without thinking of it technically. By placing the person you are talking to downstage and to the left or right of you, this will occur almost imperceptibly and quite naturally.

The closed audition

If it is a closed audition, should you focus on the auditioner? Often auditioners prefer you not to do so directly because it gives them the responsibility of having to respond to you. Generally, an auditioner would prefer to be free to observe objectively and to take notes. Always ask for your auditioner's preference, and be ready to adapt.

Making the audience work for you

If you intend to present a monologue where you are on stage alone, decide whether you think it is a public or private speech, and what listeners, if any, you require.

Many soliloquies can be played directly to the audience, and you can make the audience become whoever you wish. Richard III could look out into the auditorium and see hundreds of hunchbacks cheering him on, inspired and in awe of his current success and acts of revenge on his path to power. Hamlet can look out into a sea of deposed Heads of State such as himself, all of whom have been visited by their dead father and are as shocked and confused as he is. Leontes from *The Winter's Tale* could see hundreds of women betraying their husbands, as he believes of his wife.

This imaginary audience can change during your speech, whenever you want it to do so. This occurs in life. You begin to tell a friend about your horrendous day at work. You start by relating to her as someone like yourself a normal worker arriving at work on a normal day. When you are falsely accused of a crime in the workplace, she turns into your accuser as you let forth your sense of rage and injustice. You go to a fellow office worker for support and your listener is now this worker, as you plead for backup, assistance and solace. This is denied and you are led handcuffed from a packed and shocked office. As you look back for a last moment of threat and retaliation, your listener embodies every person who set you up and betrayed you. You step closer and whisper your final venomous revenge. When dealing with the audience, the same associations apply—use them as a screen on which to project whichever characters will release and propel you.

Deny yourself nothing!

When you choose your audience, make sure it is one to which you can reveal everything you think and feel without censorship. You can't achieve the moments of great intimacy in a soliloquy if you are speaking to a mass of unknown people. Get to know the members of your audience in detail, form a relationship with them that will allow your thoughts to become *inevitable* because of who they are and what they mean to you. Think of them as great friends, who absolutely understand you and empathise with you. If they are there for you one hundred per cent, it will allow an intimacy to exist. Think of them as *the people who hold all the answers.* This can often help you enormously as you begin to seek out answers and draw their secrets from them.

Other speeches are, and should be, private moments. For example, although Viola's ring speech can be easily played straight to the audience, Juliet's speech, 'Gallop apace you fiery-footed steeds', should be played as a private moment as she articulates her thoughts alone in her room.

If talking to yourself, find out what *part* of your character you are attempting to change. For this is the key. Hamlet's 'O what a rogue and peasant slave am I' is directed to the wimp within—the part of him that cannot spring to action and who cannot be relied upon to solve the situation. In order to affect some change *within*, the speech is directed to the inadequate part of Hamlet.

Decide what best suits your speech and choose whatever will allow you maximum range and depth.

Early rehearsals

I have said this before, but it is worth repeating. When you first begin to work on your selected piece, *do not* immediately jump up and *perform* it. So many actors do. What are you performing? You haven't rehearsed anything *to* perform! All you will be doing is raising your energy and voice and aiming for some imagined imitation of how you think the speech might be done. Time wasted without result.

First begin to understand the text, discover the ideas behind the words. Feel the language roll around in your mouth. Begin to associate with the content of the speech and allow sensory connections to begin to occur. You may need to sit for the first hour or so with all your first impressions laid out in front of you, dealing with each individual thought, letting it seep through you, and slowly gaining personal connections to them all. Remember, this should not be a clinical, intellectual or objective stage in the process. Allow yourself the time to gain instinctive and imaginative connections to the work without the pressure of making it sound *right* or *natural*. There is no such thing as 'acting properly'. Yet many student actors believe there is a right and wrong way of playing the scene. Let go chasing the myth of a scene and find your path—your truth.

The actor's journal

There are five things which I ask my students to do after the first rehearsal of an audition speech:

1. *Rewrite* the speech in your own words (particularly if it is a classical text or involves rich or dense language).
2. Seek out the *major thought* and the idea driving it. *(What is the key line?)*
3. What are the *implications* (consequences) to the ideas driving the speech?
4. What is the *character's objective* in the piece?
5. What *major change* do you wish to provoke in the audience, yourself or the character to whom you are talking?

It is important to put this foundation work in writing. An actor should be able to coherently and intelligently analyse his or her own ideas to the speech. Merely talking about it is not enough, for this can lead to vague theories and even vaguer speculations. Remember, acting can be about feelings, but when these feelings are sharp and specific and begin to involve significance and consequence, then you begin to create *meaning,* not merely emotion.

> The purpose of analysis is the emotional deepening of the soul of a part. Analysis studies the external circumstances

and events in the life of a human spirit in the part; it searches in the actor's own soul for emotions common to the role and himself, for sensations, experiences, for any elements promoting ties between him and his part.

An Actor's Handbook

We need to learn to reveal our inner connections towards a part with great depth, precision and clarity. Develop this skill early by committing yourself to paper. It will help you create detail and to work specifically.

Actor communication

You might find that the lack of communication between actors can sometimes be frustrating. There is often little freedom to approach your fellow actor to discuss the scene which involves you both. Yet if this two-way dialogue is not alive between the actors in the working situation, what chance is there that it will operate on stage? Actors must have strong illuminated inter-connections on stage, for it is only from their communication that the life of the play emerges. It is this life which will shed rays of involvement and empathy onto the audience. If two actors don't spark off each other the audience will be left in the dark. Sometimes this happens quite instinctively and then the life of the play, along with its meaning, will both emerge. But when it doesn't, don't wait for divine guidance or wallow in negative self-possession—*talk* to your fellow performer. Discuss, explore possibilities, experiment with ideas and approaches, say *yes* to as many options as possible and see where they lead. Open up a two-way dialogue between your fellow actor and yourself. Our craft is based on it.

The big break

Don't wait for it, work for it. The harder you work, the luckier you may be. *Luck equals opportunity plus readiness.* Every day, work to extend and strengthen this readiness. Nothing succeeds like preparation.

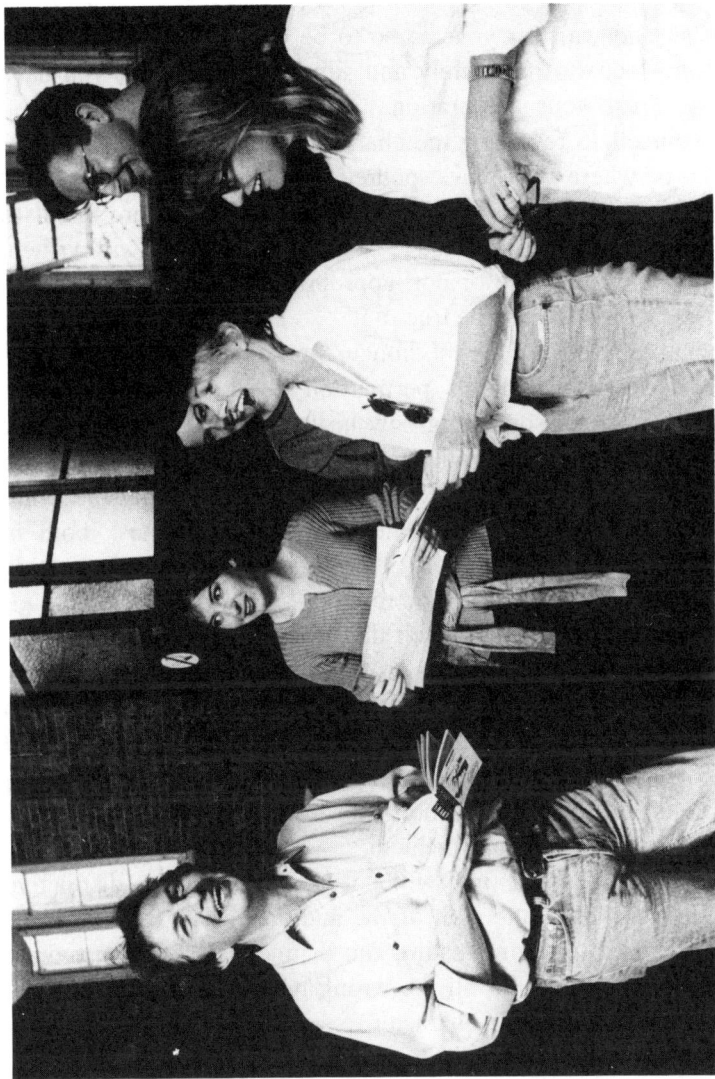

Rodney Fisher "Directing the Classics" as part of The Actors Centre Professional Series
(Photo: Stuart Campbell)

Final thoughts

As you sit and wait for your name to be called, allow your entire energy and focus to rest purely and simply, on the work you have prepared. Trust your preparation, trust your decisions, and then devote yourself to revealing the character and the unique situation. For this is where you have poured your mental, spiritual and emotional energy during your preparation. What you are about to present is your *best hunch* of the reason this speech/play was written. Right or wrong, accurate or not, appropriate or not, it is what you have made it. Trust it, and be true to it.

If you allow yourself permission to present the work you have prepared, you may find this permission gives you freedom—the freedom to discover something new in your speech—to take a risk and explore the thoughts with more clarity and rigour, connecting with the senses on a deeper level and aiming to affect the other character more fully. This, I believe, is the actor's task both in performance and in the audition situation—not merely regurgitating or recreating, but reinhabiting and reliving.

You should also remind yourself that after all your work, the hours spent rehearsing, the questions asked, the decisions and choices made and the headaches over what to wear, how to start, how to think, how to move and what to say on the audition day, you should not lose sight of those two most important ingredients—simplicity and economy. Auditioners do not want to see your hard work, they want to see the life you have created.

Actors often fear that they will not be interesting or distinctive enough to justify the attention of the auditioners and onlookers. If you try too hard to be interesting and distinctive it will only draw attention to your work for all the wrong reasons. Allow the text to speak for itself. Allow the character to speak. You are there simply to serve, to act as the conduit through which this new world flows. Do not strain and shout, do not be busy or loud, do not rush or strangle your work. Respect the character and honour his or her feelings. Trust the words, let them do their work, for they tell the story—the story we are there to hear.

It takes great skill, energy, strength and control to leap in the air, but great dancers only show us the ease and apparent effortlessness of those graceful seconds of flight. In every audition you do, find that flight.

QUICK REFERENCE GUIDE

- How do you want the audience to change during the course of your speech?
- What themes must the audience face?
- Remember the immediacy of your need—want it here and now.
- Don't go along to get the job, go along to do the job.
- What is the key line without which the speech would make no sense?
- Aim to affect powerful change in the person to whom you are talking.
- Host your own audition.
- Choose to be there, in that room, doing that audition.
- Why are these moments so important for the character?
- What do the thoughts imply—what are the consequences and significance to these moments?
- Allow the end of your speech to be as far away from the beginning as possible.
- Events are the signposts the audience follow.
- Remember to change the other person's will.
- Live the adventure of your scene.
- If you become self-possessed, you become entangled in your own effort.
- Create the appropriate relationship, then watch the words become inevitable.
- Follow your hunch—that's why it's there.
- Vanquish self-consciousness by creating interaction.

- To act does not simply mean to *be*, but to *do*.
- Discoveries promote the spontaneity which creates momentum.
- Audiences love to watch people change—adapt—regroup—and respond. Take us on that journey.
- The dynamic set-up between the objective and the obstacle produces dramatic conflict.
- Before you begin—centre, focus, harness, then begin to relate.
- Events are the result of major discoveries.
- There is no such thing to acting 'properly', so don't even try.
- An objective is one person's journey towards altering someone else's path of action.
- Respect your character and honour his or her feelings.
- Every syllable should be purpose-built—words are meaning—craft them accordingly.
- Know what you want to do in your audition, and then go in there and do it.
- Don't worry about acting—focus on relating.
- Creating specific relationships makes you into who you are and drives all you do and say.
- Whenever you're not getting what you want in your scene, try another way. Whenever you are, want more.
- Form is what is left after the truth of the content has dictated to you what is required.
- Words are the result of ideas.
- Every moment onstage should be a movement into the future.
- Emotions without ideas are meaningless.
- A full stop marks the end of the thought—why go on?
- Significance should increase as your speech develops.
- What choice best develops the idea or theme present at this moment of the play?
- What is the implication and consequence behind each thought?
- Craft your energy towards creating meaning.
- Trust the words, let them do their work, for they tell the story.
- Catapult yourself from the exposing world of the actor to the 'adventure world' of your character.
- Commit to the adventure of every audition opportunity you get.
- Respect the character through honouring his or her feelings.

The Actor's Responsibilities

What does an actor do?

- conveys ideas
- communicates feelings and consequences
- presents issues
- exposes implications
- asks questions
- creates meaning
- seeks truth

To whom is the actor responsible?

- *The playwright and therefore the play.* Explore fully, and then communicate the themes, ideas and questions that the play is presenting—in order to present the play's life.
- *The audience.* Offer them the play's life in an exciting, refreshing, intelligent and theatrical way.
- *Fellow actors.* Give them what they require on stage for themselves and their character, and develop the action of the play not only for the duration of the performance, but for the entire season.
- *Himself/herself.* Empathise with the play and the character, and make a total commitment to use your art to explore fully the best and most exciting ways of communicating the play's life, in full detail, with absolute truth.

An actor needs to have:

- A point of view, and a desire to communicate it.
- A commitment to people, and therefore to the world.
- A dedication to the power of his/her art and a determination to learn more about the use and focus of that power.
- An openness to give freely to others, and accept from others.
- A need to share ideas and to take ideas.
- A thirst for knowledge and an enjoyment in gaining it.
- A freedom to explore oneself and to act with imagination, impulse and instinct.
- An acute perception of the world.
- An openness to let the art dictate what is required.
- A perfectly tuned instrument (body and voice).
- A readiness to yield to one's own instincts and desires.
- Self-discipline.
- A love—not of yourself in the art, but the art in yourself.

An actor must at all times seek truth in order to reveal meaning.

Select Reading List

Carey, Dean, *Masterclass*, Currency Press, Sydney, 1996.
Cameron, Julia, *The Artist's Way*, Pan Books, 1995.
Hagen, Uta, *Respect for Acting*, Macmillan, New York, 1973.
Shurtleff, Michael, *Audition*, Walker, 1978.
Stanislavski, Constantine, *An Actor Prepares,* Elizabeth Reynolds Hapgood (ed. and trans.), Geoffrey Bles, London, 1964.

Australian Monologues

Welcome to the most up-to-date anthology of Australian audition material ever assembled.

The speeches in the following section offer an extensive selection of audition choices for the actor in training or the actor already working in the profession. Most are highly suitable for the *General Audition*, where the speech is required to provide range, journey, impact. They present many opportunities for you to explore a wide expressive range.

Other speeches are especially suited for the *Specific Audition*, where you are auditioning for a particular role or type of character. These speeches offer equally strong dynamics but in a more defined form. The inner landscape may cover less terrain but, when fully inhabited, a particular aspect of your abilities will be highlighted and showcased.

You will notice the following icon applied to many speeches. This denotes that the speech is also suitable for film/TV screen tests where the language needs to be appropriate to this particular audition situation. Still rich in range, these selections promote a more concentrated focus making them ideal for the medium in which they will be viewed. Some are too long, but an edited section would be ideal.

Please bear in mind that many of the speeches have been edited to create monologues of the right length which nevertheless give sufficient information to create the 'scene' or context from which

When you choose your selections, they should be rehearsed with reference to the *complete text*. Even if you decide to change the circumstances, please consult the original and complete source. This reference point will inform your decisions.

Some of these speeches are, in fact, too long for the purpose of auditioning but are valuable to work on without necessarily intending to perform them. I feel that approximately forty-five seconds to one-and-a-half minutes for a screen test, and between two and two-and-a-half minutes for a theatre audition, provides a happy medium for all concerned.

I have included a short synopsis of each play where it first appears in the book. Since the speeches are sorted by gender, this means that if there are selections for both men and women from the same play, the synopsis will appear only in the women's section (although the relevant page number is given in the men's section).

You may find it helpful to cross-reference both the male and female sections as the speeches often inform each other and give you further insight.

I trust you will find the following pieces challenging and compelling. Enjoy.

List of Monologues

Women

Men

Includes monologues suitable for film or television screen tests which are indicated by the following symbol:

The Journey students' end of year performance *Dying to Love*,
directed by Tanya Gerstle and Chrissie Koltai at The Actors Centre
(Photo: Peter Holderness)

Australian Monologues: Women

Composing Venus

Elaine Acworth

CURRENCY PRESS

Charters Towers, a faded gold mining town and home to the ore-crushing Venus Battery, 1957, the day Sputnik was launched. Like a latter day comet, the man-made satellite acts as a catalyst for a host of transformations. The play spans three decades to tell the story of three generations of women living in outback North Queensland.

PART 2: SIOBHAN CLARE, raised on a station, now married to a shearer, Patrick.

SIOBHAN:

My father had a quiet grave. He was a gentle man. Mum was always the leader, the wheeler in the marriage. Some of the other children said he was hen-pecked. I was ashamed of her. I never thought about what drew them together. You don't when you're a kid. One night there was a knock on the door. My father'd took a fall. Mum drove four hours out to him. The men didn't want to try and move him on horseback, see. She tried to send me to stay with one of the other women but I wouldn't go. I screamed and screamed. So I went in the back of the dray. It was a bright moon that night. And windless. The spear grass was rimmed in silver. When we got there my father was lying on the ground with a blanket over him and a bandage on his head. My mother took the blanket off and ran her hands down his body very softly. Then she took the bandage off. There was a funny dent in the side of his skull, near the back. The size of a two bob piece. She had blood on her fingers when she took her hand away. She moved him twice. Edged his body round to face a bit more westward. I didn't understand what was happening. She told me to move him would surely kill him. So I said why was she moving him then? And she answered that my father wanted to watch the Cross.

He wanted to see the Cross roll over. So she moved him whenever he lost sight of it and lay back down and held his hand. She said he was a man to dream all his life so he should dream to death as well.

Wet and Dry

Janis Balodis   CURRENCY PRESS

Pam and George are a prosperous, childless, middle-class couple living in Sydney. George's young brother, Troppo, is a feckless wanderer, escaping family ties, who finds himself in Darwin and teams up with Laura—childless and determined to remain so. An uneasy tension between the past and the future forebodes the loneliness of our society, yet a way forward towards a happier community.

ACT 1 SCENE 2: PAM, mid to late 30s

Sydney. The Gap. Day. The sound of surf crashing on rocks below, seagulls, and the odd passing car. PAM *looks out to sea.*

PAM:
Wet nothingness. Whatever's out there. What all those houses and units are looking at. Like so many empty faces. What are they watching and waiting for?

When I was younger I used to imagine that just over the sea were the blissful islands where men were happy with their lot, where children laughed and women were cheerful... like a margarine commercial. And then I thought... suppose the blissful islanders looked across the sea and thought the same about us. That happiness was always somewhere else. Beyond the beyond. Much better to think it was here. Some of the time. That's what's great about the view. Wet nothingness. Just like the desert. Keeps turning you back. On yourself.

ACT 1 SCENE 5: LAURA, mid to late 30s

Sydney. Hospital grounds. LAURA *comes on slowly in a wheelchair.*

LAURA:

Thin August sunshine. Hardly warm. [*Opens her eyes.*] No sky at all. One eyeful. In Darwin it turns your head full circle. Surrounds you. In the Territory I feel so big. Expanded by the heat. I'm small here... a shrivelled lump... Oh God... As we say in Darwin, 'Feel pain, get on plane.' I got on plane, I still feel pain. They must've left something inside me. Some clamp still clamping.

> [*Pause. She looks directly at the audience. A change. Aggressively up front. Mocking and brittle.*]

I had my heart set on a hysterectomy. For twenty years my uterus malfunctioned. Twenty bloody painful bloody years. 'No cure,' they said, 'except...' Do it, says I. Give me relief. Take it out. Have done with it in one foul swoop. 'Be back on the beach in a fortnight,' they said. I imagined one last bucketful of blood, and a gristley bit like a turkey neck in a jar on the bedside table when I came to. 'Surprise,' they said. 'When we opened you up it wasn't necessary. We inspected the plumbing, cleared a bit of debris and removed the odd fibroid golf ball. Lucky for you we were able to divert this tube, reconnect that one and Bob's your uncle.' Or he could become one. [*Matter of factly.*] No release. No freedom. Just sore and all my periods still to come.

ACT 2 SCENE 3: LAURA

Darwin. Beer garden. Day. The noise of a busy bar at lunch time. Someone blows into a microphone. Feedback.

LAURA:

Oh God. I forgot about the lunchtime strippers. My boss brought me here once. Just after Troppo shot through. It was his way of letting me know he thought I might be good for a bit on the side. I sat surrounded by this wall of blue singlets—and shirts and bulging thighs. The music began and this stripper emerged from the lounge. All dead-eyed and leaving nothing to the imagination. Nothing to take off you couldn't see through. No surprises. Very unsexy. She strutted back and forth to this disco beat peeling her gear off. Stilettos, stockings, garter belt, gloves, negligée, G-string. The way she took them off you would've thought she'd had them on for three days. She'd have a sip of beer here, sit in a lap there. Then she took to offering herself to guys and just when they thought they had her she'd pour their beers over them. Well in no time flat there were no takers for the golden shower and I thought one bloke was going to punch her out. Because she'd spilt his beer. She got the message and moved on to the high point of her act which involved a peeled banana and a beer glass full of cream. Unwhipped. She rubbed the cream over her tits and through her pubes. Every now and again dipping her banana in the cream and licking it off. All the time prancing backwards and forwards between the rows of blue singlets and bulging thighs. Never quite touching anyone. No one touching her. And working up to the climax. She'd stop near a table, bend over and rub the banana between her legs and on her arse. That banana copped a hiding. Till she picked on some harmless devil, one of those men who comb their thinning hair from one side of their head to the other. When she couldn't feed him the banana she emptied half a glass of cream over his head and that was the end of it. I kept having this image of a cloud of flies buzzing round his head all afternoon and wondered how he would explain the greasy patch on his shirt to his wife. What struck me most of all was the bored expressions on the men's faces. Grinning slyly but bored and wary. I couldn't understand why they came in such numbers. They seemed to get most pleasure from seeing some other poor bastard on the receiving end of a glass of beer or getting a box pushed in his face. My sympathies lay with the girl. Quite artless; but no one touched her and she seemed to be getting her small revenges.

ACT 2 SCENE 5: PAM

Sydney. Watson's Bay. The Gap. Dawn. GEORGE *turns and looks back through the fence at the coming dawn. The distant sound of a gently moving sea. Early morning traffic.* PAM *enters. She stands at some distance.*

PAM:

Remember when Troppo went to Darwin. We had a weekend away. A rare, rare event. And we went camping. Alone. Together. The bush was frighteningly quiet and we didn't speak. Nothing to say. Even when the steaks got charred on the outside but were still raw in the middle. We sat there. Crunching through the charcoal till the blood ran down our chins and elbows. We might have been eating each other. Or ourselves. And rather than speak, talk, you got up and turned on the car radio. And I was glad. And then in the tent. I couldn't sleep. You were so close and I didn't dare touch you. Even though I knew you weren't asleep. And without so much as a word, we packed up in the middle of the night and drove home. And just picked up where we left off. As though nothing had happened. Never missed a beat. Still separate. Still alone. You think we weren't screwed then? It took us years to get to that. And for years we've been like that. Is that how you plan to look after little Alex?

It won't be good enough. Not if I've had the best you can offer.

I can't give up the child no matter what... He's my son. I wanted him so dearly and he'll never doubt that I do. Our son. If I didn't think... I would have gone long ago.

After Dinner

Andrew Bovell   CURRENCY PRESS

In a suburban pub-bistro on a Friday night, five single people set out in pursuit of a good time, determined to forget their nine-to-five routine.

ACT 1: MONIKA, an office worker, mid 30s

The bistro. MONIKA *stands at the table before* DYMPIE *and* PAULA. GORDON *has just gone to the bar.*

MONIKA:

I've had an adventure. I was in the toilets crying. And all these faces kept peering over the door at me and they were the colour of rainbows. Blues, greens, yellows, pinks. I couldn't stop crying and the more I cried the more rainbow faces would peer in at me. So I closed my eyes and was about to scream when I realised I already was. Then one of the women with the rainbow faces dropped these in my lap. [*She holds out a packet of Valium.*] I took enough to stop me screaming. And do you know, when I finally stopped I couldn't for the life of me remember why I was crying in the first place.

When I got out of the toilets everything had changed. It was dark and the stars were flashing on and off. I was dying of thirst and there was this table full of drinks, so I started to drink them, all of them, until this woman slapped my face and pulled my hair. She chased me all through the dark place until I escaped through a door. But it was so bright I couldn't see. I kept stumbling into men. Men everywhere I turned. They were pushing me and catching me, twirling me around and around until I was sick on one of them. I must have fallen over or passed out or something because when I stood up, I was standing beside the coolest, greenest rock pool I had ever seen. And there were these beautiful, round, coloured fish swimming, up and back and into their holes. And and and at either end there were these men standing with fishing poles. I just had to get into that rock pool. I was so hot, I had to feel the water on my skin, so I took off my shoes.

I climbed up onto the ledge and dived in... but it was so shallow I hurt myself. Then I rolled over to float on my back and look at the sky but instead there was a circle of men's faces staring down at me. Laughing with yellow teeth, big fat red pockmarked faces, leering and breathing on me. Their hands like an octopus, all over me, smothering me. Then from nowhere two arms scooped me out of the rock pool and held me against the smoothest chest I had ever cuddled up to. With biceps like big potatoes and the squarest jaw bone, with just these tiny little prickles that brushed my cheek. And I kissed the reddest fullest lips and ran my hands through the thickest black hair. But the arms carried me back through the door, through the dark place where the woman chased me, back here, where I met another man called... Gordon, who's gone off to get us a drink.

Parts of it were... Parts of it were a nightmare.

[*She sits down. From the folds of her dress a pool ball falls to the ground and rolls across the floor. The three women stare at it.*]

ACT 1: MONIKA

A short while later. MONIKA, DYMPIE *and* PAULA *are looking at their menus.*

MONIKA:

There's that waiter. Hasn't he got the sexiest bum you've ever seen? I wonder if they realise how flattering those tight black pants are. When was the last time you woke up with a tight little butt like that beside you? Would you look at the curve of it? How do they make it stick out like that with nothing holding it up? [DYMPIE *can't stop herself peeking.*] Have you ever seen such a flat stomach? Can you imagine how firm it must be? And look, if you look lower you can make out the outline of his... Can you imagine what's underneath those tight black pants? Martin's bottom was revolting. It certainly was nothing like that.

Do you want to know what it's like to be married? Martin didn't like to do it that often. Sometimes several months would pass by before he would do anything more than peck me on the cheek. Not that I complained, mind you. But do you know how I knew when he wanted to do it? I'd be woken up in the morning by his disgusting little erection jabbing at my back. I'd lay there pretending to be asleep, hoping that Martin would go and do it to himself in the toilet. But once Martin wanted it there was no stopping him. He'd cuddle up to me and rub that thing up and down my spine, poking his tongue in my ear. The stench of his breath made me want to vomit. But instead I'd laugh and giggle, open my eyes with a smile and quickly turn on my back before he jabbed that worm into the first hole he could find.

But there's more. Because once I was on my back Martin would straddle me, and from the fly of his pyjamas, his rubbed-raw, pointy, red penis would be staring at me, dribbling his vile semen all over my nightie. Oh yes, I tried to have children but I never could, because Martin could rarely wait long enough to get inside me. That man. That revolting, lazy oaf of a man. I saw him lying there in his own shit. And I refused to clean him up. I let his own mother come in and see him like that. I told her to clean up the shit.

I haven't been crying because I lost a husband. I've been crying because I didn't lose him sooner. For all those years wasted pretending I was happy. Wasted pleasing him, never myself.

I made a decision in that toilet. From now on I'm going to please me. It's not too late. It's not too late, is it Paula? It's not too late. I'm a beautiful rose about to bloom. And watch out when I do because I'm going to... I'm going to find myself a man. Any man. I don't care. And I'm going to say to him, 'Take me. Take me back to your place. I want to sleep with you. I want to sleep in your dirty filthy man's sheets.' But in the morning I'm going to wake up and leave while he's still asleep. I'm going to walk out and never see him again. I'm going to leave him there lying in his own filth... But right now, I want to dance. Paula? Dance with me.

Aftershocks

Paul Brown and Workers' Cultural Action Committee

CURRENCY PRESS

This is story of the Newcastle earthquake and acts of extraordinary courage and love mingled with tales of stupidity and petty greed that leave you shaking your head in disbelief. Told by staff and friends of the Newcastle Workers' Club, the play goes beyond documenting how a cataclysmic event impacts on the lives of ordinary people.

ACT 1 SCENE 2: LYN BROWN, in her 40s, supervising cleaner at the Club, who has worked there since she was nineteen. Lyn was trapped for about forty minutes on a narrow ledge.

LYN:

I've lost my shoe off my foot... I was just getting up off my chair. I was going to check my staff, because they'd been on their break, and we had a rock concert that night, and I'd been doing some rosters... and that's how I lost my shoe... it was only a flat shoe, so that's all the more amazing. Everything happened in a split second... Perhaps when I was sitting there... you've got your shoe sort of half on and half off type of thing... and... oh gee... like... the rumble came, the movement of the ground, and at that stage I was on my feet because the lights went out... and that virtually would have been my job to go and find out why they went out... not to fix it, but to find out what was going on... Something's falling off the roof. I get up from the desk, walk one step, and then the lights are out. One more step, and I see all the bricks come down... just at my doorway. And everything just keeps tumbling. The big unit, the air conditioning unit, comes off the roof... just sheers straight down in front, and everything just keeps on falling. I don't scream. And as quick as it starts it stops. And I sort of stop, and look around. I know every inch of that club, but I can't orientate myself. Just nothing left there. Just quietness, you know, really it's just so still. Then the alarms and the screaming...

ACT 1 SCENE 5: LYN

LYN:

My desk was still standing there. And right next to me right shoulder, cause my office is so very small, the sides of the wall right next to me, opened up... There are cracks, two and three feet wide, and it is virtually just hanging. And the roof is... what's left of the roof, is just sort of, still hanging down there too. 'The rest of it's gotta come down. It's just gotta keep coming, and nothing can keep it up there.'... I was frightened to move, actually... 'Well, it can't stay up any longer... It's going to come down, and the rest of the office has gotta come with it, cause it was just so attached to it.' So I just tried to stand as still as I could... You know, you talk about your knees shaking, and you know... I mean mine were, and at first really quite uncontrollable. They just felt as if you were going like that, but... yes I tried to stand as still as possible. And round me the Club is gone. I can see as far as Hamilton, straight down King Street without moving me head. And up to Bull Street... There's just nothing.

ACT 1 SCENE 9: PATRON, in her 60s. A Club patron who was trapped in the collapse.

PATRON:

I only had about a ten inch square to breathe in, and I had to keep my hands up, pushing against the piece of poker machine laying ahead of me, to try and keep it from coming down. And a doctor came, and I was fast running out of oxygen, but he dug a hole at the side of me, and he passed me an oxygen mask and told me how to put it on, and then he gave me a needle, and that all I could think of was, 'Wriggle my toes.' And I wriggled my toes, and I thought, 'While I've got toes I've got feet, and while I've got feet I've got legs.' And I could hear them all talking about aftershocks... And they ordered the rescuers out... They ordered them out, as they are expecting an aftershock, and I said, 'Please don't leave me.' And they said, 'We won't leave you.' And they didn't leave me. They disobeyed their order. They didn't leave me... And all I could hear was something saying to me, 'Don't panic. Don't panic and you'll be all right. You'll be all right.' And I just clung to that.

When they started to lift the poker machines off me, of course, everything started to fall. And they stopped, and that was when they pulled me up. They were hoping to get the stuff off the top of me, to lift me up that way. Instead of that they had to come round and get me under the armpits, and pull me up through this little space. I lost all muscle on both... practically all the muscle off my... both legs, as they pulled me up through this little square... that was the only way they could get me out. And... I had a... they got me out that way. And my husband... I don't know who... they told me that I was just a mass of black and blue, and very swollen as they got me out. And later when they gave my husband back the clothes, the... the flesh was still in the pantyhose...

When it first struck, the lights went out, and I was just pushed around like a rag doll, till I came to rest... I'd had a few five cents in my purse, so I thought, here goes, I'll go down to the five cent machines and put some in... and I think I only put about three... I was there a little bit early because the buses were on strike... my husband took me in... I'd just come in to play Hoy at the Workers' Club.

ACT 2 SCENE 8: MARG TURNBULL, mid 30s. She worked in the poker machine area, and also assited on the footpath.

MARG:

Barry used to call me 'Little Passion Flower', which I thought was lovely... It was just something Barry used to make up... He'd call you anything, something that always had a... a meaning to Barry. He was actually cleaning the doors when I went into work that day, and... he said to me, 'Hello my little passion flower.' And I said, 'How are you Barry?' and he said, 'Never seen the world so bright.' And that was at ten o'clock, about five to ten, that day.

The Police rang me, I think on the Saturday, no it must have been the Friday, Friday afternoon... and they said that they'd got cars out of the Club, and would I go in to the McDonald's car park and see if my car was one of them. So I got my ex-husband to drive me in, and it was eerie, it really was incredible.

I said to the policeman, 'Is it badly damaged, my car?' He said, 'Well, put it this way darlin' if you've got a foot ruler, you won't need it all.' And I thought, 'Oh... God.' And when I went and had a look at it... the man at the towing service didn't actually want to show it to me. He wasn't going to let me in the yard. He said to me, 'Look, your husband and your kids can go,' he said, 'That's fine,' he said, 'But I don't think you should go.' And I said to him, 'No,' I said, 'I need to go. I need to have a look at it.' And you couldn't tell it was a station wagon. My tyres were shredded. It had no roof left on it. The floor was actually sitting where the roof should have been. [*Laughing.*] It was... To think that it was on top of where everybody was. Because I'd reversed my car into the back of the western wall that day, in the car park. I was about two spaces from the end of the entrance. And I overheard one of the rescue men saying that that was where they found Barry, was under that side of the wall and that really shook me up to think that my car was actually on top of Barry.

The Butterflies of Kalimantan

Jennifer Claire   CURRENCY PRESS

A strong, beautifully constructed comedy of manners about the penalties of life in the so-called permissive society. The scene is a Sunday lunch given by Kathy, a magazine writer, in her Paddington terrace house, for Sebastian, an innocent British butterfly collector and Marxist. Kathy, however, is in no mood for entertaining, having found evidence that Pete, her live-in lover, is bi-sexual. Sebastian finds himself embroiled in the world of Sydney's artists and gays and learns a good deal about the natives and their habitat.

ACT 1: KATHY, 25–35 very feminine, fragile, but a 'tigress' underneath

A terrace house in Paddington, Sydney. It is a spring Sunday morning.

KATHY:

[*to* SAL, *her very close friend*] Well, you know we were going out for dinner last night? He rang: conference about the new building—that tone in his voice, always know when he's lying. Well, I was furious. You've met Tom, haven't you? That blonde surfie? Pete's been learning from him. Surfing. [*Darkly.*] Among other things. How to say it—I just don't know. They're—at least I think—they're on together.

> [*Pause. The girls look into each other's eyes.*]

I tell you it's true. I saw—Last night I was so angry—had the instinct he would be at Harry's so I... Went and watched outside. I hid. Inside a doorway opposite. Well, after about an hour, sure enough out he came with Tom. [*Nearly shouting at* SAL *because she senses* SAL *is not going to believe her.*] He was supposed to be in a conference, remember, or having dinner with me!

They got into Pete's car, just about to drive off when the dumb blonde sort of leant over, put his head on Pete's shoulder. Pete smiled, they drove off. [*Crossly.*] And it had nothing to do with seat belts. It was a gesture of affection, I tell you.

You think I'm lying? [*Fiercely, seeing she is not going to convince.*] I know you think I'm an introverted, slightly hysterical drama queen with a flight for gross exaggeration, but this time my instincts are at work and my instincts are never wrong. Never!

I'm perfectly calm.

[*She is anything but calm during the next speech delivered preferably through gritted teeth, suppressing absolute outrage.*]

Perfectly calm. I mean, it happens every day; live with a guy for four years, have what you believe to be a good relationship—has its ups and downs, so does everyone—then one day you find he's having an affair. Not with another woman, his secretary, waitress at the bistro, oh no, nothing so simple, so straightforward. No, no, no, this man you've been living with is having an affair with a monosyllabic cretin, who speaks two words of the English language—'yeah' and 'man'—streaks his hair with Clairol and drinks milk. I mean, the insult. It's such a gross insult, gross, gross insult, Sal. [*Stopping in mid flight.*] Do they really...? Well, you know, when they... Bastard, oh the bastard. Well, I know one thing for sure—it's coming nowhere near me, nowhere near!

The Girl Who Saw Everything

Alma De Groen   CURRENCY PRESS

Liz Ransom, a successful feminist historian in her 40s, has retreated to the mountains away from the furore created by her latest book. Her husband Gareth, driving to visit her, is shaken when a terrified woman runs into the path of his car. The consequences of this event upon the couple and those around them are far-reaching.

ACT 1: LIZ RANSOM, 47

A living-room in a country cottage in the mountains. Night. Early August. LIZ *is alone.*

LIZ:

All the songs sang of dreams. Love and dreams... in a white sports coat and a pink carnation. Where did they go, the dreams? We got too old for the white sports coat and the pink carnation—but what happened to our grown-up dreams?

If I had a daughter or a son I'd ask them: what do you dream? And they'd probably say, we don't dream—what is dreaming? And I'd say, countries I wanted to see. Men I wanted to love and to love me. Work that made sense of the day, the week, the year, the life.

Passion. It wasn't absurd to have passion. It was obligatory. You were home with the Tupperware and the Hills Hoist if you didn't. Now the Tupperware and the Hills Hoist have become part of the dream, things we're afraid we might lose.

Even the rage has gone. I don't know any woman now who isn't afraid of her own rage. I wish I did. That's the woman I want to know. Is she loose? Or have they locked her up for safety's sake?

ACT 2: LIZ

The living room. Mid November. SAUL *is sketching* LIZ.

LIZ :

Any explanation nowadays is comforting. I became an historian because I was in love with the idea of continuance... of something epic and ongoing that I was in service to. But it pretty soon dawned on me that the history of the majority of humanity simply didn't exist. And when you look at the history that does exist, you realise it's been defined by one sex. The Renaissance and the Reformation were anything but high points for women. We lost nine million in the witch burnings—for crimes like making penises disappear.

Drop off, nest in baskets, and feed on corn.

  [*Pause.*]

But don't bother looking up gynocide in the standard texts. You won't find it. A whole culture is gone. Lost forever. You wipe a lot of memory when nine million people disappear.

  [*A silence.*]

Before I wrote the book I was watching a program on rape. None of the rapists viewed the women as objects of anger or hate. What they were angry about was something in themselves, or in society. Not women. Women were simply there to take it out on. And I thought, if you examine the history that still exists, if you went back as far as that goes, and you looked at the suffering of women, it could seem natural and pre-ordained. You think of primitive man witnessing a breech birth; you think of primitive man whose woman has a prolapse of the womb after childbirth, hanging down like an elephant's trunk between her legs, gangrenous and smelly—and that was common. It happened a lot. Right up until the beginning of this century. Awful things happened to women that couldn't happen to men—so why not make their blood suspect? Why not consider them impure and the object of divine punishment? Why not forbid their menstrual blood to soil the earth on pain of death? Why not consider that she offends heaven and earth? Why not—if you were a Buddhist—create a blood hell especially for women, filled with blood and filth that took 840,000 days to cross and involved 120 different kinds of torture?

[*Pause.*]

I said people's lives and destinies are genetically predetermined. I handed the enemy a stick and said, beat us, that's what we're for. It was irresponsible, a failure of nerve, and now I have to find a way to make up for it.

Blackrock

Nick Enright   CURRENCY PRESS

It's Toby Ackland's birthday party down near the surf club—and that should mean heaps of grog, drugs and good clean fun. But by morning, a young girl, Tracy, is dead—she's been raped by three boys and bashed with a rock. Who is responsible? The boys? The girl? Or the whole town? An intimate and strongly shaped human drama which examines the social forces behind the impulse to violence in individual lives. The play takes place in the present day, between late November of one year and early January of the next, in an Australian industrial city and its beachside suburb of Blackrock.

SCENE 12: CHERIE, 15

Cemetery. CHERIE *by the grave with a boom box.*

CHERIE:

It was my fault. If we stuck together like we said, you and me and Leanne, you wouldn't be here. But I lost youse all. Now I've lost you. And no-one knows how. You should hear the rumours. Someone seen a black Torana with Victorian number plates. It was a stranger in a Megadeth T-shirt, it was a maddie from the hospital, even your stepdad. All these ideas about who did it, who did it, like it was a TV show. It is a TV show. Every night on the news. I want to yell out, this is not a body, this is Tracy you're talking about. Someone who was here last week, going to netball, working at the Pizza Hut, getting the ferry, hanging out. You were alive. Now you're dead. But I know you can hear me. I can hear you.

   [*She plays a bit of a song.*]

Your song. Times we danced to that, you and me and Shana, Shana singing dirty words, remember? Mum hearing and throwing a mental... I shouldn't laugh, should I? Not here. But all I can think of is the other words.

   [*She turns off the tape.*]

You were wearing my earrings. You looked so great. And some guy took you off and did those things to you. Wish I knew who. You know, Trace. Nobody else does. If I knew, but, I'd go and kill him. I'd smash his head in. I'd cut his balls off. I'd make him die slowly for what he did to you.

SCENE 16: CHERIE

Cemetery. Evening. CHERIE *has the tape-deck. She plays the song, turns it off.*

CHERIE:

They haven't even got your headstone up yet. We're putting the tree in, but. Tomorrow. None of the guys'd give anything, even the ones that wanted to. Afraid their mates would pay out on them. We got enough, but. Leanne's Mum knows someone works in a nursery. It's going to be good. Right beside the netball courts. Your tree, forever and ever.

[*She plays the song again.*]

There you were, all over the news again last night. It's like they won't let you rest. They wouldn't name Scott and Davo, two minors, they said, just two minors, with blurry bits over their faces. They named you often enough, eh? Put your face, your name all over Australia. Now everyone's talking about what'll happen to them three. But whatever happens, they'll still be alive and you'll still be dead.

Good Works

NICK ENRIGHT CURRENCY PRESS

Nick Enright provides us with a window into the lives of two Irish Catholic families, the Donovans and the Kennedys. Spanning several decades and three generations, this compelling story exposes some of the darker moments that colour many of our family histories.

ACT 2: MARY MARGARET, 40s

1962. The Donovan house. RITA *is going.* MARY MARGARET *stops her*

MARY MARGARET:

I'm not loved. Is that the worst thing you can say to me? [*Beat.*] Look at me. I'm not loved. You think I haven't always known that? I used to wake up in the maid's room under the roof. I'd know the moment he came home. I'd hear every sound, door opening, shoes coming off, Neil creeping up the stairs, trying not to stumble, not drunk, just reeling from you. I'd hear him stumbling about underneath, I'd hear the springs of his bed as he settled, and I'd lie there and hold myself, touch myself, seeing myself burning in the pits of hell, but touching myself, wondering, what happened? What did he do to you? With you, on you, in you, how did all the juices run together, where did you do it, how many times, what sounds did you make? I knew there had to be sounds, because even on my own I couldn't stop the sounds, and they had to be bigger with two. And you two... You two together... I could imagine...

A Property of the Clan

NICK ENRIGHT   CURRENCY PRESS

The play takes place in a large Australian industrial city in the present day, between October of one year and the winter of the next year. A young girl, Tracy, has been raped by three boys and bashed to death with a rock.

JADE, teenager, Jared's younger sister

A sweetly sentimental song is heard on JADE's *ghetto-blaster, as she sits alone by the grave.*

JADE:

I'll bring this song for you. Every time I come. The paper said somebody nicked your flowers. People are really off. But they're planting a tree for you at the front of school. Tomorrow at lunchtime. Or do you know that now? I bet you know a lot of stuff now. I should have been there with you, Trace. A few times that night I thought I might sneak out. I really wanted to. Mum was reading in her room, I was watching TV, I could have just left it on, and sneaked out, come and found you. But I didn't. And I keep thinking, if I had... Would it have been different? No one seems to say anything straight. All these rumours go round, and I want to yell out, this is Tracy you're talking about. She was here last week, going to netball, working at the Pizza Hut, getting the ferry. She was one of us. I wish I'd kept them earrings...

[*She plays the song again, then turns it off.*]

I woke up that night. Faces looking down at me. I should have known... when I went round your place on Sunday, and saw the cop-car outside, and the guys from Channel... I should have realised. You were calling to me. That nightmare. It wasn't one. It was you calling. Because all the faces. They were guys' faces. And I knew them all. The cops came round our place last night. Mum was spewing. They're interviewing everyone who was at the party. Seventy kids they're going to talk to. But no one can talk to you. You can talk to me whenever you want to. Please talk to me.

JADE

JADE *sits at the graveside with flowers.*

JADE:

I got your message, the day your tree was pulled up. Jared's girlfriend Rachel, she came into the yard with it, and everyone thought she was really off. They give her heaps. A couple of us tried to plant it again, but I think it had been out of the ground for too long. I'll go back after Christmas and see. It's like nobody will let you rest, Tracy. When Scott finally owned up, and Davo and Wayne Hanley, and it was in the papers and over the TV what they did to you, I thought that had to be the end, they'd let you rest now. But I keep hearing you, in the night. I know you're not resting. Because of what happened after. These three guys all say they did those things, terrible terrible things, but they didn't... after that, you went away, you were walking. Well, staggering. They said you were heading off home. What happened after? If you'll tell me, I'll tell. I want you to be able to let go. Funny Christmas. We had our phone number changed. My Dad was hassling Mum. Yelling things down the phone. Great Christmas present. What else? Jared was going to help me get up on his board, but he's never home. I went round your Mum's to say Merry Christmas and that, but she wouldn't open the door. Funny thing is, they reckon someone saw Scott bringing flowers here. You really liked Scott, didn't you? You thought he was really cute. Like John Stamos, you said, if you half-closed your eyes and his hair was a bit darker. He brought you flowers. But him and Davo and Wayne Hanley... I dreamed the beer, you know. And the cigarettes. Not the rest. I'll leave these here for you. Nobody better nick them. I love you, Tracy.

JADE

JADE *stands at the graveside in school uniform.*

JADE:

I'm not coming any more, Tracy. No, I'll come on your birthday. But I don't want to keep coming all the time. It's a new year, and I want to... you know, get on with... things. I want you to stop talking to me. I want to know that I can close my eyes at night, and just forget about the stuff that's happened. Don't get me wrong. I've felt really special. But now... Sometimes I think you've gone away, and then, like when Scottie and them went to court, it'd be like you were talking to me every night. And now they've charged Ricko, it's all on again.

I want a quiet year, Tracy. I still love you. You're still really special. But I want to make some friends. I mean friend-friends. I don't think I want a boyfriend. Not just yet, anyway. Not for a while. This year everyone's saying you got to start looking for a boy you like. And hopefully one that likes you. I'll see how that goes. I suppose you'll be watching. I know you'll be watching.

The Gay Divorcee

Margaret Fischer   CURRENCY PRESS

Gretel embarks on a journey toward emotional and spiritual liberation as she attempts to come to terms with life, relationships and love.

SCENE 15: GRETEL

At the pool. GRETEL *changes to reveal a swimsuit.*

GRETEL:

I swim every day, I do Yoga and I'm on a diet. Not a crash diet, but one where you change your childhood eating patterns. I've lost three kilos in three months. And I've been a thrill seeker. I went on a seven-day horse trek with a group of women, even though I hate horses. But the 'Finding the Real You Within You' workshop was the best. Brilliant. Great for self-esteem and makes you feel so positive about everything. Isn't it amazing the things you get back into when you're being single?

My God, look at her thighs. They don't wobble at all when she walks and her stomach is totally flat. Oh no, it's crowded. I hate it when it's crowded—so competitive for a place in a lane. Oh, the water's freezing. That's okay—it's good for circulation. Oh, it's filthy—look at all the Band-Aids. Ah, what's a Band-Aid or two?

[She gets into the water and begins to swim.]

I have a desirable body. I am totally gorgeous.

But you're a boring lover.

No! I love and approve of myself.

You're symbiotic.

I am not! I am joyous, happy and free.

I am joyous, happy and free.

You're not! You're lonely and scared, and no good.

No, I love and approve of myself.

Whatever I need will come to me.

[She bumps into another swimmer.]

Hey! Yes, I know this is the fast lane. Me too slow for the fast lane? Well, you've got flippers on. Stuff you! I'll swim in the fast lane as long as I bloody well like. Hey, I'm talking to you. Yes you, the woman with the fair hair and the mock Olympic swimsuit. And what are you staring at? Why don't you do something useful and fish out all those Band-Aids in the pool, and the hair and the snot!

[She gets out of the pool.]

The chlorine level in this pool is outrageous, the opening hours ridiculous! The training squads are incessantly occupying lanes one to five, there are hordes of recreational swimmers in the only three lanes left, and the canoe polo team is constantly in the diving pool. What about the rights of single swimmers?!!!

Gee, 'Finding the Real You Within' workshop said it was good to express anger. That was probably meant to happen.

SCENE 12: GRETEL

Party. Sounds of chatting, tinkling of glasses. Party music. GRETEL *eats during the scene.*

GRETEL:

Hi, Julie, great food. Oh, I'm fine. Oh no, it's okay to be here. I've been reading a great book that says going out and being social is really important at this stage. Hey thanks for not inviting Rita. It would be too hard. Yes, I know she's your friend as well. I really appreciate it.

Hi, Heather. I'm coping. Look, Rita isn't selfish. She's a triple Piscean. She's exploring other parts of herself. You see, I'm an obsessive compulsive, and the combination can get overwhelming. I've been reading all about it. I've got the book here. You see, we're in Stage Three, and its characteristics are re-appearance of the individual, taking risks and dealing with conflict. An affair is one way of re-appearing as an individual, and then there's this thing called 'limerance' which is all the excitement of new passion, and in a long-term relationship, 'limerance' changes, so established couples need to acknowledge this, and then there's... Oh okay, I'll lend you the book when I've finished, if you like.

Hi, Fiona. Oh, pretty good. Yes, we're still together. Oh yes, we've got a commitment to working it out. Well, we have a non-monogamy contract. So you saw Rita with Sarah at the dance. How were they? They looked very close. Thanks for telling me.

Jeannie, I'm glad to see you. Look, just because I came over and was a mess for a week doesn't mean you have to hate Rita. I don't want people to take sides. Well, I think non-monogamy can work. I'd rather be monogamous but I still think there needs to be freedom in relationships.

[*She eats voraciously.*]

Look, I can take it. It's a challenge.

[*More eating.*]

You see, I want a long-term sexual relationship, not a series of three-year ones or a non-sexual long-term one. Rita... Rita's confused. I've got this book that says... What? God, she's here. Julie said she wouldn't be here.

Oh no, here she comes. Hi, Sarah, what are you doing in town?

[*aside*] Fucking Rita.

A workshop? The Seven Habits of Highly Effective People.

[*aside*] I feel like spitting in her face.

How long are you here for? Ten days!!

[*aside*] That means ten nights of earth-shattering sex with Rita.

Oh, a trip to the wineries. Bit of a wine buff?

[*aside*] She would be.

Sure, it's Rita's car too.

[*aside*] I hope she gets decapitated in a fatal accident.

Enjoy yourself.

[*aside*] Oh my God, why did I say that?

SCENE 2: GRETEL

GRETEL *is alone in bed reading 'You Can Heal Your Life' by Louise Hay.*

GRETEL:

[*reciting*] I'm totally safe, I'm totally safe, I'm totally safe…

I went to find her to say—let's go home and see the New Year in on our own—and I couldn't find her. Rita always tells me if she's leaving a party early. And then I couldn't see Sarah either, and then I felt sick and sort of cold and detached, and I thought—right, they're off somewhere fucking. Stop it! Create positive thoughts. I'm being an idiot—Sarah's my friend from Sydney.

They were talking incessantly all night. I had a funny feeling I was intruding. Oh no, that's ridiculous. Rita, where are you? Maybe she had a terrible accident, and she's in a casualty ward too injured to tell the doctor our phone number and my name. I'll ring all the casualty wards. Don't be stupid. I'll clean my room, keep busy.

[*She indicates a book on cats.*]

She gave me this for our third anniversary—*to my gorgeous, adorable cat lover.* That was just after she'd got her new kitten who got very sick and we were constantly at the Vet's together. The Sheridan sheets we bought as wedding presents to ourselves—the most expensive. The shop assistant said they'd outlast cheaper brands.

They must have been in the car. I didn't check the car. I can just see it—they're all over each other like Sharon Stone in *Basic Instinct*. They drive straight to where Sarah is staying, and rip each other's clothes off before they even get to the front door. They're covered in sweat and whispering incredibly dirty things in each other's ears and biting each other's... Stop it!

I'll make some New Year's resolutions for me. Wax my moustache, re-join the gym, love my body, go on a diet—no sugar, fat or carbohydrates or protein.

Maybe that's why this is happening. Sarah is slim and mysterious—I'm fat and obvious.

Rita's probably licking the inside of her thighs—which are thinner than mine—and Sarah's turning her on better than me. Stop it!

Rita's probably just dropped Sarah off, had a hot chocolate, then she got a flat tyre, went to ring me but the phone box was vandalised.

It's five-to-twelve, Henry. Rita, I want you to be here. This isn't how it was on our first New Year's Eve together.

Burning Time

Nicholas Flanagan   CURRENCY PRESS

Outwardly talented and successful, the Cavanaghs inhabit Melbourne's more affluent suburban environment. But beneath the veneer lurk pain and fear, which, ultimately, conspire to tear the family apart.

ACT 1 SCENE 13: MARY CAVANAGH [née Kelly] (KEL), 35, actor, Dr Dion Cavanagh's wife.

The Cavanagh house.

KEL:

[*to her husband*] You 'seem to owe a lot of money.' You *seem* to? Oh, Dion, one can only be mesmerised by the complete authority with which you conduct your affairs. You 'seem to owe'... you're like patient of the week at an Alzheimer's convention—

First you very nearly kill my child—and now you want to take away my home. It's incredible! What is the matter with my life? I'm surrounded by morons and cretins. You're eldest son is an imbecile, and that baffles me—or it did that is until it's become painfully fucking obvious where he gets his inspiration.

This is my home, Dion, my *home*. It's about all I've got. And you want to take it away from me? You're not doing it. I won't abide it. You are not taking my home to settle some tawdry tax account. Go to prison—you will not take my house. You will not take my house.

I feel like I'm *in* a Dr Seuss book. Short on the green eggs but right for the ham—he's standing right in front of me being Bula Blase and saying, I'm having a little difficulty. Little! You have a difficulty of *monolithic* proportions, and I'm not talking about tax. Don't just stand there like Boris fucking Karloff. Say something! My husband the Collins Street psychiatrist, ladies, has a little difficulty—nothing serious—nothing that one of his Doctor friend's lobotomies couldn't alleviate—just a little taxy waxy thing, you know—so he's going to sell the house and we're moving to a modest little cottage in St fucking Albans! It's because they're all suicidal over there. Why? Go to St Albans and you'll understand. [*Yelling.*] They need us!

[*Picks up an object and hurls it through a window.*]

I think I am finished, yes. Don't you have somewhere to go?

ACT 2 SCENE 10: KEL

VINCENT*'s apartment.* KEL *is covered in blood, like something out of a bad horror movie.* VINCENT, *her son, enters.*

KEL:

He wouldn't go. I hit him with the meat cleaver. I tried to wash the blood off the floor.

Oh, he's alright, you could drive a tractor over his testicles and he wouldn't notice... he wouldn't shut up... he kept saying how much he loved me... and waving that, that hand at me saying, 'Is it the hand, is it the hand. It's the hand, isn't it?' And I'm saying, 'Of *course* it's not the hand. I don't care about the fucking hand.' He wouldn't leave me alone... and there was a gin bottle there—who left a gin bottle there?—I thought maybe I'd have a martini, just to drown it all out—just the one—just the one.

And I drank the martini but there wasn't any Vermouth so it was gin really, not even a martini and I kept seeing you—your face when you came back from Sydney—only a baby—You were looking at me—just looking at your mother. And I got frightened—and Harry's saying talk to me talk, talk to me—and I'm thinking, my little boy— and Harry's saying, 'It's because I'm deformed isn't it, that's why you don't love me—it's because *I'm deformed.*'—and he's coming at me and waving the hand saying, 'Isn't it—isn't it? It's because I'm deformed!' And I couldn't bear it any more, so I said, 'Yes. Yes *Yes.* It's because you're deformed, you unfortunate cripple!' Just to shut him up. But he kept coming toward me—with the hand— waving—and Dion's watching too—and Michael, but I couldn't see his face—and I'm screaming at Harry, 'Don't come near me or I'm going to hit you with this meat cleaver'—I don't know where I got it from—and he still kept coming at me—touching me with his fucking hand and he wouldn't stop and I told him to stop or I'd I hit him with the meat cleaver—but he kept coming and I hit him. I hit him. [*Cries.*] You'll never forgive me, will you? You'll never forgive me.

[VINCENT *comforts her.*]

Help me… God help me. Please! [*Breaks down.*]

Jerusalem

Michael Gurr   CURRENCY PRESS

Vivien Rickman convenes a volunteer group of prison visitors. Cameron Rickman is a member of the parliamentary Labor Party. Each strives to create a new and better society. Oliver Rickman is their son. He travels. They each begin to question their ideals and, by looking inwardly, to discover that perhaps the new world needs to be created from within the self. This searching play generates a deep sense of questioning about the world in which we find ourselves and the power within each of us to change it.

ACT 2 SCENE 6: NINA KLEMPER, 30s, Oliver Rickman's girlfriend

VIVIEN RICKMAN's *house.* NINA *and* MALCOLM, *a member of Speaking Terms, a voluteer prison visiting service.*

NINA:

And what is that idea? That everyone gets the disease they deserve? Yes, I am interested in it. And I'm particularly interested in the fact that you never hear it from the parents of a child born with its brain hanging out of its head. Karma? What goes around comes around? There's something very nasty hiding in the idea of karma. It's another way of not thinking. People get what they deserve? Sounds like the Liberal Party with a joint in its mouth.

 [*Beat.*]

All bad deeds are accounted for? Really? In my experience there are great numbers of very bad people leading very happy lives. It's a pretty false comfort, wouldn't you say, to think they'll all get a spank in Hell. To think they'll all come back as a piece of dogshit.

 [*Beat.*]

Surely the point is what we do now? Who we become, how we behave? To leave all the judgement up to God or the karmic compost—that's a terrible impotence isn't it? Adults, grown men and women, with a dummy in the mouth. And look closely at this, Malcolm, look at the people who glue themselves to these ideas. For the happy and healthy these ideas are a way of feeling smug. Fifty cents in the poorbox and the knowledge that the poor will always be with us. And those who actually suffer? What are they saying? I am suffering because God wants me to? I think of those American slave songs, so uplifting, and I want to be sick. In my training they take you around the wards. There was a woman, both breasts long gone into the hospital incinerator. She tried to hold my gaze while the sutures were taken out. Until the hospital chaplain came sliding across the lino. And her pale fierce eyes slid him right back through the curtain.

 [*Beat.*]

You see I don't believe that justice is something you light a candle for. It's just the way you behave.

[*Beat.*]

But that's me. Will you tell Vivien I called in? Malcolm, I've enjoyed our little talk.

[*She extends her hand.*]

Only Heaven Knows

Alex Harding   CURRENCY PRESS

A tender fresh musical set in the exciting and bizarre world of post-war Kings Cross. Tim, a young writer, leaves an unsupportive family in Melbourne and arrives in Sydney to explore the temptations to delight a war-weary population. At the end of his musical odyssey, Tim must choose between his love and an offer to try his luck with the international theatre circuit.

ACT 1 SCENE 6: GUINEA, a nightclub singer, late 30s

Sydney. Summer 1944.

GUINEA:

[*to* TIM] Don't you ever—ever—say that to me again. You think I don't get my share of looks—accusations. A single woman living around here, singing in a club, doing my best to make ends meet—don't you bloody say I've got it easy! Looks on the street—what's wrong with a pretty dress? I earned it—why should I wear makeshift clothes? So what if I've got some blackmarket eggs? I laid 'em myself didn't I—don't you dare say it's different for me just because I'm a woman—to hell with you!

[TIM: I'm sorry—I didn't mean...]

GUINEA: And that's the trouble—people don't mean to say what they say, yet they go ahead and say it just the same, bloody fools.

[*Silence.*]

Look—what you've done is nothing to feel ashamed about. Christ almighty—people don't stop making choices just because there's a war on—you've made yours—be proud of it. You're not the only one. Lana's been given so many white feathers he's going to make a

boa! It's not your fault—the war. You're not responsible! Jesus—
those nasty bastards—let them come around here, I'd give them a
mouthful. If they want to fight, then let them do it—let them go and
be heroes if it means that much to them. I'm sick of it! Sick of it!
Jesus Christ you're a kid.

[*Silence.*]

ACT 1 SCENE 9: GUINEA

GUINEA*'s room.* TIM *is reading a message written on a napkin.*
GUINEA *is putting on her make-up, getting ready for work.*

GUINEA :

[*She gives him a worldly-wise look.*]

Relax will you for Christ's sake—it's only dinner! Let's have a look.
[TIM *gives her the napkin.*] Discretion is assured... This your first
date? With a feller... There's been others then...

I never liked mine much—my husband—although it wasn't too
bad in the beginning. The sex was good—that always helps! I tend to
overlook everything else if that works! But he hated me working—
singing in the club. Not at first, but he began to get very jealous,
especially when he heard other blokes talking about me. He was the
barman. He'd say I'd been flaunting myself up there on a stage—for
Christ's sake, if you're on a stage, you've got to have some
personality, something that makes an audience like you. I've got
plenty. He didn't like that. We'd get home, he'd start a blue, so I left
him. I mean what's the point? He didn't like it, but bugger that! The
boss got rid of him when he started causing scenes—I was more
important the boss said—nice eh? He still comes into the club—
usually with some nice looking sheila on his arm—but there's no
trouble—not anymore. Still good-looking. Always sends me over a
drink and we'll toast each other from across the room. Cheers
Harry—Cheers! You miserable old bastard. I was about your age
when I met him.

I was auditioning at the club—jeez I was nervous! 'Next.' Oh
Jesus it's me! I'd got on a nice floral print frock and some frangipani
in the back of my hair—at least I smelt good if nothing else!
'Name'—uhm—Jennifer Wilkins. Jennifer Wilkins! It just blurted

out! It was my mum's name, and I loved her Tim—my dad too, but his name wasn't Jennifer! And I sang—opened up my mouth and I let rip! Harry came over when I'd finished and says, 'Girlie, that was fantastic! You wanna know something? I reckon you're worth more than a pound a week—I'd give you a Guinea!' That's how I got my name see!

Yeah—me and Lana probably die there. That's where I met Lana—he's the sort of—you know—do anything type, cleans, waits on tables—good mates me and Lana. I caught him one night in my dressing room getting into my make-up. 'Get your own bloody lippy Lana Turner—times are tough'—the times he's been in this room, cut and bleeding—punched silly by some bastard who hated him 'cos he's queer. You'd better go—you're going to be late. [*She hands him back the napkin.*] Discretion assured—the fact that those words have to be written down on something as simple as a dinner invitation. You have yourself the best time.

Table for One?

Claire Haywood   CURRENCY PRESS

The male shortage: media myth or reality? What has the sexual revolution really achieved? 'His Pants for Her': a subversive marketing ploy designed to undermine men? These and other contemporary questions are raised as Jenny, Nick, Robert and Fran stumble through the singles scene in this comedy about sexual politics.

SCENE 4: JENNY, an editor, 35. Warm, witty and friendly personality if slightly cautious in relationships. She excels at her career. An optimist.

JENNY:

That's it! No more booze, no more late nights, no more coming home in the morning smelling of somebody else's facial scrub. Gary used a brand called 'Mostly Men'. I ask you. Mostly men? No wonder the relationship didn't work out. I have this friend Nora. She writes the beauty column at work. She says I've got a serious image problem. Somebody should tell her about 'The Beauty Myth' before it's too late and she turns into the 'The Collagen Kid'. Personally, I think I just attract the wrong types. Lobotomized apes, unweaned intellectuals and social retards: I swear I'm a magnet to them. [*Sighing.*] I don't know. I guess all the real men choked on their quiche back in the eighties. I feel like I'm living in a war zone. Women are getting madder and men are rushing off in droves to bonding sessions. [*Sarcastically.*] Poor things! It must be terrible to find out after twenty thousand years that you aren't the King of the Jungle after all. I tell you, the whole scene terrifies me. I really am better off out of it. Yes! Today is the first day of the rest of my life. I have abused my body for the last time. It's celery sticks and rice cakes from now on and the first place I'm headed is the gym.

[*She heads off and then stops.*]

After I go on a water diet, shed five kilos, buy myself a halfway decent leotard and criminally expensive pair of Reeboks and wait for cellulite to come into fashion. [*Beat.*] After all, I do have my ego to consider.

SCENE 13: JENNY

JENNY:

I don't know. It's like the whole thing is one giant rollercoaster ride. You know what I mean? You fall out of one doomed relationship but you lick your wounds and get back on. You tell yourself it's not so bad being single again. After all, eating takeaway six nights a week saves on dishes and the personals column in the paper has always been good for a laugh. Even the deep and meaningfuls with your cat are beginning to sound intelligent. Then suddenly, out of the blue, Mr Maybe shows up on your doorstep. He's just some guy you slept with once. You know, one of those memorable nights when you can't remember a thing? You give him a bed for the night— unfortunately it's yours, and before you know it, you're looping the loop again. The big C rears its ugly head: commitment that is, not cancer, 'though it might as well be. The silences between you grow malignant, the phone goes uncharacteristically quiet and you find yourself… standing around in comedy clubs, looking at your watch a lot. Can I buy you a drink?

SCENE 17: JENNY

JENNY:

I don't care, I don't care, I don't care, I don't care. I don't care. I don't care any more. I just realised that today. I am officially past caring. It's over, gone, finished, kaput. And do you know what? I don't care if I never get involved with anyone again. I woke up this morning in my big empty bed and I looked across at the pillow and I thought: what difference does it make if there's a dent in it or not? I mean that's all love is. No more than an impression in kapok that can be shaken out in a second. Fuck men!

The only trouble is, I like them. So where does that leave me? Back to the seventies, playing bimbotic games in fern bars after work? Or Pinteresque conversations in crowded coffee shops feeling the silences sink like stones. Alison Wiley is full of shit! So, she's found some sensitive hunk who takes equal responsibility for the kids, the dishes and her orgasms, but what about the rest of us? It's as if the sixties never even happened. I get so angry these days. I for one, didn't burn my bra as an offering to the Gods of Perpetual Solitude. Is that all it boils down to: fear of growing old alone? Sometimes I go through that particular movie. Usually on Sundays, late at night. I get these sudden nightmare images of old ladies in bowling uniforms wearing their loneliness in too many badges; heading home to empty houses that smell of closed doors and cats. Hot flashes of immaculately dressed female executives at the tops of tall buildings waiting to jump. 'Superwoman Smashed To Smithereens on Sidewalk' scream the headlines; distilled panic at the thought of going into a restaurant and having the waiter ask: table for one?

The Passion... and its deep connection with lemon delicious pudding

Sue Ingleton   CURRENCY PRESS

An epic voyage of self discovery leads a woman named Silver through a fantastic world of vibrant images and events drawn from the legends and fables of many centuries. Along the way she is transported back and forth between the suburban and the mythic.

ACT 2 SCENE 19: SILVER, a mother

SILVER:

Your son has been killed in a motor car accident. Your son has not been killed in a motor car accident. Not. Where's not? I want to hear one tiny three letter word. NOT N–O–T. To identify the body... To identify the body. What do I say? Ah yes, I remember this part—I grew this leg and that arm. I can identify those lips they're the same as mine see? Where's his right arm? I grew him a beautiful right arm. He would put it round me, he would clutch at my breast with his fingers, chubby perfect fingers, cherub arms, my boy, my beautiful boy. Your face, this is your face, no beard, still no beard my golden boy. Oh God, all that work and time and effort! He's brand new! He's been getting ready for life—not death! Bastard Death! Cruel Bastard Death! He's in perfect condition and death has mauled him, torn him in two—his body was so beautiful, let me tell you, I saw it! I witnessed its growth. Sweet body. I kissed it every day. I couldn't stop really. I wanted to eat him most of the time— then he grew and stretched up to the sky—his shoulders, his back—a winged Pegasus! Long legs, arms that would never fit shirts, feet that would never fit shoes... how did I give birth to this great golden boy! How did I do it? He was so full of love. The hard part is my darling, *this* is what I knew. This body. But you've gone. This isn't you. This never was you. The joy, the love, the breath of laughter, the light in your eyes. That was you. That's what you gave me, that's not *here*. [*She looks at his body.*] So all these things here I've lost— but all the things missing I've got. That gives me something to work on.

What Do They Call Me?

Eva Johnson   CURRENCY PRESS

The play encompasses an Aboriginal woman, Connie, and her two daughters, Regina and Alison, and the complicated intersections of the politics of gender, race and sexuality. Eva Johnson delineates a shameful history of black oppression, but with a tone of determination, survival and hope in the search for identity.

REGINA BRUMBIE, 38, Connie's elder daughter

REGINA *is addressing her adoptive mother.*

REGINA:
Why? why did you lie to me?
why didn't you tell me?
why did you lie to me all these years, Mother?
to protect me?
FROM WHAT?
who am I?
when you adopted me, who gave me to you?
who is my real mother?
what is my REAL name?
NO, nothing's wrong, I just want to know
things are happening I don't understand.
The other day I walked into a place for a drink
and the man behind the bar leered at me and said
'We don't serve Boongs here.'
He was talking to me, Mother
I couldn't believe this was happening to me.
'Who, me?' I said, 'Are you talking to me?
Can't you see I'm practically white?' I shouted
'My father is a white man, just like you
that proves I am not a primitive
I was *not* made in the bush
for your information, my name happens to be

Regina Penrose Hill.'
He laughed at me.
For the first time in my life, I felt ashamed
degraded, dirty, ugly, yes, *ugly*, Mother.
Why? why did you hide me in this false white skin?
were you ashamed of me? did you hate my black skin?
well, my whiteness has let me down.
No, I'm not over-reacting
I'm totally confused and I'm angry
you made me believe that I was someone else
you lied to me, you lied to me
so tell me, Mother
am I still a Eurasian?
or is that a fancy name for BOONG?

ALISON BRUMBIE, 35, Connie's younger daughter

ALISON:

Sara, remember when we first met?
We were travelling on that Greyhound bus to Alice
I wasn't aware of you on the bus till it broke down.
God, everyone panicked
but you were just magic
you organised everyone, and somehow managed to keep the women
together in one group.
I was fascinated, I was playing 'spot the dyke'
when the other bus came, you know I sat up the back
and watched you all the way to Alice.
Three weeks later you rang me in Adelaide
remember that revolting, revolving restaurant?
you were nervous? God, I could hardly speak
then you started your conversation
on the philosophical, healthy outlook and advantages of
'Unconditional Love'
I had no idea what you were on about
I was just so impressed, you had it all together
… and here we are, six years later…
Happy Anniversary, Sara.

The Gun in History

Tobsha Learner   CURRENCY PRESS

A gun passes through three generations of the one family. Each puts it to a dfifferent use. The play studies the nexus between sex and violence.

PART 2: YOUNG WOMAN, about 21, tense, originally from the country

Hotel room, King's Cross, 1953. The YOUNG WOMAN *stands staring out at the audience. She is smoking nervously. A* YOUNG MAN *enters quietly.*

YOUNG WOMAN:

Did I write to you? I'm still at that damn factory. You can probably smell it on me dress. Strawberry. September's usually a Strawberry month, then we've got Apricot, then Peach... I hate jam now, won't have it in the house. Just the smell makes me puke. Strawberry. It gets under your skin, doesn't matter how hard you scrub. It's in me hair too. Sometimes when I'm asleep I dream that I'm swimming in this sea of strawberry jam, the weight of it is pulling me down, then just before I'm about to drown this submarine starts to break through the red waves. And it's you, somehow I know that it's your submarine. Then suddenly I'm on board but all the sailors are you, at least they've got your body, your hands, but when I look at their faces, they're all blank... I did forget what you look like you know. Sorry. It's been over two years. I wish you'd been here for the birth. Not that you would have been allowed to be with me, just near me. Mum said I was real good. I hardly screamed at all. Don't tell her but secretly I thought I was going to die, you'd know all about that, wouldn't you?

[*Beat. The* YOUNG MAN *stands, they are breast to breast.*]

I often thought about this moment. I'd imagine you standing there, so close. The width of your shoulders, the smell of you coming up from under your white shirt. I'd close my eyes, and it would all be there. Your black hair, the oil in it, the taste of your skin pressing against my lips. Your salt on my tongue. And for a moment I'd have you. Silly, isn't it?

[*For a minute their eyes meet. She moves away.*]

I don't really know why I came here. Because it was expected. Because your mother, my mother, expected it. I thought maybe if we touched we'd know each other again. But you smell different, wrong. I'm sorry. I didn't mean to change. I was hanging on, waiting, waiting... But things started to take a shape of their own. Suddenly I saw how small the houses were... The one you wanted to buy, I'd stand outside and put myself inside looking out. The burnt grass, the azalea bush in the corner. Year in, year out. The same words. The smell of silence. I hate it.

He touched me once, reaching for a batch of jars. Red currant. It wasn't meant to happen. I was leaning back and our arms brushed each other. Red currant. I'm sorry. It wasn't meant to happen.

He's waiting for me now. In another hotel near Central Station. He's waiting for me to phone.

[*She hesitates then leaves. He walks over to the table and puts the end of the gun in his mouth. Blackout.*]

Wolf

Tobsha Learner   CURRENCY PRESS

Tobsha Learner captures the flavour of four decades of social change as she traces the women in the life of Daniel Lupus from his first sexual encounter as an adolescent, his years as an art student in the late sixties, his career as an artist and teacher a decade later and as a graphic designer in the late eighties.

ACT 2: ZOE, a University student

1969. The kitchen of a commune in Balmain. DANIEL *is sketching.*

ZOE:

[*to* DANIEL] You would have liked him. He was beautiful like a girl, only his hair was lighter. We were twins. We used to do everything together... Oliver, after my uncle. He hated it. All the kids used to call him Ol.

He comes to see me sometimes, you know. When I'm really out of it. It happened the other night. I was just lying there, listening to music when he walks in through the door and sits down. We didn't say anything, we just think to each other. It's really cosmic because there is no fear, just this feeling of warmth, then we're remembering together. Playing in the swimming pool, listening to father and mother argue and then we're back in the bedroom with the music thumping through me. And he takes my hand and then...

Blood seeping from under his khaki jacket. He doesn't know that he's dead, see. He needs someone to guide him.

The Rain Dancers

Karin Mainwaring   UNPUBLISHED

Kat is a young woman who has spent all her life on an outback station with only her mother and her grandmother for company. After twenty-five years her father arrives. Knowing that there is some secret that will explain the girl's naivete, he bullies her until she explodes. This is her revelation.

KAT

KAT:

I was playing with Doug behind the tank-stand. We were bored. We were playing with a lizard we'd found, dead, in the dust. We'd poked at it with sticks trying, I think, to worry the life back into it. All we'd done was worried the flies out of it. It was full of them. There were ants too. They were going mad.

It was the weather... hot and still and humid. Everything was flat. Like the earth knew that a great weight of water was about to fall upon it. And the smell... as if the rain coming, for it was, was a hand that held the earth in its palm, like an orange, squeezing it, fragrance spraying out like zest.

The lizard was flat too. But that was the insects pulling its mass away from it. Doug and I knelt in the dust... sticks discarded and watched it... and from this frenzied fight for food came order... the soft bits were triumphantly carted away first... then ants with big claw heads came to saw and rip away the harder pieces.

We pretended we were ants and ate some. It was hard to see what they were getting so excited about. Doug pretended a maggot was a witchetty grub. He ate it. I couldn't.

And then it started to rain. Drops like maggots splattered around us lifting the dust into the air so that, for a second, the earth hovered under a red haze.

I looked down the front of my dress, it was soaked, pink... viole I think. I remember it had a shirred bust... not that I had one to shirr. I always thought that was something you did to eggs. You would not believe what I thought ladies had in their dresses. Mine had nothing but dead lizard stains smeared across it.

My dress was wet. I could see my underpants. They were white, waisted Cottontails. Like these. Not very sexy I admit. Although Mum tells me there are some dirty men who find the sight of grown women in undies like these exciting. She calls this a fetish. She says they are perverts. They have a fixation.

Doug had no such fixation. In fact he preferred me without any underpants at all. Like this. We both thought this was very funny. Nobody else did.

The rain was falling in sheets, like iron, slicing through the air. It was so much like being slapped that, by the time I realised I was being slapped, it was too late to transmute the tears of joy that streamed down my face to ones of sorrow.

And that was the last time I saw a man, boy, male, until I saw you in the dirt outside.

Blood Relations

David Malouf CURRENCY PRESS

A family group gathers at Christmas about the dynamic and manipulative patriarch, Willy—a man with many pasts. They are joined by two inquisitive characters bent on uncovering his secret. The revelation uncovers a further mystery of guilt and reconciliation

ACT 2 SCENE 4: CATHY, 22 year old daughter of Willy, a 77 year old Australian of Greek origin

CATHY *and* EDWARD *watch* WILLY*'s ashes being scattered on the sea from a plane. They stand close together.*

CATHY:

I'm confused by all this, Willy. I'll have to think of you from now on as a different person. One I only half knew. Because half of what you told me wasn't true, was it? Whatever 'true' means. It didn't happen the way you told it. The funny thing is, I feel closer to you than ever, now that I know the whole story. It explains things I couldn't explain in myself, or connect to you, or to my mother. What a sad, sad world I came out of, Willy. I wish you'd told me earlier. I would have wept for you. And for her. And for those others. Did you think I wouldn't forgive you? I would have. I'm weeping now. I'm happy—I can't help being—but I'm weeping too. Look: Hilda's roses: this is what she's been growing them for, all these years. And my tears.

Milo

Ned Manning CURRENCY PRESS

Milo and Di live on a hobby farm—he is a pipe dreaming visionary while she cuts the mustard in a high powered job in Foreign Affairs. A visit from an old mate and drought battered farmer, Toby, and his long suffering wife, Peg, precipitates a thunderstorm of pent up fury.

ACT 1 SCENE 2: PEG, married to Toby. Works the farm with Toby.

The kitchen table after dinner. PEG *and* DI *are having a drink.*

PEG:

Personal, economical. You name it. We'll be lucky to get through another year. It breaks my heart. It's like a huge black cloud has descended on our place. Nothing makes any sense any more...

I don't know, maybe we should have sold out years ago but Toby wouldn't hear of it. The last twelve months have been unbearable. The worst of my life. I literally went off the air for a while. I couldn't stand it any more.

I was pregnant, we'd had a dud wheat crop, terrible season, plus the fuckin' interest rates. We'd borrowed to do some fencing that had to be done. When the wheat crop failed we'd had to borrow more. Then Jock carks it. Toby went for weeks without talking. He was like a zombie. We fought. I belted him in an effort to get some response out of him. It's pathetic. Here was I, eight months pregnant, belting into him. Dunno what the fuck I thought I was doing. When Toby's in one of his silent moods there's only Artie to talk to and as much as I adore him, not much change to be had out of a baby. I try to talk to Tobe but when things are this bad he just withdraws. Just as I'm about to pack up and piss off he arrives home with some little gift.

I, I uh, I had a bit of a fling with the Stock and Station Agent a while back. Before Artie came along of course. I never told Toby. He was flat out harvesting. I felt bad about it but, you know what? It was really exciting. It was like a little adventure. I think it stopped me going crazy.

It wasn't really serious but, in a strange way, it made me feel special. And really horny!

[DI *goes to* MILO'*s dope tin near the bath. She takes out a ready-rolled joint. She lights it and shares it with* PEG.]

I used to run into him in town when I was shopping. He's really nice. A bit more three dimensional than most cockies. He treated me as though I had half a brain. Anyway, Tobe was working really late and getting up at sparrow fart so I hardly ever saw him. I was looking after the rest of the place: the stock, sales, anything that didn't involve the harvest. We had a few drinks after the sale one day. I started getting that feeling, you know that feeling. I won't go into the gory details but you can imagine the rest. We ended up like a couple of school kids in the back of his ute.

After that we'd meet in town when I was shopping, spend a few hours wildly fucking, then I'd head home with the groceries with a big smile on my face.

That delicious feeling of guilt and excitement... a dynamic cocktail. Like wagging school.

Steal Away Home

Phil Motherwell   CURRENCY PRESS

Jack Stewart is a petty thief whose world is thrown into confusion when a chance encounter leads him to question his parentage and reveals his hidden Aboriginal forebears.

PAT, a middle-aged woman known as Aunty Pat to the drinkers at the Morning Star Hotel. She is an elder in the Aboriginal community.

PAT:

The news spread far and wide through the bush when the white man came to our land. We heard that dead people were coming back from the sea, with skin white like pipe-clay. We felt that each of them must be linked to us in some way. That each would find his place among us. They showed us such wonders...

[*She plays with a bottle as though she has never seen it before.*]

You see this sea-shell the white man left behind? Never found one like that on our beaches, smooth sides, dirty-looking brown colour, but you can see inside. Funny that we don't find them around here. What sort of fish would live in there? Wonder how he comes out through such a small hole? Some kind of jellyfish, maybe? Wonder what they call him?

While we were still dazzled by their trinkets, the white man was fencing off all the water, leaving us thirsty.

They dared to take our children away from us...

You can't tear a kid away from his people like that—give him nothing in return.

A kid attacked me one time, a white kid right out of the blue. He wouldn't have been more than four years old. He just flew at me—calling me all kinds of filthy names, belting me with his little fists—he knocked a full bottle out of my hands and smashed it to smithereens...

He flew straight past me and threw himself down in the middle of the street, crying his eyes out, screaming that he wanted to die. Wanted a car to run him down... I'm down on my knees picking up the pieces...

I look up and he's watching me put the broken pieces in the brown paper bag. Next thing I'm rocking him in my arms and he's cried himself to sleep... His mother had no time for him, neither did his dad. He's heard them talking and he wanted to die...

White people watch over their children too. They love them in their own way, and dream of a good life for them... 'My son will learn to work and save, our wealth will grow in his hands, and our name will be respected'... We want something different for ours. We want them to share with each other, look out for each other. We sing charms to make them generous.

Atlanta

Joanna Murray-Smith   CURRENCY PRESS

Atlanta is named after the NASA spacecraft orbiting Perth at the moment of her conception. She stands out from her confident, well educated friends through her awareness of a deeper, darker side of life. Sensing this awareness, her friends are stirred in different ways, particularly after Atlanta's death. The play probes the nuances of friendship and the ways we deal with loss.

ATLANTA, 29, a poetic, disturbed young woman, haunted by the past but infatuated with the future. She belongs uneasily to the world of the group, always somehow dislocated from the modern world and admiring it.

ATLANTA *is alone.*

ATLANTA:

I was walking through fields. They were beautiful European fields, green and covered with red Poppies. There was a path through the fields. I wanted to walk through the grass, but I heard my mother's voice up ahead of me telling me to keep to the path, that the grass was too wild to walk through. I couldn't disobey my mother. I was walking along the path and I turned to look for my mother, but she wasn't there. On either side of the path there were little mounds of earth with trap doors in them. When I bent to look closer I heard voices. I called: 'Mother.' And a voice came out of the earth. It said: 'I'm here, darling. I'm in here.' It was my mother's voice. I called through the door: 'Come out, mother!' and I tried to open the door but it was locked or jammed. She called out to me: 'I can't come out, darling, but you keep walking, keep walking through the fields.' And I said: 'But when will I see you?' And she said: 'We can't come out, but you can speak to us even though we're buried under the earth. We're all here. Your father is over there, down the path. Your grandmother Rose is three mounds down.' I walked further along the path and I spoke through the earth. I said: 'Hello Grandmother.' And she said: 'Hello Atlanta. Pleased to meet you.' Suddenly I thought— how terrible, how awful—everyone buried alive! So I ran back along the path and all along the way voices were calling out to me, calling out for me to stop. And when I came to my mother's mound I called: 'MOTHER...! MOTHER...!' I dug away the earth around the door, clawing at the dirt, pulling it away, trying to get her out. But there was so much earth. And then I saw the earth move a little and I pushed my hand in and I felt something soft and alive. So I took hold of it and I pulled. And out of the earth came a bird. It was a seagull with a broken neck. I was standing holding a dead bird in my hands and one of the feathers dropped from the bird and floated down and when it touched the earth it turned into a poppy.

ATLANTA

ATLANTA *is alone.*

ATLANTA:

Something in me just reaches a point where the only way it can be satisfied is to imagine breaking glass. I want to physically propel my body through a window, I want to break the glass with my limbs. I want to walk straight through. Straight through glass. But I never do anything, because actually I'm a terrible wimp and absolutely detest blood and guts of any sort. I never saw *Platoon* or *The Deer Hunter* or anything like that because I absolutely cannot stand blood, even fake blood. So the actual reality of cutting myself is pretty revolting and I don't do it. But I imagine it. And one day, well, I wouldn't be surprised if I actually got up off my bottom and did it! Coming out from under the glass, from seeing life through the past, through other people's lives... Can I break through it? Can I live my own life? Breaking through glass... There's something so beautiful about it...

Moments of falling. Something grows up inside of me, like a monster blown up with air. It takes me over like some diabolical orgasm. I go walking through glass, that is what I do. I go walking and the glass breaks all around me and somehow... I get through it to the other side... and there is light there, light there and hope...

Honour

Joanna Murray-Smith   CURRENCY PRESS

Gus and Honor have a comfortable, middle-class, middle aged marriage. What happens when that marriage suddenly stalls? When shared values and responsibilities no longer coalesce? When the opportunity arises for one life to be renewed, but at the expense of the other's happiness and security? Gus leaves his wife of thirty-two years for a younger woman, Claudia.

SCENE 12: SOPHIE, 24 year old daughter of Honor and Gus

SOPHIE *has met* CLAUDIA *for the first time.*

SOPHIE:

[*to* CLAUDIA] I wish—I wish I was more— [*Beat.*] Like you. Like you. You're so—you're so clear. You seem so clear about things. Whereas I'm—I'm so—I can never quite say what I'm—even to myself, I'm so inarticulate. [*Beat.*] Some nights I lie awake and I go over the things I've said. Confidently. The things I've said confidently and they—they fall to pieces. [*Beat.*] And where there were words there is now just—just this feeling of—of *impossibility*. That everything is—there's no way through it—

[*Pause.*]

[*progressively breaking down*] I used to feel that way when I was very small. That same feeling. Not a childish feeling—well, maybe. As if I was choking on—as if life was coming down on me and I couldn't see my way through it. What does a child who has everything suffer from? Who could name it? I can't. I can't. [*Breaking.*] But it was a—a sort of—I used to see it in my head as jungle. Around me. Surrounding me. Some darkness growing, something—organic, alive—and the only thing that kept me—kept me—*here*—was the picture of Honor and of Gus. Silly. [*Beat.*] Because I'm old now and I shouldn't remember that anymore. Lying in bed and feeling that they were there: outside the room in all their—their warmth, their—a kind of charm to them. Maybe you're right and it was—not so simple as it looked, but they gave such a strong sense of—love for each other and inside that—*I* felt—*I* felt loved. And since I've gotten older I don't feel— [*Weeping.*] I feel as if all that—all the—everything that saved me has fallen from me and you know, I'm not a kid any more. No. I'm not a kid any more. But I still feel—I need—I need—

[*Pause.*]

Sorry.

Love Child

Joanna Murray-Smith   CURRENCY PRESS

Anna is a film editor with a political conscience and a collection of Helen Garner. She lives in a stylish house with all the designer trimmings. Billie is a soapie actress and proud of it. She doesn't believe in causes and never reads anything well-written. This first encounter between mother and daughter could change their lives forever. It's a scene Billie has played over and over in her mind. For Anna it's a shocking surprise.

ANNA, a film editor, Billie's mother

The play is set in ANNA'*s designer home.*

ANNA:

[*to her daughter*] Of course later generations have had to reinvent us. Somewhat shabbily. To justify their own apathy. I look around me now and I feel sad that—Well, it was just such an amazing time. It sort of gets more and more amazing—as if it was some kind of enclosed time. Sort of unto itself.

I was at university and I sort of fell in with a group—and they were right at the heart of what was going on. I'd never encountered anything like them! I'll never forget the first time I saw Douglas Hatfield smoking these enormous reefers up the back of the caf. I thought he was Jim Morrison and Jean Paul Sartre rolled into one. He—he was sort of the reason I got involved. I was such a timid thing and they were—they were so fierce! I was attracted to their— well, I don't know. They believed in justice. They believed in fighting for... Where would we be without the sixties? It's like we rose up to claim the future...

It's amazing how the myths sneak up on you. We were completely caught up in the moment. We were very active on campus. Vietnam and all that was raging. We had a conscientious objector staying with us for a month—what was his name? Fred? No, Frank. Frank. He introduced me to Patti Smith. Anyway, he kept trying to crawl into bed with me. I nearly blew the whistle!

I nearly got chucked out of uni. We barricaded the doors leading out of the Dean's office. He had to call security to get out. We'd painted his station wagon with... something. That was the night we—My God, the Rolling Stones were playing at Kooyong. I had to hitch and... I don't think I ever got there... Astrid was devising a play about patriarchal—No, no, that was another time... There were all these gorgeous women running around with all these—well, they were such drips now that I think about it! We were all on the pill and it was—it wasn't like now—it was messy, all those relationships. But I was under a spell—Parents, parents' friends, the suburbs, all those boring expectations just crashed.

BILLIE, a soap actress, Anna's daughter

ANNA's home, a little later.

BILLIE:

[to her mother] It was one of those things that poisoned my blood so slowly, I didn't recognise it. I always denied that I wanted to know. I always said: If she doesn't want me, I don't want her. [Pause.] You. [Pause.] Isn't it funny? All the 'hers' are 'yous' now.

[ANNA looks at BILLIE, finding this terribly difficult to hear.]

Then one day I was watching a movie with a friend. Ridiculous really. A kind of Hollywood tearjerker. Ordinary People.

Very emotionally manipulative—the way those American films are. Well, of course they are—that's why they work. And this child in the family is in so much pain. And the actor was fantastic. Everyone was fantastic. Mary Tyler Moore was the stitched up mother who couldn't cope, couldn't love, couldn't be loved. And the child was the walking illustration of the mother's disability. And the whole thing just... shifted something in me. I felt this huge... ball, rolling inside of me and I thought well, this film isn't my story, but this mother, child, family, tragedy, feeling, unfeeling, all of it: that's me. That's this great, grief inside of me. [Pause.] I waited. I knew what I had to do and that made the waiting tolerable. Just knowing that I had to find you was in itself a relief. When they died, I couldn't help it—I just felt like I was about to soar...

BILLIE

ANNA's home, a little later.

BILLIE:

[to her mother] You made sure! You! What was it you made sure of, exactly? Where were you? What did you secure for me? You have no idea! You wouldn't know the first thing about what was good for me, what I had, or missed, or lost! There are all kinds of liberties I might have had if my parents had been of my blood. I could have hated them and bitched about them and left and come back and left, I could have betrayed them and abandoned them and returned and fought—all those privileges of a blood connection. I could have pushed to be free of them because I would have known that I could never be free. We would have been blood. Temper or whim or anger—nothing could have budged that one fact. If it's not a blood tie, nothing's dependable. All those shifts of feeling are so much more dangerous, because there is nothing to stop you from walking away. There is nothing... biological... to beckon you back. That's a big strain to live with. Somewhere good manners came into it. I couldn't be a real child, because I might hurt them and frighten them and frighten myself. So don't tell me you 'looked into them'. You didn't look anywhere. You didn't know anything.

BILLIE

ANNA's *home, a little later.*

BILLIE:

[*to her mother*] I thought you'd be so... hungry for me. That you would sit me down and feed me soup and tell me boring, comforting stories about your Indonesian wallhangings and you'd be so proud of me. Because I am successful. And I am attractive and slim and clever. And reasonable. And you would... hold me.

[*Silence as* BILLIE *and* ANNA *stare across the room at each other.*]

You're not my mother.

[ANNA *looks at her.*]

Do you feel that way? Do you feel that there is a tremendous space there. Not social. Something, you know, down deep in the chromosomes, something so... crucial—that we cannot see it or name it.

[BIILIE *looks away.*]

I will raise my children myself. So that when they are twenty-five, they don't have to be standing in strange living rooms, introducing themselves... I'm sorry if that upsets you.

I am what I have made of myself. I have dreams full of little children in tiny shoes. I dream the caramel smell of their soft skulls and their sweet see-through skin. And the children all have a particular expression in their eyes and when I catch a glimpse of myself in department store windows, I recognise it. Do you know what I dream of, Anna? I dream of myself.

ANNA

ANNA*'s home, a little later.*

ANNA:

[*to her daughter*] I didn't know what to do when Ed left. I wanted to be free. I thought I knew. It had to happen. But it felt as if my head had moved faster than my heart. I've been so skilled in taking all the facts and weighing them and making the right decision. You know, like a chemist. Like an alchemist. As if this thing inside me can be put in its place, this, this place where... where the feelings are kept.

　　[*Pause. Silent tears as she breaks.*]

Yes, I dreamt of you... I dreamt of a tiny baby crying in non-existent rooms. I climb out of my bed and walk through corridors searching for you and this terrible... this terrible realisation that I have had a child that I haven't been caring for, I have left it somewhere and forgotten it. And the dread! The loss... I have *longed* for you. For years I've lived in front of windows, catching glimpses of you through all the different parts of me. My heart. My head. My eyes. Sometimes just sensible thoughts: what school you're at. How tall you are. And then others... others too... Wondering what might have happened if I—And all the time, the knowledge that if I let go, I will lose myself. Like a giant wave that will fall over me and I will drown...

　　[*She drops her hands.*]

When I got your letter, I spent long hours thinking about a future I never thought I would have.

　　Don't you see—all those years, all that time, it creates these tiny divisions, like borders, like borders on a single territory. But you are mine. I am yours.

BILLIE

ANNA*'s home, a little later.*

BILLIE:

[*to her mother*] As a child I had these stomach pains that used to just take me over. Seize me up. No doctor could find the cause.

Psychosomatic. Agonising pain—like, like an ulcer. Doctor after doctor my parents took me to. And they were sweet people, my parents. Sweet and stupid and so unlike me, it was a joke! All those years wondering what my pain was. And then when they sat me down one day at the kitchen table and told me I wasn't really theirs—suddenly it all made sense. And I knew. Just like I told you. That I had to find my mother. And then the Adoption Service told me: She's dead.

[ANNA *is staring shell-shocked at* BILLIE.]

And it happened so slowly. That this feeling built. This—look, it sounds like madness, but it was as if all the fences that keep thoughts neat and orderly and real inside my head fell apart and there were no barriers to what might be... And the thought just came to me. What. What if. What if I. What if there were. What if there were *another* mother? Another mother. Sort of the same age. Who gave her daughter away. Her daughter the same age? What if she could become my mother? What if a daughter could possess a mother simply by naming her?

And then the details fell into place. You can access medical records. It you're a doctor. And Stuart was a doctor. And that sweet weak creature loved me so much that he would do anything for me. Like find out who else gave birth to a daughter that day. What other mother gave away her child that day? And perhaps a mother could be made simply by a daughter appearing out of the past to say: I am your daughter. As if she were really her mother. As if she really *were* the mother. The *real* mother. The *right* mother? What will the chosen mother say when she opens the door to meet her daughter? Will she say: No. You're not Billie. After twenty-five years, *will she know?* And if she doesn't know—does she deserve to?

[*It all begins to dawn on* ANNA *what* BILLIE *is saying.*]

I looked through the medical records at the hospital where I was born and found a woman, called Anna. Who gave birth to a little girl called Billie on my own birthday. The very same day. In the very same town. Who also gave her child away. A woman who had never been repossessed by her real daughter. And so it was. That I found a free mother. A mother who had not been handed back her history.

[*Silence as* ANNA *stares, overwhelmed by shock.*]

Capricornia

Louis Nowra (from the novel by Xavier Herbert)

CURRENCY PRESS

A saga of life, set in the Northen Territory, circa 1929, Norman journeys into the heart of his own darkness.

ACT 3 SCENE 2: HEATHER POUNDAMORE, a hotel owner

In prison and waiting to be hung, HEATHER *speaks to* NORMAN, *his Aboriginal cellmate, of his father.*

HEATHER:

We were going to be married. I hadn't been in Port Zodiac five minutes before I met him. He was brash, rubbed everyone up the wrong way. But he had something. He came to Port Zodiac as a clerk, like Oscar. He bought himself a pearling lugger. He was always reckless. The Aborigines have a word for it. *Myall.* Wild creature. I loved him. I was naive and innocent then. Someone sent me a parcel. In it was a burnt cork. I asked Mark to tell me what it meant. He couldn't tell. He said it was a joke. So I asked a friend and she told me that they say that when men up here go combo he can never be with a white woman again unless he blacks her face. When I heard about it I confronted him and he admitted he had been with black women. That was it as far as I was concerned. I couldn't bear him to touch me. What a waste! What a waste of years! Now I think to myself, black women, white women, what difference does it make? If it had been a white woman I would have forgiven him. Absolutely stupid.

I wanted to tell you about your father and me. I knew a couple of things that you didn't know when you came to Capricornia. Your father killed a Chinaman—He ran away. Vanished as far as most people were concerned.

[*A beat.*]

But he actually didn't. He spent a lot of time fishing, trepanning under another name. I learnt to forgive him. As I do now.

[*She looks around into the police station.*]

Mark...

[JACK RAMBLE, *a maritime captain, appears.* NORMAN *immediately understands.*]

Crow

Louis Nowra   CURRENCY PRESS

An Aboriginal woman named Crow has been fighting the Government for years to win back a tin mine that is rightfully hers. Mercurial, stubborn, wilful and irreverent, she never gives in, even if at times she is her own worst enemy. The play is set in February 1942, just before and during the bombing of Darwin.

ACT 1 SCENE 2: CROW, mother to Vince and Michael (Boofhead)

Verandah of THOMPSON'*s house. Twilight. The sound of cicadas, etc.* THOMPSON, *a lawyer, is having a gin and tonic.*

CROW:

Don't you ever say that. About blacks and whites living together. That Compound is filled with kids whitefellas created. Yet all a man's got to do is just live with a black woman and you all laugh at him, turn your back on him—cos he's living out in the open, living honest. Everyone turned their back on Patrick, cause he was with me—living in the open—you did too. No, you all looked down on him and me. When he went to have a drink at the pub, no one would serve him. Yet all those men go slinking around creating all those kids in the Compound. We were alright out there by ourselves. I mean, he wasn't perfect, being a man, being Irish and all that—I mean, I used to think blackfellas were bullshitters until I ran into a few Irish fellas. Christ, they lay it on thick. He called me a goddess, a black Madonna, the fire of his loins—and that was only on the first date! I have Vince by him and think, well, it's all fine and dandy, he's working at the abattoirs, and next moment he's saying he's bought a gold mine—for peanuts. I did cause to utter, Mr Thompson, such pearls of wisdom as, 'Why would anyone sell a goldmine for peanuts?' But would he listen? He spent every penny on it. We go out there in the backblocks, we go inside with a torch and there it is—the whole cave sparkling like the Milky Way. Well, we're laughing and dancing and crying, deciding what dreams to make real... when a piece of gold falls on me. Just a flake, then another flake. The fella who sold it to us had done the old trick, put some gold in a shotgun and peppered the mine shaft... so we were left with a useless mine. So he drinks for a week, singing those sad Irish songs, don't the Irish have any happy ones? I nearly throttled him. Then some old prospector comes by and spots something and says, 'That's tin.' So, it's party time again. We didn't realise it would be all backbreaking toil for years. Everyone talking about us here back in Darwin—Pat living with me and not hiding it. But we eventually made a living, nothing grand, but it was an honest living, Mr Thompson.

[*Pause.*]

I worked every day for that mine, it's mine and our son's.

[*She downs her beer.*]

Thanks for the beer.

[*She goes.*]

ACT 1 SCENE 8: CROW

Outdoor cinema. Night. Canvas chairs everywhere, some on their sides, some open, some closed. THOMPSON *sits in a chair, pouring whiskey into an enamel cup.*

CROW:

Listen to me! Or I'll clout you! I come here five years ago to get back what was owed me—And immediately they took Vince and Michael from me and stuck them in the Compound. Hundreds of kids in there. Sleeping on concrete floors. For Vince it was bad enough. I mean, him and me, weeks after Patrick died, ran that mine by ourselves.

He was the man of the household and they shove him in there. You know what they did to Michael? You know him, he's special, he's got a lot of stuff we don't know about in his head. Cos of that, he makes a lot of mistakes. They stuck him in the sweatbox. He doesn't like things closing in on him at the best of times. They stick him in the sweatbox. Corrugated tin box, size of a dunny. Leave him in there for a week. Shoving food into it like he's some animal. The Boss of the Compound calling him Crazy Face. I couldn't do nothing for him. Now, I can. You can! If you don't, I'll tell everyone about Lily. I'll tell everyone that you've been fucking me. You won't be able to walk down the street without people staring at you. In court they'll turn their backs on you.

I want my son back. Get Michael out of jail, get me the mine and you can kill me.

[*Silence.*]

Whitefellas taught me very well. You'll get him out tomorrow.

[*Pause.*]

Get my son out and you can kill me.

ACT 2 SCENE 4: CROW

The Governor's house. Morning. The living room has been directly hit by a bomb. CROW *jumps up, furious, as if she's going to hit* THOMPSON. *She suddenly puts out her hand. He steps back.*

CROW:
Shake it—go on, shake it. It won't bite.

[*He shakes it gingerly.*]

That's the hand that shook Napoleon's. My husband shook my hand and said, 'That's the hand that shook Napoleon's.' He had shaken the hand of a man who had shaken the hand of a Frenchman who, in turn had shaken the hand of a Frenchman who had shaken Napoleon's hand.

[*She advances on* THOMPSON *and strokes his cheek.*]

These fingers have touched the cheek of my mother, who in turn has touched her mother's cheek, who in turn touched her mother's, stretching back and back, for thousands of years. These fingers have touched cheeks thousands and thousands of years old. I cannot tell you how many thousands of years because it is so many. Where we're standing was where mothers touched the cheek of their daughters for thousands of years. Now it's gone. This land belonged to us but was taken. I am not going to let these mongrels take the land that I worked with Patrick. I am not turning the other cheek. They can slap my cheek all they like, but I'm not going to turn it. I've learnt that. I'm gonna find my papers and keep them. After the war is over you and me are gonna fight them all over again.

The appeal was rejected behind our backs. Bet you they decided it last night over drinks—like a whim or something. Got here this morning nice and early and some clerk told me. A clerk! Look, Mr Thompson. I know I am stubborn. Got a bee in my bonnet, buzzing around. Stupid more than half the time. I do give cause to utter to myself: just give up, but I can't. When they took it from me and then my sons I could have caved in, given up and I did for a time, feeling real sorry for myself and then I thought, I gotta fight. Like Vince in the ring. Got to fight. I'm not gonna be forced to be a wanderer in my own land.

Radiance

Louis Nowra   CURRENCY PRESS

Three half sisters have drifted about as far apart as it's possible to drift, but when they meet again at the ramshackle house on stilts where they grew up, it's to do more than bury their mother. The play is set in North Queensland.

ACT 1 SCENE 2: NONA, the youngest sister

The living room. Afternoon. The three women are having a glass of champagne, having just brought their mother's ashes back from her funeral.

NONA:

Mum said he was really handsome. People called him the Black Prince. Every night I went to sleep dreaming of him. I know he was a bit of a bastard for leaving Mum, but, you know, he was my Dad. I'd never seen him, not even a picture but I knew I'd recognise him. He'd be tall, handsome. The Black Prince. 'Course, he wasn't there in Ayr. But when I saw the bucking horses, men trying to ride them, the bullocks, and the smells and crowd, I sensed him, sensed this would be the type of place he'd be. I took up with this bloke. Went with him from rodeo to rodeo thinking I would come across dad. That one day there would be this man, this guy, standing tall in his cowboy boots, leaning against a verandah post. You know, the silent type. He'd be grinning and I'd see him in me. Our eyes: they'd be the same and he'd recognise me, recognise that he had created me. Then I found out that the bloke I was with was married with four kids so I came back here. And in I come, I walk in and there's Mum in bed with this guy. And she smiles and hugs me like I'd never really been away all those months, so I thought, she's OK by herself—time I pissed off again, I knew I could look after myself. [*A beat.*] Maybe, now, the Black Prince'll hear about Mum dying and track me down, eh? [*A beat.*] And we'll all get to meet him.

ACT 1 SCENE 3: CRESSY, the eldest sister

Later. Evening. The women have been going through some of their old belongings and memories.

CRESSY:

[*to* NONA] Men and me don't get on. I had a man who used to stay. Sort of. I thought he stayed. There were no signs he was there... but I knew he stayed... I was on this disastrous tour of Europe... I took on a role when my voice wasn't ready for it. Every night I'd go out and try to sing it, but the music kept on overwhelming me. I felt like I was drowning. Every night I drowned. One morning I woke up and saw that all the furniture—writing tables, drawers, chairs, were all piled up on top of each other. I thought it was a practical joke by the musicians—a musician's idea of humour is a car accident—but the next morning, in a new city, there it was—all the furniture piled up again. Then the next town. I never heard a thing. I'd wake up in the morning, and there it'd be—these towers of furniture. I began to wake up in a sweat, wondering who was coming into my room at night and doing this while I slept. I blamed everyone, the musicians, the hotel staff, but it kept on happening. Maybe it was a poltergeist—But it wasn't. It began to affect my singing. Because while I was singing, I was thinking of what was going to happen that night when I slept. At the last moment, I'd change rooms and lie awake waiting for it to come in. Eventually I'd fall asleep and when I woke up—there it would be... my furniture piled up in the middle of the room. I didn't know what to do. I had someone sit with me all through the night. That helped, because it didn't come. Then one night I slept by myself and I woke up in the morning, not in my bed, but in the corner of the room. It had come in, lifted me out of my bed and put all the furniture on the bed. I was petrified. I didn't know what to do. I thought I heard it in the bathroom and so I cowered in the corner, huddled up in my blanket for hours, until my manager came and got me. I was late for my performance. The first time ever. I got her to check the bathroom but there was no one there. There was no poltergeist. I had done it... in my sleep. Overwork and strain, I guess.

ACT 1 SCENE 3: CRESSY

A few minutes later.

CRESSY:

[*to* NONA] She knew where I was. Where Mae was. All she had to do was visit. Once. Not good enough. Not to have a father and your mother not wanting to see you—

On visiting days, some parents would come, even from interstate and there I'd be, me and a few other girls with no visitors. And because we had no visitors the nuns would get us to do the laundry. To pass the time. To pass the time! There we were, us girls in the steam and stink of the laundry, with its smell of starch and dirty clothes. At first I would make believe we were in hell and I'd curse the nuns, say that I'd fuck the devil, but one day I saw a picture in one of the nun's magazines. It was a film star playing a Polynesian princess, wearing a sarong, hibiscus in her hair. She looked so beautiful, so exotic, so far from the laundry. And so I pretended to be her. I'd wrap a table cloth around me, put an hibiscus in my hair and sing to the other girls. They'd applaud me and I'd do it again and again, until I thought I was that princess, pretending the copper steam was the steam of a volcano I was about to throw myself into and sacrifice myself to the gods. But instead of throwing myself in, I won a singing scholarship. I came back here on the way to Sydney.

Mum said the wind was coming up from the island. The ancestors were telling me not to go. I walked out that door and made it as a singer. She didn't fight for me.

ACT 2 SCENE 1: MAE, the middle sister

The mud flats. The same night—early hours of the morning. The three women have been up all night.

MAE:

Shut up! I came up here. She was ill, but she was disappointed it wasn't you, or you. She lived like a derelict. I told her lies. [*To* CRESSY.] You were overseas, you'd be home soon. [*To* NONA.] You had an important job down south. [*Yelling.*] You understand! You understand how every time I told those lies why you weren't here, I hated you. I hated your selfishness. I hated you! And yet, I looked after her. I cleaned and washed her.

I came here because I was afraid. And humiliated. To go to court, to be called a criminal... do you know how humiliating that is? I came here because I wanted to know. I wanted to know where I came from, how I ended up the way I did. I'd take her down to the beach and I'd point to the island. I'd ask her: what happened, how did my great great grandparents get thrown off the island? She wouldn't answer. I wanted to know about my father. My relatives. About her. [*A beat.*] Sometimes she and I would talk. Not much. Sometimes she even said thank you when I bathed her. [*To* CRESSY.] I couldn't leave her. Too much of a sense of duty. Same old Mae. Isn't she a trouper? Isn't she just the best?

ACT 2 SCENE 2: CRESSY

The mud flats. An hour later. A distant glow from where the house is on fire.

CRESSY:

[*to* NONA] You were created from dirt—your father was dirt! He never raped her. [*A beat.*] It was me. He raped me! [NONA *gives an astonished laugh.*] Under the house.

[*Pause.*]

Under that burning house. [*To* MAE.] Me. Me playing under the house. He grunting like a pig. Hands under my dress, stabbing me in two. And I am moaning, moaning in pain, Nona.

[*Pause.*]

He was just one of Mum's boyfriends. If he walked down the street I don't think I'd even recognise him. He was going to drive away but his car had no petrol, so he went and bought a can. Mum laughed at him coughing and spluttering as he sucked on a tube to get it flowing into the tank. Then she went into town. I was playing under the house, and had forgotten him entirely when suddenly he was there putting his hands up my dress. I said no, but he hit me across the face. I struggled and screamed but he was too strong. He forced me up against one of the house posts. As he was doing it he kept kissing me with his mouth smelling of petrol. The pain. All this awful pain through my body like he was stabbing me in two. It was so excruciating that I bit into the post, wanting to bite it in two. He was grunting like a pig, biting me in the shoulder, his saliva in my ear. When he finished he warned me not to tell Mum but I wasn't quick enough in answering him, so he shoved the handle of a screwdriver up my rectum—I was crying out in agony—and he warned me that if I told anyone, anyone, about what had happened he would come back and put the screwdriver right through me. Then he drove away. I stayed under the house for hours crying and crying, trying to clean myself with some old rags. I didn't tell Mum. Then a few months later I realised I was having that man's baby. I tried to keep it from her until it was too late. You know what happened when I told her— she hit me. She said I was lying. That it wasn't her boyfriend—that it was one of the local boys and I was blaming him. She didn't believe me.

[*Pause.*]

I hated Mum for not believing me. But at least she kept you, pretended you were hers. [*Motioning to the tin of old photos.*] That's not your mother. I'm your mother, Nona. You were born because your so called Black Prince raped me.

Falling from Grace

Hannie Rayson   CURRENCY PRESS

Three women in their forties: one in medicine, one in the media and the other a business manager—power and authority in female hands. Best friends in a professional world, they are witty and erudite, passionate in pursuit of success and relentless in their pursuit of passion. They juggle careers, children and lovers. Their friendship is about to be tested over the question of public morality and the struggle to see who should be its guardian.

ACT 2 SCENE 3: MIRIAM ROTH, early 40s, gynaecologist and head of a medical research team trialing the drug, Zed 400

MIRIAM ROTH'*s rooms at the hospital.* MIRIAM *is in conference with her friend* JANET BROCK, *an investigative journalist.*

MIRIAM:

OK. If it turns out that all the results from the animal testing and all subsequent laboratory trials over two years were universally incorrect; that the pharmacology teams involved from three countries—that's the U.S. and Britain as well as us—if they're all wrong, as is the Australian Drug Evaluation Committee which is the most stringent in the world—so if we've all stuffed up—then yes—we're culpable. But let me just contextualise this for a moment and talk about what's at stake here. It's not just *my* research or *my* career we're talking about. If this tumbles over then we're seriously putting back the cause of women's health, twenty or thirty years. It's as simple as that. You see, the people who make decisions about what gets funded and who designs medical research are nearly all men. That's the way it is. Medicine as we know it is based on the assumption that maleness is the norm. OK? And this is understandable. Men know about what happens to men. And they fund what they're afraid of. The medical profession is very focussed on dramatic intervention. So a lot of resources are devoted to coronary and intensive care units and high tech hospitals. If we were serious about reflecting female needs, more of the resources would go into primary care and prevention. That's why when men get involved in reproductive medicine they go in for I.V.F. and playing with high tech toys. All the other stuff, like PMS, endometriosis, pelvic inflammatory disease, post natal depression—that's not where the action is. Never mind that PMS effects a vast proportion of the female population. Never mind that some women spend four or five days every month in such a state of illness and depression that they're suicidal. And do you think they care that this has a profound impact on equality issues? PMS makes some perfectly competent women unable to hold down a job. So you see for us to have got them to take something like this seriously enough to invest two million dollars is probably one of the most radical things this hospital has ever done. And to think that the whole struggle could be sabotaged, just because of this one G.P.... I can't tell you how wrong it is. The thing is, when you're dealing with such a conservative male hegemony like the Medical Board you may never inspire their passionate commitment to a project like this, but at least we'd secured their confidence. Now if that gets eroded... we're stuffed basically. I'm sorry to lay this on you but I have this rage inside me... and even though I don't know you very well, I have this feeling that you really do care about what's at stake here.

ACT 2 SCENE 13: SUZANNAH BROMPTON,
41 years old, editor of *Metro Magazine*, mother of Tessa, divorced from Hugh

SUZANNAH*'s ex-husband,* HUGH, *has just entered.*

SUZANNAH:

Don't give me any of your holier-than-thou fucking bullshit. I'm sick of it. I'm just so sick and tired of it. You know, you go on and on about all the things that are wrong with me, but the fundamental difference between you and I is that you've got a wife and a family. You've got someone there for you who really does care that you're OK. But I've been battling it out on my own for ten years. And no-one gives a shit.

You know what? I'll tell you something. I went down the country last weekend because I decided it was time I did something with that money Dad left me. It's not much, but it's enough to buy myself a little house in the country. And all this time, ever since I was a kid,

I've wanted to do that. Somewhere not far from town where I could have a vegetable garden and maybe some fruit trees. And a little cottage garden out the front with a lavender hedge. It's a little fantasy. Pathetic as it may sound. And so there I was in Castlemaine looking in the window of the real estate agent and all of a sudden I started crying. I was standing there in the main street with tears streaming down my cheeks. I couldn't stop myself. And do you know what it was? It was this real grief because I wanted to be doing it with someone else. And there isn't anyone else. [*Silence.*] I don't know why I told you that. Just to make myself look even more pathetic than I am already.

The Garden of Granddaughters

Stephen Sewell   CURRENCY PRESS

Max, a world renowned Australian conductor, returns unexpectedly to Melbourne with his wife, Moriley, for a family reunion. Their three adult daughters, Michelle, Fay and Lisa, are in various stages of decline, success and reproduction. Their granddaughters are full of hope, promise and childhood dreams.

ACT 1 SCENE 4: FAY

In the street. FAY *and her sister,* LISA, *stride on.*

FAY:

So what do you mean, 'Irving left me'?—Let's get one thing straight: Irving did not leave me, I left him; and I left him because he was a snivelling little slimy rat, NOT because he was a fat lecher, because as a matter of fact, Irving is not fat, and even though he's a conniving, deceitful, faithless scum-bucket, my sense of self-respect does not allow me to lower myself to demeaning accusations about his weight, hair-loss or state of personal hygiene; and as for what I do with my life in this delicate period of grieving following the irretrievable breakdown of my marriage; that, according to my therapist, is no one else's concern other than my own. So if you so much as mention anything to Mum and Dad about Morty or anyone else I may or may not be involved with at the moment, in no matter how fleeting or jocular manner you might do it, I'll cut your ovaries out, you got me...?

Look, Mum and Dad are only here for a few days and then they won't be back for another three years—We'll go to the zoo with them tomorrow, take them to the opera, do whatever they want; and nobody has to squeal, nobody has to turn it into a family psycho-drama; all we have to do is shoot the breeze, have a bit of fun together and they can just go away again as happy as Larry and none the wiser—Isn't that the way we should handle it?

[LISA: Isn't that a bit like lying?]

FAY: Of course it's lying! What do you want to do? Tell them the truth? Look at us! After fifteen years, you're still a struggling artist without two cents to rub together, my husband's about to go to jail for either carnal knowledge or grand larceny, hopefully whichever carries the longest sentence; the only one who's made a success of her life is Michelle, and even she's about to blow a gasket if she doesn't stop trying to be Super Mum—You call that a triumph of family dynamics? With a report card like that, it's a wonder we're not all being chased by people with butterfly nets. I'm not saying we're bad people, Lisa; I'm just saying we don't quite come up to scratch as *The Brady Bunch*.

Believe me, Lisa, this is the only way to handle parents: don't tell 'em what they don't want to know and they won't feel like they've got to do something about it. It's the sole basis of happiness in the contemporary family.

ACT 2 SCENE 2: FAY

Mietta's restaurant ante-room/dining room at night.

FAY:

[*thoroughly incensed, to her sister,* LISA] Yes, well at least I *was* married; I took the plunge, didn't I Lisa; and for your information, I loved Irving, and for as long as he came home at night, I was faithful to him, and that's the truth, Lisa: for nine years I was the perfect wife, and alright, we didn't have kids, but that wasn't my fault because what I found out in the final Gotterdammerung was that he didn't want kids because he'd been chasing every skirt he could catch since the wedding day when he'd found time to pork one of the flower girls on the way to the reception, and couldn't see any reason why he should start tying himself down now; that's what the bastard did to me: stopped me from becoming a mother so he could kick up his high-heels with whatever piece of fluff happened to blow across his path; so if I seem a little desperate in getting a man, Lisa, that's the reason: I want kids; I desperately, passionately, want kids and my time's running out because that prick wasted my life! [*Pause.*] I'm not a trivial person, Lisa... And apart from that, I've got quite a lot of fucking to catch up on.

ACT 2 SCENE 5: LISA

Mietta's restaurant dining room.

LISA:

[*to her sister,* FAY] You think I'd touch Morty Schwartzkopf? The name on the bottle of a brand of shampoo? You need your head read, Fay.

You've made some pretty outrageous bloody-minded remarks in your life, Fay, but that one's really got to take the cake. If you think I'd touch that greasy little meatball in a dinner suit, you not only need your head read, you need a complete overhaul from top to bottom! Not only am I not attracted to him in any way, but I find his very existence a blot on the dignity of the entire human race. Vain, pompous, arrogant, with the dress sense of a hedgehog and the subtlety of a chain-saw, he has got to be the most personally disgusting, violently backward, pettily boorish and thoroughly repulsive excuse for a man I have ever met. I wouldn't touch him if you threatened me with twelve hours of Richard Carleton tapes. I wouldn't date him if he and Paul Lyneham were the last two men in the world! Morty's the kind of human Lego set that makes a bag of wet cement look exciting! He's revolting, Fay! Absolutely, unashamedly, irredeemably revolting; and the very idea of him and me together makes me physically sick! How could you? The man's a human fur-ball!

ACT 2 SCENE 13: MORILEY

The kitchen at night. MORILEY *is standing by the radio. Her husband,* MAX, *her daughters,* MICHELLE, LISA *and* FAY, *and her teenage granddaughter,* PAULA, *are looking at her. After a pause,* MICHELLE *attempts to speak.*

MORILEY:

Shut up, I've heard enough. [*Pointing at each of the women.*] You're wrong, you're wrong, you're wrong and you're wrong. [*Proceeding to lay down the law.*] We did not come here to check up on you, and we did not come here to interfere with your lives. If you wouldn't listen to us when you were five years old, I don't see why we should expect you to start listening now. Whether or not Michelle got her picture on the front page of *Truth is* completely beside the point. It is now and it was then, and what prurient interest a pack of dirty old men might have had in the youthful exuberance of a generation that set out to challenge and confront the world on the point of nuclear extinction seems quite irrelevant beside the huge strides this country made as a result of their efforts. As for Fay and Lisa, their lives are theirs to live, and if they don't have a proper moral sense now, I don't see how they'll ever get one; but for everyone's information, I happen to believe that they know exactly where they're going and have no difficulty in distinguishing right from wrong and are living according to the principles in which they believe. [*To* MAX.] As for you, you're the father and ring-leader of three of the most quarrelsome girls who've ever been put on the face of this earth, but I'd like to remind you that no parent is responsible for their children forever, and one day you have to wake up and see that they're adults... They're adults, Max, our babies are adults, and now we have to respect them; the decisions they make and the lives they choose. Our role as guardians is finished... [*To her daughters.*] We're here to love you, that's all; to love you and to take pride in you and to watch our grandchildren grow: that's the final pleasure of our lives, and that's why we're here. It's for the children, all our lives were for you children, and now it's for the grandchildren, our granddaughters; and we love every one of you as our future and our hope.

The Family

Jill Shearer

CURRENCY PRESS

Sarah, newly appointed to internal investigations, is an intelligent and principled graduate police officer. She soon uncovers a long-buried case that implicates her police officer father as an accessory to police corruption. Thirty-five years of denial and guilt have left heavy scars beneath the skin of the family and she has to decide whether to pursue an investigation that will bring disgrace upon her father and possibly destroy her mother. The play is set in present day Brisbane.

ACT 1 SCENE 2: SARAH, 35, a Police Inspector

SARAH *and* ALAN'*s apartment.*

SARAH:

[*to* ALAN, *also a police officer*] No! It's simply the wrong time. No matter what your mother, your sisters or your aunties might say. I'd have to drop out for a minimum of four months and frankly, I'd want more time. When it does happen I want at least a year, a year to get to know our baby. That can't happen now. And don't start on biological clocks. Yes, I'm thirty-five... but there's still time. [*Silence.*] I know you don't like me working in Homicide. Huh. Look at me in my sleep sometimes and wonder. [ALAN *moves away, almost violently.*] Homicide? It never appealed to me either. I was sent there. My first murder, my first body, I was physically sick. I had to leave them and walk off into the bush. You're right. I have changed. You have to. Small things. The victim's handwriting, a half-used lipstick... and children, tiny ripped T-shirts... horrible... scuffed shoes. Know what protected me? Helped me? Unravelling the truth. Looking into people's eyes and gradually beginning to know when they were telling the truth, the half truth. It's like a giant jigsaw. Each new piece brings you closer.

It's still the most important thing. It's what the Law's supposed to be about, isn't it? Being willing to stake everything, to swim upstream if need be. But not at the cost of our life. Never that. Yes, I know you're not happy with what I'm doing now but it's my job.

ACT 2 SCENE 3: SARAH

SARAH *at home. She has an old report and is trying to decide whether or not to read it.*

SARAH:

[*to* ALAN] He 'might've known her. Might've seen her around.' Alan, Dave was at my christening yet Dad can't remember whether he was in Vice with him or not. He might still be a Sergeant, but he's always had a memory like a steel trap. Me, Emma, we never tried to lie. He'd remember. Trip us up. Yes, he's been under stress, but he hasn't changed, not that much.

Suddenly I couldn't sit there a moment more. [*She stands, hugging herself... cold. Shakes her head.*] Something. Maybe I imagined it. [*Pause.*] Hunting dogs. It was dreadful. All the time we were talking images kept coming. Him throwing me up in the air, birthdays... candles. Silly, trivial things and yet something else was still in me, registering, like a machine, a clock I couldn't turn off. His eyes. Like someone else's. At times as if I was interrogating someone whose cunning... was always keeping one step... The way he started moving his head. [*She puts her hands to her face. She stares at the report.*] Something.

Report into the death of Ann Marie... It took ages to find it. Row on row of them. Dust. Mould. See? Everywhere the smell of... death. No one to battle her case, eh? No public to get upset about her death. In the end... suicide. Prostitutes have no feelings. Right? [*Picking up the report.*] And yet it hardly feels like a real person any more? [*Laughing.*] What happens to us? Before I entered the Service I'd read the news. Murders felt like they were real. Flesh and blood. A photo in the newspaper, a relative on telly... and I'd cry. Cry. I trusted people. Now I believe no one.

Hunting dogs, that's what we become. No wonder you and I, we can't love. Feel like we should. [*Silence. She stares at the report.*] So what am I to do? Alan? Let sleeping dogs lie?

ACT 2 SCENE 4: SARAH

SARAH *is with her parents,* BARBARA *and* FRANK, *and* EMMA, FRANK*'s younger daughter, at their home.*

SARAH:

So there were no bruises. No autopsy either. Burial took place next day. Witnesses not interviewed, the few statements that were taken. Here... unsigned. How the hell did they do it? Get away with it. [*Pause.*] No lineup called. Ill-written reports. More pages ripped out. [*Dropping the report on a chair.*] Collusion, collusion. And they called that an investigation. Ah, but a year later someone must have asked something. Another investigation. See? [*Reading.*] 'And was it true that, although you were barely a member of the Force at that time, they set you up with one of the girls?'

'And was it also true that even although you had left the branch... that for more than six months after... [BARBARA *stands.*] ... you continued the affair with the girl known as... Ann.'

[SARAH *takes her mother's hand.*]

That last time we came down. Remember Mum? The Police Motorcycle Stunt Team led by Sergeant Frank Stevenson. Mum and I down near the fence. And then we heard it. The roar of exhausts, louder... louder. Twenty motor bikes in formation, revving, growling, like demons on a leash. Then they began moving in across the clipped grass. Back and forth in intricate manoeuvres. Suddenly you broke away. The crowd fell silent as ten men appeared, carrying a huge platform. They began fitting it on to your bike, onto you. Strapping bars of steel onto your back, across your chest, your neck. Then they began climbing on it, crawling on it, making way for more... more... until finally thirty-five men stood upon it! You were part of a huge cross. A crucifix of bike... men... and steel! The crowd went quiet as you revved, roared the engine up, then cut her back and carefully began your circuit. Like a wave, the applause, the shouts as slowly you rode by us. And I... [*To* BARBARA.] adored him... loved him.

ACT 2 SCENE 4: BARBARA, wife of Frank (a Police Sergeant)

A short while later.

BARBARA:

[*to* FRANK] Someone had beaten her up. A week before, as a warning I suppose. I read it in the paper. You left it. On that page! Left breakfast. Stood up one morning without a word, like it had been between us for months and went to work... and left that page, that picture on our kitchen table. Six weeks. You met her six weeks after we were married. Lying in bed, hearing him come in. And then smelling it... her, that perfume. Pretending to be asleep. You'd brush my shoulder and I'd want to scream, 'Don't touch me! Get out of my bed. My...'

> [*He tries to reach her. She backs away.*]

We stayed together. You did in those days. And then suddenly it stopped. I never smelt... her... it... again.

I used to lie awake, wondering what had become of her. Strange, in the end it became almost like an obsession. As if I... knew her. Cared about her. We stayed together. I was pregnant. Where could I go? [*To* SARAH.] Something changed, got better the day he held you. He wanted you! He seemed almost glad of me. And then they brought him back here again and I wanted to scream, 'It's not fair.' What you've done to him! To me! Back from clean air to that... job! And then that Inquiry. He wasn't guilty then. [*Half laugh.*] Not then. I know that. [*Pause.*] I've always tried to keep busy. That helps.

[*to* FRANK] But for so long, here, the memory. It was like something... another body... between us in the bed. I went to church more. It can be... a comfort. We managed.

> [*Silence. The lights dim briefly. The family,* BARBARA, *move to stand alone, staring outwards. Silence. Lights change to blue.*]

The colour of the sea at this time of year is turquoise. Grading out beyond the breaker line on some dull days to shades of deepest blue. Frank says that's where the tailor are.

State of Shock

Tony Strachan   CURRENCY PRESS

The story of Eddie Thomas, based on the true story of Alwyn Peter, a Queensland Aborigine charged with murder in 1979. In September 1981 an historic legal precedent was set in the Queensland Criminal Court when Peter was released on parole. After a year of gathering expert evidence, his defence lawyers presented a case showing that men like Peter were shaped and destroyed by their artificially created environments on Queensland reserves.

ACT 2 SCENE 2: MRS JENNY BOB,
Eddie's grandmother, in her 60s

The visitors' house at the reserve at night. O'CONNOR, *the Director, is drinking.*

JENNY:

My sister cannot see my face any more. She can't see the trees or dust from the kangaroos. When she looks up, she can't see the clouds like white camels walking across the blue sky. No, Director. My sister doesn't see the sun sinking into the sea at Yambala. It's night all the time for her now. You can see these things, Director, but you are blind too. You sold my family and my people for thirty pieces of silver when you took us from Yambala twenty years ago, and three years ago you sold my sister's eyes.

I have talked for so many years to you for improvement in our lives, but you never change, because you are empty inside. Why you shaking your head, Director? You got something inside, you got a belief? Do you believe in Jesus Christ? No. You believe in your family? Maybe your wife. But I see no love for woman in your eyes. You believe in your Parliament? Or this British justice? I don't think so. What about the land? Aaah, yes. Yes, you believe in the land, don't you? Make a hole in it here, dig up over there, take the oil or bauxite, then put the money in the bank and finish with it. [*Pause.*] This land is bleeding, Director. You cut into the body, pull out the bones and leave the bleeding flesh. This Cape York land cries out. I have heard it.

ACT 2 SCENE 3: JENNY

Prison cell. Daytime. JENNY *enters and stands looking at her grandson,* EDDIE. *He turns away.*

JENNY:

You wondering where your grandmother been, eh...? She been sitting in her broken down old chair outside her little house, thinking. Six weeks. That old chair just held onto me, Eddie, wouldn't let go. I talk to it, I say, 'My grandson he's in Stuart Prison, I got to go down and see him.' And the chair say to me, say, 'That grandson of yours, he's no good; he kill beautiful girl, a girl he loved.' 'That don't matter,' I say, 'He's down there in that prison, no one to talk to him...' But still that old chair don't let go of me. 'He just another one drank too much and kill his own family,' it says. 'Hundreds like him all over this State, this year, year before, next year... Forget him,' says my chair.

[EDDIE *turns to look at her.*]

But it's hard to forget, boy; hard to forget you are part of me, no matter what happens... Six weeks I was sitting like this. Then I got a letter from the court people in Brisbane. And I showed that old chair the letter. That chair put on its glasses and it read what the court people wanted to do. It saw that they wanted to find out all about your case so everyone can understand properly about all this killing, and about reserves and about Yambala, our country. This letter said, 'We want to know Eddie's story.' And you know what? That old chair, it thought a little while, and then it let go of me at last... And I got on the Fokker Friendship and come to see my grandson.

[EDDIE *rises, goes to her and is enfolded.*]

I hope you have some forgiveness for an old woman.

ACT 2 SCENE 3: JENNY

A short while later.

JENNY:

Eddie. Your gran'pa told you a story. You forgot. It is a story of children, long time ago. You see, one morning they went off from camp to look for Blue Emperor butterflies. They were out quite a while and they saw all kinds, but couldn't find a blue one at all, see. Then the eldest boy saw one bigger than anything from his dreams. He shouted to the others and they all chased the Blue Emperor till they reached a big lagoon. The butterfly went here, then there to all the bushes and flowers round the water's edge. They sat watching it for a long time and they were very happy. Then they heard a noise like thunder. It came closer and closer, and the eldest told the other children to get ready for the rain. They all looked up in the sky, but nothing. Then they saw a man on a big horse with white legs, galloping through the trees, and a dozen others coming behind. These men on their horses galloped straight into the children. The oldest boy rolled into the water and he watched as the bones of his brothers and sisters and cousins cracked and broke under the horse's legs. He lay very still in the water as the blood of his family flowed into the lagoon all around him, the blood of those eight little children. The man on the red horse took out his knife and cut his initials and a big number eight in an old tree by the water's edge. There are many trees like this in this country. [*Pause.*] Your gran'pa saw all that. He came out of that lagoon and lay down for three days. His legs couldn't carry him away. [*She pats his hand.*] We are all children of that red lagoon. You found your story now. You will never forget. [*She stands.*] Time for me to go. Goodbye, my boy.

Barmaids

Katherine Thomson   CURRENCY PRESS

Nancy and Val know how a good pub should be run. When they step behind the bar they are in control. The 'first-ins' and the 'all-days' know who might cut off their beer and turf them out. But Nancy and Val are professional barmaids who recognise the value of service and loyalty. They look after their regulars. Then one day The Arms is bought by a syndicate and accountants start hatching new schemes to bring in more customers.

ACT 1 SCENE 5: NANCY, 40s, indefatigable. Married and divorced three times. Loves her customers, being a barmaid she sees as a long-term career. Partial to a drink she has worked in 'The Arms' for twenty-odd years, and is eternally optimistic. She floats, she flirts. She prides herself on the clarity of her speech and the fact she still has her hair set on a weekly basis.

The front bar of a hotel in a port town or city in Australia.

NANCY:

Oh my god. Oh shit. I'm insane, I'm insane, I'm insane. I don't do too many things I could get locked up for. But this'd have to be one of them. Tuesday. Unpremeditated. Which is what you say when you want to get off.

Well all right I did put the brick in the car. I *was* driving to the house of the creep who still hasn't called me with the brick right next to me, sitting on the passenger seat. With a note. And a rubber band *if* I felt like attaching the note to the brick which I did. But my intention—and this was only if any throwing was going to happen which I still wasn't sure of 'til I got there—my intention was perhaps to throw it more or less to his front porch or... through the windscreen of his poncy RX7, but until I got there, and I'll stand up and say this in court—please don't let me go to court—until I got there I had not even considered the option of sailing it through that huge plate glass window that is, I admit, basically the entire front of the house.

[*Pause.*]

It was a firm type of note, he'll know it was from me. 'No one fucks me around like this. I hope for your sake you've got amnesia.' Just sort of lobbed it. Left my hand before I knew it. My only hope is it didn't hit the dog. It was pretty much where his little cushion is. Anyway... first rule of the bar. If you want respect you have to earn it. First rule of the bar.

ACT 2 SCENE 1: NANCY

THE FRONT BAR.

NANCY:

I'm sorry? What's it to you where I slept? What if I did sleep in my car, it's my car I can do what I like in it. Of course I didn't sleep in the bloody car, don't be ridiculous.

I suppose I'm still working here. [*She announces to the clientele as she pours beers.*] I'm going to the ladies, no idea how long I'll be gone, you're getting one drink so sit on it because for all I know I could be in there for bloody ages. I don't have any change so yez can all pay me back later which I'm sure'll make you feel better. [*Pause.*] And when I come back I'll be nicer to you... sorry.

[*She takes her handbag and Hungry Jack's coffee to an area which suggests cubicles and basins. She stands looking in the mirror, lonely and trying not to cry.*]

The worse thing, who can say what's worse... the worse thing is how she had really really long legs. I've never had long legs, how do women *get* them that long. 'We got the note and Alan realised it must be you.' Oh really. Oh that's a shame. I was hoping scrotum-breath wouldn't have had a chance to read it because it would have waddicated him on the side of the nut and sent him into a coma. 'He's been meaning to speak to you I think.' Longlegs is incredibly calm. She's wearing a rock on her finger. Someone from the darts mob caught my eye, I remember that. I'm supposed to be getting the show on the road but I'm not telling Longlegs that's what I'm doing. I think I've been mocked enough for one night thank you. Well, I ask... because she's calmly taking it all in her stride, 'Did you... it seems you already knew about me... wasn't the note on the morning brick even a bit of a surprise?' Wasn't I just a teeny-weeny bit of a shock— because I certainly didn't know you existed. 'Actually,'... she says... 'I did know he'd been seeing an older woman.

[*A pause as* NANCY *contemplates strangling her.*]

But once we'd finally announced our engagement... well of course he stopped. Of course he's fucken stopped. I did happen to notice that my love life had more or less clunked to a standstill. I want him, I want him, I want him, I want him, he makes me feel about twenty and laugh, he never shuts up and what he says you can listen to and he's only three years younger let's not build this out of all proportion. I don't say any of this. I don't even say Outside, I'm Going to Have You, because what I realise, she doesn't even see me as competition. There's no fight to be had. She's discussing this only to prevent future window damage. As if this old chook'd be a contender. As if shit-for-brains'd be interested in her. Not when there's perky little me around. Fair enough I was confident at her age but these young tarts'd run rings around us. 'I can see you're upset. I'm sorry you've been hurt. I just wanted to clear the air.'

[*She becomes somewhat obsessive about finding an emery board.*]

I could smash every window in his place, that could clear the air.

[*Pause.*]

Wouldn't have thought fingernails could just snap off from grief... I should have known... he could charm the birds out of trees. Oh fuck Jenny Craig! I'm sacked I know I'm sacked. [*She looks upstairs.*] Come down and tell me, I know I'm dead.

[*She tries to cry and can't.*]

Cried myself out obviously.

The Night of the Missing Bridegroom

Linden Wilkinson   CURRENCY PRESS

A woman loses her husband on her wedding night but finds much more. A contemporary satire about the possibility of passion.

ANNIE, the Bride

The forest beyond the house. The sounds of the reception in the distance. NEIL, *the New Man, semi-naked, wearing a set of deer antlers on his head, has been performing a tribal dance as a storm approaches.*

ANNIE:

[*to* NEIL] We love each other. We really, really, really love, love each other. But his career sucks me dry. How long will it be before I can just sit down with a good book and not be tormented by our shared fear of his imminent failure? Life's cruel. The only genuine power you have is the power to withdraw affection, withdraw support. I looked at him all through the ceremony. Please, just make an effort. I thought, after all I've done for you. Nope. Mr Cardboard

Cutout. I started to cry. Isn't it silly. I've always thought weddings were such a joke, a show... but... just like holding a newborn or watching a coffin slide into the furnace... there's still a moment of incredible awe, a moment of disconnection.

ANNIE

A short while later.

ANNIE:

[*to* NEIL] I'm just angry, that's all. Why should I have to do everything... organise today. Smile all the time, save his neck... like where do my boundaries of responsibility end?

I know you think it's my fault but I have tried. I've taken a serious look at my underwear drawer, for example. But, I'm very sensible. I'm an organiser. I organise syllabuses. Syllabi, for the Education Department, so, you see, I just can't get past the convenience of Cottontails.

[NEIL *takes her hands.*]

That's an extraordinary concept. Men's groups. I thought they just stood about in lines. If you'd said you ran men's lines, I'd find it credible.

I don't dance... I haven't danced for years. Max displays a kind of heavy jungle influence and I get nervous on behalf of everyone's furniture. Some things you can't replace.

[*He begins to remove her gloves. She hasn't experienced tenderness for a long time and talks herself out of weeping.*]

Men's groups. How chic. All over the world groups are... reclaiming the night. It's a phenomenon. It's even hit my stuffy old workplace. Imagine. There's a woman, really... quite competent... she goes moon dancing once a month. She's gay now but she has children, which is quite a satisfactory way of going about things. If you're that way inclined. Which I'm not. I don't think. Not that I haven't thought... about things... There have been some long nights. Max doesn't travel all the time. This woman wears ankle length socks, so, really, you can't believe everything she says. I mean. What kind of perspective do you have on the world if you dress like that... dear Mr Deer... But she says she orgasms for the duration of the

festivities. On and on. She is so blissfully happy... A whole night under the eye of the full moon. She said the first time it happened she thought moths were flying out. She wonders why I don't try it. They do it in public parks. For heaven's sake.
[NEIL: You're trembling.]
ANNIE: Now isn't the body the darnedest thing.

[NEIL *looks at* ANNIE *then kisses her.*]

ANNIE

ANNIE *is alone.*

ANNIE:

If I lived in another century, I'd have so much structure to crush me... from my nipped-in waist to the threat of perpetual pregnancy... and I wouldn't have all this freedom to make so many bad choices. If I lived in another century... I'd... I'd be in my room, the fire burnt low... but not the fire in my heart. [*Gasps.*] Beads of sweat on my brow, I'd jolt from my empty bed, unable to endure the agony of separation any longer. I'd loosen my hair, it'd cascade down. A defiant toss. Coal-bright eyes. I'd lower my bodice. I'd take charge of my body, flaunt convention. Risk all for one mad, shameful night of passion. Open the door. Not a sound. A smuggler's moon. Clouds scud, scud, scudding across an inky sky. Up the wooden stairs. Dash along the hall. Bare feet on bare boards. Hardly breathing. Cashmere shawl draped across my all but naked shoulders. I'd run as I'd never run before, carried along by the wings of desire. Oh! That such hope could be born of such desolation! I'd knock... 'Yes?' he'd answer huskily. I'd thrust open the door and there we'd stand, eyes locked. Then... suddenly... he takes me in his strong, tanned, muscular arms and—

Australian Monologues: Men

Janis Balodis

Wet and Dry   CURRENCY PRESS

For play description see page 100.

ACT 1 SCENE 3: GEORGE, mid to late 30s

Sydney. Back Patio. Night. GEORGE *is by himself.*

GEORGE:
Another day. Another late summer's night. Not many stars. Sydney.
Winding down with Johnnie Walker. [*Drinks. Laughs.*] The old man
wasn't much of a worker. Not much of a swimmer either. But he
could drink. Good thing he worked for Resch's. This one day he had
his allotted couple of gallons for lunch and climbed into an empty
vat to sleep it off. Usual story. The afternoon shift pumped the vat
full of beer. No-one heard the old man. His mates reckoned he
wouldn't have yelled. Would've tried to drink his way out. It was a
lingering death. He had to get out twice to have a piss. Moral: if you
can't swim make sure you haven't had too much to drink. It was
about that time that Alex took up swimming. Not because he was
worried about ending up in a vat of Resch's – he was hardly twelve.
It ran deeper than that. It was his way of blocking out the old man.
Drunk or sober when he got nasty the old man used to tell Alex,
'You're not my son.' Tried it on me when I was about that age but I
was a dead ringer for him. 'Who'd want a piss pot like you for a
father?' I used to say. He could never catch me. And I moved out
first chance I got. I didn't know Alex was copping it. Alex took it
pretty hard—not his dying—being told, 'You're not my son.' He
hasn't been able to drink Resch's beer since. [*Drinks.*] That's how
the old man would have liked to go. In a vat of Resch's. Actually he
was riding home, pissed as a parrot on his push-bike and fell into a
stormwater drain. There was no water in it at the time, and he broke
his neck.

ACT 2 SCENE 1: GEORGE

Sydney. Back Patio. Evening. GEORGE *by the back fence.* PAM *comes out to him with a can of beer.*

GEORGE:

Three months... What can I say? Congratulations. [*Pause.*] I never thought I'd miss that bloody hound over the fence. Bloody thing going for your throat after leaving a cunningly placed turd for your feet to skid on. An apt reminder of the sort of world we live in.

Congratulations. Good luck. Against the worst possible odds you finally did it. All on your own. Well good on you. Now I'm down on the mat with the shit on my shoes, rub my nose in it.

I had nothing to do with it. Did my bell ring? Did the earth move? I must've fainted. Nothing had happened. Nothing was going to happen. We saw all the experts and half the loonies, and the line between them is marginal. We've run the gamut from medication to meditation. The Valium relaxed me so much I couldn't get out of bed let alone get an erection. The vegetarian diet gave me terrible wind and under hypnosis I regressed three lives to discover I'd been a eunuch in a harem. That really boosted my ego. We've consulted the horoscope and the tide charts. Prayed to all the gods and mammon burning everything from incense to a big hole in our bank account. The only thing we haven't done is smear ourselves with chicken entrails. We can't make babies.

ACT 2 SCENE 5: GEORGE

Sydney. Watson's Bay. The Gap. Dawn.

GEORGE:

When I came back last night I sat in the dark of my office and was a good father to him, taking good care of him, being there when he needed me and... you weren't in the picture. It wasn't enough. I had to keep coming up with new toys new games. For myself. I didn't know who he was. I haven't really seen him. For what he is. I don't know what he wants. My son. But he needs his mother. That much I know. And I said to Alex, I'd be his father. I do want him. My son. He's my son. Maybe he'll show me to be a better husband. Our son.

[*He turns to look back through the fence at the sea.*] I was wrong. Last time. I want to admit that I could never forgive myself. Till now… Look at the state of this fence. When some little kid crawls through that it'll be too late.

After Dinner

Andrew Bovell   CURRENCY PRESS

For play description see page 103.

ACT 1: GORDON, a bank worker, mid 30s

The bistro. GORDON *is sharing a table with* STEPHEN, *a fellow employee at the bank.*

GORDON:

[*to* STEPHEN] I thought we might just talk. You see I haven't had the chance to talk about it with anyone yet. When Brendon was kind enough to ask me to join you for dinner, I became quite excited. The thought of spending an evening with two of my fellow men excited me.

Yes, you see I don't think I've been out with just men since I was a teenager. I've been looking forward to it all week. I thought that if anyone could possibly understand how I felt then it would be another man. The separation hasn't been easy for me. I've been a little battered by the whole thing. We had to sell the house of course and I've been living in a small flat ever since. I've isolated myself from the world, so to speak, but then again I had to Stephen, I had to. After all the bitterness, the disappointments and rejection, there's only one thing left to come back to, Stephen. Yourself. Only the very sad thing, the pitiful thing is that there's no guarantee you'll like what you find, when you get there. Can you understand that, Stephen?

I don't like myself very much. When your wife leaves you and makes you feel like you're not worth the ground she walks on, then you're not left with a very high opinion of yourself. And you need to talk to someone. You need to tell someone you've been crushed.

You need to shout before you go mad, before you hurt someone or before you hurt yourself.

That's why I've come here tonight, Stephen. I need to shout. I need to tell someone. But not just anyone. Certainly not a woman. I need to tell a man. I need the support of my fellow man.

Men do have emotions, Stephen. And they can express them if only they're allowed to. Believe me, a day has not passed since she left, that I haven't wept like a lost child. Collapsed on the floor in a heap of uncontrollable tears...

I'm sorry. I've made a scene. Don't misunderstand me. I'm not a homosexual. I only wanted to talk. Yes, I'm sorry. My mistake.

[*They reach an awkward silence.*]

Aftershocks

Paul Brown and Workers' Cultural Action Committee

CURRENCY PRESS

For play description see page 106.

ACT 1 SCENE 4: STAN GILL, about 40. The Bingo and Hoy caller at the Club. Stan rode a floor down and was injured quite severely.

STAN:

I rode the floor down. And as the concrete hit the floor, [*Clapping hands.*] I've sorta BANG with the concrete floor, and BANG up again, and I'd say what's happened is the chairs've come underneath, cos I ended up all tangled up in chairs, and me arms up in the air and stuff like that.

Whereas just before that, okay no worries, Howard Gibson and me, we yak yak yak... about these globes that needed replacin'... The old ducks, they can't see... so you know what Howard's like. Well, Howard always does those things for me, and if I ask him, then sorta, they're done straight away.

I remember I looked at him, while it was going on, we could hear this massive roar, this sorta, huge, like a bloody underground train coming... and then we stopped talking... There was three big, long slow waves, and the whole floor just collapsed, and he musta seen it and bolted for an opening. Yeah, Howard went east, and I went west.

I never been close to death... I knew I was... the first thing that struck me, as the floor started to give way, and I went down with it, the first thing that hit my mind was, hello I'm dead.

I sorta looked up. Everything was coming down. Then it gave this great big puff! Like the air and everything, big puff of wind, and the whole... big dust thing went straight up in the air, went straight back up. And when everything sorta got quiet, that's when they all started screaming, I could hear all the people screaming. The ones who were actually trapped, y'know.

All the bloody sound gear was lying everywhere. I could see all these wires hanging down and apparently I started yelling out. I don't remember doin' it but I was, y'know...: 'Fer Chrissakes will somebody get me out of this fuckin joint.' [*He laughs.*]

I just heard someone yell out, 'Get jacks, get jackhammers, get the ambulance, get the police, get the lot', words to that effect. I wouldn't have recognised the voice. 'Mate I've done something to me back', I said, 'I don't care how much you hurt me, but for Chrissake get me out of these chairs.'

And the most vivid thing I remember about it... I couldn't move cos me back was too sore... I ripped me shoes off thinking that might let me get out of the chairs a little bit better and what terrified me the most was when I looked up and the bloody dance floor was still there. How, I dunno why. Like all around the whole dance floor, everything just come down. You got this massive... you been to the main... you been up in the main auditorium...? Well that dance floor's still there. I dunno how it stayed there, but that dance floor was actually still hanging there.

ACT 2 SCENE 6: JOHN CONSTABLE, early 20s. A cleaner under Lyn's supervision. John took part in a number of rescues, including Lyn's.

JOHN:

I've gone to the basement, and then all of a sudden this girl's come up, one of the girls from work experience, and she's gone, 'John! John! Jennifer's down there. Go help her. Go find her. She's in there somewhere.' And I've gone, 'Nooo.' I've known Jennifer for years. I used to give her heaps as a kid. I used to throw rocks at her and things like that... so I've gone in looking for her.

All they can see is just a little bit of her head. And I see this little gap about this wide. And I stick my head down, crawl down face first, and I'm totally right up to my ankles into this rubble before I get to her. And then this SES guy just grabs me by the ankles and just holds me, you know... and I get to her, and I start caressin' her, 'How ya goin' Jennifer? What are you up to? What are you doing down here? What's happening?' [*Laughing.*] 'You tell me what's happening.' 'I don't know what's happening either. I've come to help ya.'

I go straight down, and I go right under, so I can reach me hand straight up underneath her ankle. And I feel all it was was her shoelace, so I'm sayin', 'It's okay Jen, it's only your shoelace. It's all right.' She says, 'Oh...' [*He makes a big sigh.*] ... A big sigh comes out of her head. And they pass down these jaws, and I put it underneath the brick... well it wasn't brick, it was a whole slab. I'm comin' in from that way, and they're digging from this side... They're gonna start cutting the door out. 'If you cut the door out, everything's gonna collapse on her'... And then this, I don't know who he is, he's a yobbo anyway. I'm sayin', 'Her leg's clear.' And this SES guy says, 'The leg's not clear,' and I'm saying, 'Her leg's clear, there is nothing on it at all. Her foot's clear, I can move her foot.' And this guy says, 'No, her leg's not clear'... Anyway, he's put another jaws in on the other side... but as he's lifting it it's unstable, and I can see it's gonna go, and I grab the slab, and as I try to hold the slab, 'crunch', and the whole thing just falls straight back down on her leg. 'OH'... tryin' to hold on to her leg [*Miming the action, reliving the effort.*] and she's just letting out this almighty scream, you know, and I go, 'Oh no', I say, 'Quick, get it back under there', and he puts it back under there... And anyway, he's lifting it back up straight away, and he gets it off her leg, and he says, 'Oh her leg's clear now.' [*Laughing knowingly at the stupidity of the yobbo.*] 'Her leg was clear the first time.' And he says, 'We're gonna drag her out, and as we drag her out, you straighten the leg, and then support it as it's comin' out'... [*Cynically.*] ... right... 'Oh here we go', and he starts just draggin' her out, she's a bit frantic to start, see. And I've started straightenin' out her leg and… and as I'm straightening out her leg, I go to about there [*He indicates on his own leg.*] and she starts, 'Ahhhh.' [*He is mimicking her own guttural scream.*] It's okay Jen, in five minutes, you're not gonna feel a thing, you won't have nothin' to worry about. It's all right. It's okay.'

ACT 2 SCENE 12: JOHN

JOHN:

Sunk the piss, mate. Straight onto the piss. I sank piss for seven days straight, I mean I did not sober up. I mean I woke in the morning, and I'd sink piss again. I was… for some reason too scared to face what happened, and what I had gone through. And then the seventh day or the seventh night, I'd said, 'Ah fuck this. I'm going out back for a spew.' You know. I was a changed person. I was more arrogant, more short tempered. Just pissed off with everything. Anyone tried to hassle me out… 'Fuck you'… straight up 'em, you know. And on the seventh day I'd… went out the back and just sat down and thought about it, and then bawled me eyes out… first time I'd cried in years. And really hit me like a ton of shit, eh. It all just came down all over me, like a sheet, and that was it. Bawled, and bawled and bawled.

I remember me and Wayne Dean are both running for the truck at the same time saying, 'A, a, a, a,' like this. And Wayne Dean was closer than I was, and he's sort of turned around and seen it. I was in mid-stride, and Wayne Dean, he's come right up shouting and stopped it just before it ran over her head. It was unbelievable. And we got the ambo driver that was just about to run over her head, we got him to take her away.

I dreamt that all the graders and excavators and all that were as they were pulling down walls… there was other parts falling down where people were. And I dreamt that I'd found the core of the earthquake. It was in the basement of the Workers' Club. What it was, was just this deep hole. I'd got all the bosses together and I said, 'Listen, this is where the earthquake comes', and they've gone, 'Bull', and I've gone, 'Shhh, you'll have to keep quiet. If you talk too loud it'll start an earthquake.' They've gone, 'John, John, we want you to prove it.' And I've started down into this hole, and it's rumbled everywhere [*He makes a rumbling sound.*] and I've just darted into this little tunnel I knew come up near the door, the Union Street door. And my girlfriend's there. And I've said, 'What are you doing here? You're not supposed to he here.' And anyway I've gotten her out And that was it... I'd found the core of the quake... And I'd just left all the bosses in the middle of the Club and I'd escaped my own way.

Kingaroy

Martin Buzacott   CURRENCY PRESS

The Carnival comes to town, and with it the usual assortment of drifters and oddballs. The host of the rodeo championship finals at his horse stud outside Kingaroy is Rhett Perkins: Aboriginal, Vietnam veteran and former country and western singer. Upon this stage, the heavens conspire to draw together a group of individuals who, although strangers to one another, are interconnected by a distant and extraordinary past.

ACT 1: WAYLON GOONBUNGEE, rodeo star

A homestead on a horse breeding property outside Kingaroy, South Queensland, 1992.

WAYLON:

You've got to feel the earth reachin' up to you, and the place where everything's quiet and... I don't know... and sorta powerful. Because when you're up on the beast, it's like there's... well, it's like a battle for ya soul. You've got some guy, up above tryin' ta catch ya by the hand, and another behind ya snappin' at ya heels. And they're both real jealous for ya and that. You know, they want ya real bad. Thing is, ya don't wanna go with neither of 'em. What ya wanna do is stay right where y'are, in touch with the earth. Like not wantin' to die I s'pose. Ya just think three things. First of all, be positive. Sounds simple but it's the hardest thing. Second, use ya spurs whenever ya feel yaself tippin' over. Third, keep hold o' the rope. Whatever happens, keep hold o' the bloody rope! That's all that goes through ya mind.

ACT 2: RHETT PERKINS, horse breeder

RHETT:

There's a legend among the blackfellas. It says the shootin' stars are the souls of the dead returnin'. And, if ya open up ya world to 'em, the family ya lost'll come right on back to ya. I never believed it. Then when the meteors started flyin' night after night it was like the spirits callin' out, pleadin' to the last bit of blackfella in me. Didn't know if they was real or not, but there was somethin' from long ago drivin' me to it. I claimed the rodeo for meself, eh. I got the Carnival world of free spirits ta come into this place—and all o' the dead returned. I was answered. [*Triumphantly, in wonder.*] Blackfella live again. Blackfella still got spirits. Blackfella got his self-respect.

And tonight maybe the heavens'll be quiet at last. We'll watch, and we'll wonder why.

Scales of Justice

Robert Caswell   CURRENCY PRESS

Australia in the early 1980s.

ACT 2: DETECTIVE INSPECTOR KEVIN PETERS

Drug Squad room. Night.

PETERS:

You are all aware there's a lot more heroin on the streets now, more than ever before. Official estimates put the number of addicts in the nation at twenty thousand, but you know and I know that that's bloody conservative when you add the middle-class users to the street junkies. This Police Force is in the middle of a crackdown on organised crime, and the media's not buying it. We have to stay one jump ahead of the bastards. We have to get results and we have to be seen to get results. Now, Sergeant Miles has received certain anonymous information concerning a dealer by the name of Maynard. It is believed that Maynard is in possession of three to four kilos, and that he's armed and dangerous. One of the first things impressed on me on taking charge of this squad was the soundness and the reliability of Sergeant Miles' sources, so that's how you can expect to find Maynard. I'll now pass you over to Sergeant Miles to brief you on the suspect's whereabouts, points of entry and so on.

Let me remind you, especially those of you new to Drugs, of a directive from the Police Minister's office. The Minister wants the likes of Maynard through the courts, he wants to make an example. Hit him hard and hit him fast. No excuses tonight, fellas, don't stuff this one up.

ACT 2: ASSISTANT COMMISSIONER PHILIP THOMAS

RSL Club. Night. THOMAS *and* INSPECTOR BOURKE *sip beer at a quiet corner table.*

THOMAS:

We've got a real problem on our hands here, Jim. I'm getting the nod from the Minister, he doesn't want that particular prosecution to go ahead at this stage. I know we've been after the bastard for a long time but I'm sure we can get him another way. But if we put the pressure on now he's going to blow. He knows Roach and you remember what happened there, he knows about that, he may or may not be able to get it out, but if he does, it's going to hurt your Prosecutor's Branch.

We don't want a bloody enquiry, with headlines and politicians crawling all over us. You and me have worked too hard for too long. Not about to have all that stuffed up by one lousy crim. He's more trouble that he's worth. I think we better go through that evidence and find some problem.

Kafka Dances

Timothy Daly   CURRENCY PRESS

Inspired by the letters of Franz Kafka to his fiancée, Felice Bauer, the play draws on elements of Kafka's life and family, his struggle to form an intimate relationship and his overwhelming drive to write. The action takes place during the life of Franz Kafka. It shifts between the Kafka family home to the Yiddish Dream Theatre.

SCENE 10: FRANZ KAFKA, a thin man aged 30–35

FRANZ:

What I'm about to say, I, I have no doubt at all in my mind that you'll reject as, as completely absurd and typical of a, a man in my extreme state of, of nervous intensity and physical weakness and, and as I say, should this, this offer be unattractive or, if as it surely must he to you, then I, I hasten to assure you that I could never, ever in a million, hundred million years, though I know I won't live that long, God forbid, but metaphorically speaking, I swear that I would never hold it against you for a, for a moment should you correctly feel that such a proposal was absurdly unattractive to a person like you, who after all is in the prime of health, enjoying the best of social life in Berlin with a wonderful family I've, I've had the privilege of meeting, a position in your, your company that's far superior to any position, I could possibly hold now or at any time in the future, and prospects of a, a happiness that would make me envious were it not for the fact that the person who is the, the recipient of all this good fortune is also the most, the most deserving person I can possibly imagine, and I, I can only say that if marriage is ruled out now or in the future, then I would retire into some dark oblivion where I would never, ever forget the kindness you've shown in ever being able to love a person who has, has never found the least reason to love himself, and I understand, I do, because a person like you deserves a husband who loves her so completely that he would never torment her in the way that, that you would be tormented if ever you were so rash and foolhardy as to consent to be my wife, and I, let me repeat, I'm ashamed to be mentioning such an outrageous proposal if it were not for the fact that you have always been so kind and generous that even the biggest fool in the world doesn't feel himself a, a little wiser for having been in your presence. [*Pause.*] Is that clear?

The Girl Who Saw Everything

Alma De Groen CURRENCY PRESS

For play description page see page 111.

ACT 1: GARETH RANSOM (GAZ), 50

A living-room in a country cottage in the mountains. GAZ *is talking to* LIZ, *his wife.*

GAZ:

What's happening to me, Liz? I've spent my entire life putting a neat little frame around everything, haven't I?—the best paintings, the perfect clothes, the right car—as if it made sense. There is no sense. It's random, it's violent, it's cruel. You were the only meaning in it all—and where are you these days?

Why aren't you with me? What are you doing up here?—apart from planting cabbages and listening to bloody birds you can't identify! You say you're thinking things through, but there doesn't seem to be any result on the way, does there? You're simply hurting us! I'm your husband! I miss you! You could come and work in the business. It's out of control. It really is... I'm out of control. I've been fucking that girl—woman—girl. Carol. From the accident. The inquest. She's a librarian. I didn't know what else to do. [*Pause.*] I've been pretty upset. [*Pause.*] And Carol could see that. [*Pause.*] And she was upset too.

I worry about her. It's been worse for her than it has for me. She doesn't sleep well. I think she broods. I think she's looking for a major life change.

I've been trying to do the right thing by everybody, and that's the whole problem—it's not possible. No matter what you do, you end up exploiting women, because there doesn't seem to be any way not to! [*Pause.*] But at least I had a real response to my own need. And to somebody else's need. [*Pause.*] So what happens now? Do I go the way of television, newspapers and mirrors? [*Pause.*] I've been having an affair, that's all. If I hadn't gone and blurted it out, nothing would have changed. [*Pause.*] I never meant to tell you. It simply came out. I don't know why. I feel like somebody up there's dangling me on a string and watching me dance.

Bad Boy Bubby

Rolf de Heer   CURRENCY PRESS

A powerful and disturbing 'De Profundis' story, the film follows Bubby's escape from the subterranean depths of a brutalising and hermetic childhood into a world that at times seems more brutal and damaged than the hellhole from which he has emerged. Despite encountering persecution in equal measure to protection and encouragement, Bubby the fool—the idiot savant—eventually finds his way to redemptive love, encountering along the way many of the major joys and ills of the modern human condition.

SCENE 94: THE SCIENTIST

Scientific Hall. Day This building is cathedral-like, but rather than religious artefacts, it is filled with monuments to science and technology—an extraordinary array of complex equipment that seems almost to have no sense. THE SCIENTIST *is leading* BUBBY *through, waving his arms about as he talks.*

THE SCIENTIST:
You see, no one's going to help you, Bubby... because there isn't anybody out there to do it. No one. We're all just complicated arrangements of atoms and subatomic particles. We don't live, but our atoms do move about in such a way as to give us identity and consciousness. We don't die... our atoms just re-arrange themselves. There is no God. There can be no God. It's ridiculous to think in terms of a superior being. An inferior being maybe, because we, we who don't even exist, we arrange our lives with more order and harmony than God ever arranged the earth. We measure. We plot. We create wonderful music. We are the architects of our own existence. What a lunatic concept to bow down before a God who slaughters millions of innocent children, who slowly and agonisingly starves them to death, beats them, tortures them, rejects them. What folly to think that we should not insult such a God, damn him, think him out of existence. It is our duty to think God out of existence. It is our duty to insult him. [*To the heavens.*] Fuck you God, strike me down if you dare, you tyrant, you non-existent fraud. [*Back to* BUBBY.] It is the duty of all human beings to think God out of

existence. Then we have a future, because then, and only then do we take full responsibility for who we are. And that's what you must do, Bubby, think God out of existence. Take responsibility for who you are!

SCENE 133: STEVE

The Houses of God. Day. STEVE *sings a short burst of a muezzin's prayer. He is framed by an Islamic design. He lectures* BUBBY.

STEVE:

Beautiful, isn't it? Fantastic. And yet this mob have been trying for centuries to clingwrap this...

> [STEVE's *dialogue continues unbroken. The background at his feet has changed. There is a star of David and representations of the Jewish faith.*]

... mob, even though they share the same god. Mind you, this mob have been getting pretty good at clingwrapping lately. And this...

> [STEVE's *dialogue continues unbroken. A Christian background.*]

... mob's got the same god as well, but they've had a fair go at clingwrapping that first mob, they've been trying to clingwrap that second mob for a good couple of thousand years, and...

> [STEVE's *dialogue continues unbroken. The painted background depicts an Aboriginal camp.*]

... they've pretty well succeeded in clingwrapping just about all of this mob, who never did much clingwrapping to anyone but themselves. And then...

> [STEVE's *dialogue continues unbroken. A Hindu backdrop.*]

... there's this lot. A different god altogether. You'd think that would help, but it doesn't. See this mob clingwrapped about half a million of that first mob, forty or fifty years ago, and they've been at it ever since. They've all done their fair share of killing or being killed, and it's all pointless. The thing is Bubby don't be like them. No matter how mad you get at someone, don't kill them... ever.

No more excuses. No more clingwrapping. Okay...? Bubby?

And don't mention it to anyone. We look like all being rich and famous soon enough, so let's not spoil it.

Royboys

Barry Dickins

CURRENCY PRESS

You will barrack for them, hate them and eventually form a strange attachment to them. They are the fate of man. The play follows the fantastic footballing fortunes of the battling Noble family. Like the club they worship, the struggling Nobles have no real home, not much money, but lots of heart. Their one ambition in life is to have a Royboy of their own. Instead they have a daughter who in the beginning hates football but finally goes on to become the first ever Roygirl.

ACT 2 SCENE 3: RAY NOBLE, father of a football family. A passionate alcoholic obsessed with footy. A man of 60.

The set is a battered old cranky weatherboard dump with a raked bottleheap on a raked stage.

RAY:

[RAY *reaches out and clutches his only daughter,* GAIL*'s arm. She jumps.*]

[*softly*] Come on, darling.

[GAIL *remains completely glassy throughout* RAY*'s speech; utterly unmoved. She seems rigid and embalmed.*]

[*staring into his daughter's eyes*] Why'd we have to go to Tokyo, anyway? We ought to be home, our old home, sweetheart. Saint Georges Road. Wind in the trees. Possums in there too. Remember the old bridge over the Briquette yard? What's the caper? You look different. Completely crazy. I come to bring you home. I come to tell you I love you. I miss you. I do. You're my hero, did I tell you that? Ha! I must have! I look up to you and respect you; do you know that? I want you to be a writer. But a funny one. Do you love this peanut, do ye? Remember when you went through the old gate at Saint Georges Road, darlin'? It was like being born. You were such a happy little girl. All you did was eat and sleep and laugh. In that order. There was order in the old days. Marlboro were six bob for ten years. Milk was tenpence a pint. Come back, darlin'. Come home with me. We'll hop on the milk cart and trot home among the stars.

[RAY *gets up slowly, and puts on his old battered hat.*]

The Custodians

Eric Earley CURRENCY PRESS

A small outback town with a large Aboriginal population during Australia's bicentennial year. Conflict exists between the police and the Mission community, resulting in the death in custody of a local Aboriginal man, Paul. Police Sergeant Alec Ross, close to retirement, is an old war comrade of Paddy, Paul's father. Ross is torn between friendship, his sense of justice, self interest and the demands of his superiors.

ACT 2 SCENE 5: ALEC ROSS, Police Sergeant, late 50s

Late morning. Police station. Senior Constable JOE SMITH *enters. Sergeant* ROSS *is reading* JOE'*s statement.*

ROSS:

Sit there. [JOE *refuses.*] There were men, women and kids in that riot. Get it into your thick head, you created this situation, you're answerable. I don't have to clean up your shit, drugs or a hanging. This statement... [*Pause.*] From a Senior Constable? No. On a death in custody? No. A date, times, excuses... wake up Smith, this is the eighties, we're custodians, supposed to keep blacks alive, not let them hang themselves or... Whatever happened. I want to know. An Inquiry'll want to know.

[*Throws the statement across the desk.*]

You're an idiot. Why put him in solitary wearing long socks? Why the blood washed off, the cell hosed? Why all the bruises on his face and chest? Why wasn't a doctor or an ambulance called? Why racial discrimination, Paul jailed, Bluey freed? Give me answers to those questions, Senior Constable Smith. Take this garbage...

[*Throws note book, etc. across the desk.*]

Get out, fix it now!

ACT 2 SCENE 5: ALEC ROSS

Police station. Senior Constable JOE SMITH *enters with statement.*

ROSS:

The Riot Squad Inspector spoke highly of you, wants you to join them. He was very impressed with the way you waded into the mob.

I think I can understand your frustration with the blacks; I've had 'em up to the neck, I'll probably put in for a transfer myself. Thankless bloody lot, after all I've done for them... he suicides and they turn on a riot... What really happened that night, Joe? You can tell me now, off the record like... the heat's off.

[JOE *holds out the statement.*]

You haven't left any little things out? Like, did you see him eating fish and chips in the pub? Did vomit come from his mouth when you sat on him? Did you have a shower and sleep well that night? What did you have for breakfast when you woke up? What does yer wife think about it, eh? Is she all on edge? Are you going to put up money for Bill's bail. He's in there, sweating it out. If Giotto had her way you'd join him. So, it's all in here? Everything? [*Pause.*] Yes Joe, he told me the adrenalin flowed every time he tackled you on the footy field... he was a wild one, must've been hard to handle, eh? [*Looks at the statement.*] Everything?

[ROSS *jumps up. Pushes* JOE *into a chair, holds him there by the shoulders.*]

Liar!

[JOE *tries to rise.* ROSS *thrusts him back into the chair.*]

Sit, you mongrel! You gave Bill and Simpson a hiding and got nothing outta them. You locked Paul up to find where he'd hidden yer dope, you were ready to belt him till he squealed, right? He saved you the trouble... Never told you a thing, did he? Didn't say a word, did he...? Why not Smith? Why not? He was dead or close to it when you dumped him into the cell right? You sat on a prisoner with a gutful of beer and chips, he was asphyxiated... choked in his own vomit! You panicked... you strung up a dead man... heavy, eh? Idiot! You could have got off with accidental manslaughter in the course of duty.

Blackrock

Nick Enright CURRENCY PRESS

Play description page 113.

SCENE 17: BRETT RICKETSON (RICKO), 22

Beach. JARED *sits on a rock.* RICKO *approaches.*

RICKO:

I did. I fucken killed her. Shana come on to me, then she backed off. Spider says it's a full moon, heaps of other chicks down the beach, take anyone on. I knew which ones were up for it, mate. We both did. We checked them out together. And they were checking us out, weren't they? You and me and every other prick. The whole fucken netball squad. So, I get out there. Wazza's getting head from some bush-pig up against the dunny wall. One of them young babes, Leanne? I don't know, comes running up to me, calls my name, Ricko, hey, Ricko! She grabs me, pashes me off. She's on, no she's fucken not, she's with some fucken grommet, he takes her off down the south end. I head towards the rock. I hear my name again. Ricko. Ricko. It's Tracy. Tracy Warner. I go, right, Jared was here. It's cool. I'll take his seconds.

   She's on her hands and knees. Says will I help her. She's lost an earring, belongs to Cherie, she has to give it back. There's something shiny hanging off the back of her T-shirt. I grab it, I say, here it is. She can't see it. I give it to her. I say what are you going to give me? She says she's going home, she's hurting. I say hurting from what? Guys, she says, those guys. Take me home, Ricko. Tells me I'm a legend, says she feels okay with me. Look after me, Ricko. Take me home. Puts her arms round me. I put mine round her. I feel okay now, Ricko. She feels more than okay. I say I'll take you home, babe, but first things first. I lay her down on the sand, but she pushes me off. Oh, she likes it rough. I'll give it to her rough. Then she fucken bites me, kicks me in the nuts. My hand comes down on a rock…

A rock in one hand and her earring in the other. [*Silence*.] It was like it just happened. The cops wouldn't buy that, but. Would they? Now if I was with you... Will you back me up, mate? You got to. You got to. Please. Please, Jazza.

SCENE 24: JARED KIRBY, 17

Blackrock beach. Day. New Year.

JARED:

I was here. Sitting up here. I saw the way it all began. You said you wanted to know. I tried to sleaze onto Tracy. Toby dragged me off her and I went off, had a swim, then sat up here, having a smoke, having a think, a think and a smoke, and starting to feel okay. Back at the club-house Gary's band was bashing some poor bloody song to death, but out here it was quiet, totally still... and then I saw. Down below me, between me and the ocean. Davo and Scott pissing themselves. Toby Ackland dragging someone by the arm. 'Come on, Tracy. Come on.' She was sort of half-giggling. He pulled her down on the ground. Then she wasn't giggling no more, she was like some animal in pain. Like he's got a hand clamped over her mouth... Scottie and Davo start barracking. Cheering him on. Fighting about who's going to be first with the sloppy seconds. I let it all happen. [*Silence*.] They headed back to the party. She went stumbling off down that way, towards the rock. And I turned and ran the other way. I could have gone down there. Any time. I could have taken her home. Only I wouldn't. I didn't.

A Property of the Clan

Nick Enright   CURRENCY PRESS

The play takes place in a large Australian industrial city in the present day, between October of one year and the winter of the next year.

BRETT RICKETSON (RICKO), Jared's mate

RICKO:

[*to* JARED] I didn't hear any names. Forget you even saw it. Nobody knows you were there. None of them three know, do they? [JARED *shakes his head.*] It's just the way things happen. The way she came, with a bottle of bourbon, and her little earrings bobbing, and her tits poking out of her T-shirt. She was up for it. She was always horny, mate, a horny bitch. She was always a bloody moll. You've seen her 'round. You've called her that and worse. She was a slut, mate.

You're so bloody full of what you been through. It was my party. Three times they been 'round our place. I've had to go through their bloody lists and say who was there and who wasn't, and who was in the band, and who bought the grog, and who was with who and how were the invitations issued, Mr Ricketson, and I'm bloody sick of it. Wipe it. All right? I'm up Queensland, the local cops start cruising the van, and say they've been advised I shouldn't leave Black Rock for the next few weeks and would I please turn round and drive home. How does that make me feel? Just because it was my party? And I was so shit-faced most of the night I couldn't even remember my own name. I'm going down the Hero. I haven't heard anything, mate. Not a word. Not a name. Not a single fucking name. Get it?

RICKO:

Brett Christopher Ricketson... Nineteen years old... 23 Waruna Street, Black Rock Point... Unemployed...

It was easy to catch up with her. She didn't hardly know which way she was going. One point, I thought she was going to walk into the sea. I sort of steered her back, but she pulled away from me. The way she'd always done 'round me. So there she is, carrying on about being pregnant, and hurting, and all this shit, when all she was was blind and legless... I said I'd had my eye on her for months, and how come she was putting out for everyone and not for Ricko? She said tonight was her first time, which had to be bullshit, same as everything else she ever said. I knew heaps of guys had been through her... If it was the first time, how come she always carried on like she was the greatest little slut in town? And she just looked at me, and started walking off. Saying she had to find her other earring. Earring. That's when I lost it. I grabbed her, and pushed her down on the sand... [*Silence.*] She was a total moll. A real little cock-teasing whore. Ask anyone. But I still feel like shit. And when I read in the paper that all them doctors, they reckon she was a virgin the night she bought it, I thought there's something wrong somewhere. There's gotta be something wrong somewhere. Something really wrong. People have to act the way they are.

JARED ELPHICK, teenage schoolboy

JARED *is waiting at the beach in his wet-suit. His friend,* RACHEL, *approaches.*

JARED:

The world is totally fucked. Why did she have to be the way she was? People don't do things out of nowhere. Ricko's life is ruined. Total. Total wipe-out. Fifteen years locked up because she didn't know the limits. All because she was out there, and said what she said or did what she did, and wham. It's just one moment. Wham. Could have been a fist or the back of his hand. And she would have copped a few bruises, and no-one would have heard a word about that night. But she got him going and he put his hand out, and there was a rock. And she's gone, and he's gone. Fuck. Fuck. Wham! [*Silence.*] Look at me. Why won't you look at me? Say something. Say something bitchy. Get back at me. You're never short of words. Say something. Fight back!

You got to listen to me. I'm going away tomorrow and I want to tell you. I was there. Not at the end, not with Ricko. But when the three of them… I watched. Saw it all. Well, heard it all. Everything you read in the paper. But afterwards… They pulled their duds up and headed back to the party to tell everyone how they'd paid out on Tracy. And she went stumbling off home. I could have gone down there. Any time. I could have stopped them, maybe. Only I wouldn't. I didn't. But afterwards, I could have taken her home. And then she never would have died. She would've been raped, and bleeding, and all that, but she would've been alive. She'd be alive. Not dead. And I sat up on the sand-hills and watched her disappear down the beach. She was heading for the water. I turned and ran the other way.

Burning Time

Nicholas Flanagan   CURRENCY PRESS

For play description see page 122.

ACT 2 SCENE 12: VINCENT, youngest son to Dr Dion Cavanagh (psychiatrist) and Kel Cavanagh (actor)

The hospital. KEL *is immaculate, composed, waiting.* VINCENT *enters. Pause.*

VINCENT:

I can see it burning. The film box burning—'up in flames' as you said. That's how I dream about it. Burning. And the pine tree. I dream about that too—the pine tree we set alight in front of our house, remember? We put all our toys on it. Set it on fire. Why did we do that?

I'm just wondering why no-one bothered to rescue the film box from our house when we moved. Why no-one gave a shit. Why no-one was interested in when we were happy. [*Pause.*] Remember the one with the Superman costume? And the one at Johnson's farm when Liz Johnson ran up the hill?

Yeh, the nude scene. [*He makes soft sounds of destructive burning.*] The box of film. I see it burning every night. Every fucking night. [*Pause.*] It's such a fucking waste. It's like it never existed. You were never married—we had no childhood and Dad never went to the war—never came back—he was never there—he never lived.

And have you? You're just like him, you know—a shadow in your own existence. Burning time. The lights are burning you see. It's the cost. The measure. How much is this artifice going to cost? What price do we pay for all this illusion, this bullshit. Because that's what illusion is—a nice word for bullshit. The invoice is in, and we can't pay the bill, so we just burn the film and pretend we were never there, that we never incurred the cost—but we did and we're gonna fucking pay—we are paying. [*Beat.*] Like the toys. Burned, gone. They were never there. Didn't exist. The pine tree is in flames—the make believe is consumed by fire. But we don't have the footage of when we used to smile.

We have a right to happiness, don't we? We're not in a fucking war zone; we're not under water sucking on a reed for air being strafed by bullets—that must count for something. But it doesn't—for some reason it doesn't—so we burn up anyway—shoot smack, corrupt our bodies, stand for nothing—stand for *nothing*— [*Pause.*] I... I don't want to blame anybody. I just want to see those films ... just one of them. Because I don't remember. Mt Martha. I don't remember.

Just film, burning...

God's Best Country

Gordon Francis   CURRENCY PRESS

A confrontation between the new and traditional owners of a pastoral holding in the Northern Territory Kimberley. In the harshness of the far north, each character battles to retain possession of the precious land. In an essentially hostile environment the radio receiver is the only immediate link to the outside world. The setting of the play is the homestead on Red Lily, a remote cattle property in the Top End.

ACT 1 SCENE 3: PART, a part-Aboriginal in his early 40s, employed by the Aboriginal Development Commission

The homestead. Sunset.

PART:

Well, here's one version you *can* believe, because I was there. I saw it happen. It was just as the papers said—like something out of Vietnam. They hit Leaning Tree with helicopters first—three, four, maybe even five choppers, all making low level passes over the camp—terrifying the women and kids. Then they moved in with Toyotas—bull catchers full of red neck ringers and squatters, all blasting away at the sky with shotguns and rifles, rounding us up as if we were scrub cattle. Anyone who tried to resist was beaten up. Look.

[*He parts his hair, showing his scalp.*]

That's how I acquired this little memento. When they had everyone yarded up on the edge of the lagoon they brought in the cattle trucks: filthy stinking cattle trucks that hadn't been hosed out in God knows how long. Then the fun really began. They started using goads on us to get us up the ramps and into the trucks. That was the highlight of the day. Ramming an electric cattle prod up a stinking blackfella's arse was a lot more fun than ramming a stinking blackfella's humpy with a bullcatcher. We were herded up the ramps and into those trucks like we were animals and then made to stand there ankle deep in cowshit and watch while Horse's bully boys brought in the bulldozers and flattened the entire camp.

[*He begins to pace around the room.*]

Their land; their need for their land. It seems to be something that's very difficult for a white man to grasp. Their hunger to be part of their land, to be one with it is so great they're prepared to go to any lengths to get access to it. Red Lily is a lot, lot more than just a cattle station to the Gungunnu. It's something infinitely more complex and spiritual... Red Lily is their spirit well, their life force, the very essence of their being. They draw all their power from it.

[*He looks out over the lagoon.*]

Whatever it is about this place, this country, I can feel it too. Perhaps not so strongly as the Gungunnu, but I can feel it. That's why I joined the walk-off, I suppose. One day I suddenly realised that *they* were my real kin, that I belonged with them in the filth and squalor at Leaning Tree, not here in the homestead with the Holy Family. Before I knew it, there I was at the head of the whole bloody clan, waving the land rights banner and leading the charge.

ACT 2 SCENE 1: HORSE, a cattleman, in his mid 30s

The homestead. Dusk. HORSE *enters on the verandah, toting the ubiquitous rifle.*

HORSE:

Treacherous black bastards, squatting on *our* land, giving us the big fucking run-around. 'We sorry, Boss. No boys today. Maybe tomorrow.'

It sticks in my gut. The old man let them get over the top of us and I didn't stop him. [*Imitating Dad's voice.*] 'They'll come back, soon as they get sick of living on bush tucker.'

It's no bloody game. Bastards are up to their old tricks again... Middle of the cattle season... Million dollar contract at stake... They thought they'd squeeze a couple of hundred square miles out of us. But what they never reckoned on was the support we got from the rest of the battlers round here. We yarded that mob, culled 'em, dipped 'em, tested 'em... right on schedule, all two thousand head behind barbed wire, waiting to be trucked to the port... All clean as a whistle—no ticks, no TB, no bluetongue, no brucellosis... Cleanest mob of cattle never shipped to Singapore, I reckon.

You know bugger all—bugger all about cattle and even less about blackfellas. That contract would have put this place back on its feet again for the first time in forty years... The old man couldn't believe his luck when we landed it. It killed him. The night they cut those fences and bushed that mob, he was a dead man. When we broke the news to him next day he didn't say a word: just walked out onto the verandah and sat in his chair, and that's where he stayed until he snapped his hobbles. He broke the first rule he ever taught me—first rule everybody learns in this country: never let the blacks get over the top of you; always show the buggers who's boss.

ACT 2 SCENE 1: HORSE

A little later.

HORSE:

[*to his sister,* TWEETIE] What do you mean—yesterday's enemies? What's that, another of your half-arsed economic principles? You're all the bloody same: patronising, supercilious Southern bastards— come up here still wet behind the ears, think you've got all the answers—filling the blackfella's heads with all sorts of fancy notions.

They had no right to cut those bloody fences. And as for *you*, you're worse than him. You should know better. But no, you live in this bloody dream world all the time. Afternoon tea parties and tennis on the lawn, that's what you want. Happy niggers corroboreeing away all night long, bringing their runny-nosed kids up from the camp for you to doctor... The little missus, doling out tins of bully beef and handfuls of boiled lollies on ration days!

It's *war*. Only they're not fighting with spears any more. They're using *our* weapons. That's what makes them so bloody dangerous. That mongrel half-breed out there was the brains behind the walk-off. *He* torpedoed that shipment.

Christ, he's only been here a couple of hours. Back into your pants *already is* he? He *used* you. Set you up; same as me and the old man. You were just another patsy.

What is it about that bastard? Even the old man refused to believe it. The night the stock inspectors get here all two thousand head get mixed in with a mob of wild buffalo. Any other time and we could have run them back into the paddocks and the bureaucrats would have been none the wiser. *But not when it happened under the stockies' noses!*

That bloke from the union, he didn't know a thing about quarantine. But our ex-head stockman did. But what always had me buggered was where he was getting his information. He always seemed to be that one jump ahead of us—and, the coppers. Stock squad couldn't pin anything on our clever yellafella, because he's got the best alibi ever. While the young bucks are out with the wire cutters that night, he's under the old paperbark tree hanging out of his sweet little Tweetie-Pie!

[TWEETIE *tries to smash* HORSE *across the face but he grasps her arm and twists it, forcing her to her knees in front of him.*]

You were his alibi, Tweetie. You were his source of information. I know. Coppers told me...

[HORSE *releases* TWEETIE *and starts to exit, stops and gestures up at the photographs.*]

This family's been fighting the blackfellas for this country for close on a hundred years. We sell to them now and it'll be the finish of everything these old blokes worked and fought for.

Furious

Michael Gow   CURRENCY PRESS

A family secret, a terrible betrayal and an obsession to rewrite the past combine in an explosive cocktail of fact and fiction. A stranger, Chris, has come into Roland's life and he will never be the same again.

SCENE 9: CHRIS

ROLAND*'s place. There's loud pop music from sixteen years ago.* ROLAND *wears a heavy jumper and fingerless gloves.*

CHRIS:

Roland, have you ever felt like you were two people? More than two, ten, fifty? I never felt like one person until I met you. It's always been in my head, the stuff we do and not just that, all kinds of stuff I've imagined doing. It's like what I want to do has always been just over there, all I'd have to do'd be reach for it, but I have to stop myself, too scared. So there's the me at home, studying, eating dinner with Mum and Dad, sailing on the weekend, rowing practice, church. And then there's the me at the beach looking at bodies all the time, me in the showers at school, me every night alone in bed. But here I know where I am. It's like I'm all here all at once, at the same time. So if I shut up, complete silence, I can stay, I can keep coming back? Have you got a spare key? I can come and go and if you're working you won't even have to stop and let me in. You can stay in your room. You won't know I'm here, until you need a break, a breather. Otherwise, silence, study. Here, see, this is me studying.

SCENE 17: CHRIS

ROLAND*'s place.*

CHRIS:

I called around twice before. No-one home. I just sat in the milkbar and stared at the ocean. Thought if I just sat there you'd walk past.

I hated the way I just couldn't see you. I worried about you. I worried that you'd worry. About me. But I didn't do anything desperate. Thought about it. This guy I have to see, he sees these other kids. They've tried. Not me. First few times, I was waiting for them to strap on the wires and turn up the voltage. Make me stare at ink blots for hours. But nothing like that. Just questions. Boring more than anything. But I put up with it. Kept quiet.

Only one person knows I'm here, this girl who goes to the same place. But I trust her. She's great. Getting here was very interesting. Had to cover my tracks. Cover up the cover-up. Make up stories to back up the stories I told them. It's worked up till now. But I won't risk it again. I can't see you. Not for a while. Like a few years. But I learnt how to do it, cover up. Lie low. Like I'm a counter agent sent over to the enemy pretending I'm on their side. Then one day I'll get the call and start my work. And they have no idea how dangerous I really am. They were unbelievable in the sessions we had together. Mum was like this crazy woman. Same nice clothes, same jewellery, same hair do. But crazy. Dad just silent. Nothing. And when we got right down to it, the thing they hated most was that they've been robbed of grandchildren.

If I don't go I'll be late. All my careful stories'll fall apart. You look after yourself. Off I go, into hiding.

Only Heaven Knows

Alex Harding   CURRENCY PRESS

For play description see page 126.

ACT 1 SCENE 6: TIM, aged 18

Sydney. Summer, 1944.

TIM:

[*to* GUINEA] It's not their fault—they didn't ask for me—I didn't ask for them—I felt—I felt I had no right to be there, not any more. Peter went off to the war, and at first things seemed easier, but then Aunty Maureen got a telegram—Peter was on his way home, he'd trodden on a land mine and lost both legs. From that day on I felt I was a constant reminder of their son, but it was me running around on two legs, not him. Aunty Maureen was alright, we'd talk. We'd listen to the wireless. I loved the plays best—I'd like to do that one day—write plays. Could I listen to your wireless sometimes Guinea? I miss it. Do you think that I could get a job in the theatre—or on the wireless?

I'd go with Aunty Maureen to the army hospital to see Peter. I hated it. Other blokes there—the same age as me—half dead, screaming. Peter would be crying all the time—he wouldn't say anything. Everywhere was pain and I was terrified—that they'd make me stay there, that I would never get out—I felt guilty because I wasn't in those beds, I was free—I was—free. And my uncle would look at me and behind his eyes would be the word 'coward'... I'll never go back, never.

ACT 2 SCENE 14: ALAN, ocker gay man

Sydney. Winter/spring, 1956. GUINEA*'s backyard.*

ALAN:

[*to* CLIFF, *his best mate*] I've begun to play a game with myself—silly—but, I look at myself—in the mirror—each morning, and I stick out my tongue and say 'fruitcake!'—and then look away very quickly! Then I look again, 'fruitcake!'—then I smile—make—myself smile. This morning I used the word 'queer'—it didn't hurt... 'Queer... Fruitcake... [*Much softer.*] Queer'... I've packed away the parents! I didn't want to see them in the first place, but the doctor insisted. When I rang my father, he wasn't too keen—he insisted we meet on neutral territory—The Paragon in Katoomba of all places! [*Silence.*] 'You're looking very well dear—isn't he Frank—Frank?—do stop fiddling with the table cloth, and straighten your tie!' says mum—and he said, 'What do you want—money?' 'No father I don't. I'm going to have electro-aversion therapy, I've decided that I no longer wish to be queer.' Well—the whole restaurant came to a standstill—ears strained from every conceivable place! 'That's very nice dear,' says mum, 'Will it hurt?'—'Only on Tuesdays and Thursdays—my appointment days.'

'Be a bit like a cattle prodder, I suppose,' says father, 'the cream gateau looks nice.' The doctor loved them, thought they were marvellous old stock. I'll never see them again, Cliff—what for? Let it all—rest—it's over—it is.

Blood and Honour

Alex Harding   CURRENCY PRESS

The play is a record of one precise period in the history of AIDS. It reflects the courage, fear and desperation of those facing a fatal illness without the unconditional support of the community.

MICHAEL YANG, of Asian origin, mid 20s, Colin's lover

MICHAEL:

[*to his lover,* COLIN] I watch you sometimes while you sleep. I remember once, a ray of sunshine across your face. You looked incredibly peaceful, settled. Remaining quite calm, I wondered—as you sat sleeping in the new lounge chair that we bought so you could sit in the yard comfortably in the sun—whether, if I left you alone for too long, I'd come back and you would be dead. You would be *free*, finished with this virus. This killer, it would have no further need of you. Both of us share you now in this time of life, of death, but I'm stronger than it, *feel* stronger than it. We're fighting back.

MICHAEL:

[*to* COLIN] And it laughs, you hear it? In the corner of our bedroom there's a chair. I often imagine that it sits in that chair watching Colin and me as we sleep or whenever we have sex. Jealous, angry, *evil*. It stalks the house reading personal letters, shitting on the floor, tormenting the dog as it sleeps. It is *wilfully* clever, this virus, and very complex. [*A church congregation is heard singing.*] And Christians! Kissing, licking its unwashed arsehole. Fervour! Passion! More lives! More! More! Fred Nile on his knees baying to the moon, his tongue servicing that unwashed arsehole. His sort all over the world on their knees giving it the gift of life, of love—bastard *devils* all. [*Music and sounds fade. To* COLIN.] Do you suppose that people think… that I infected you? Don't die.

MICHAEL:

To see what was underneath the towels of all the guys that I fancied! The ones that came into the men's changing rooms down on the beach. It wasn't my fault that some hunk came into the sheds every three minutes. I wanted to see! I wanted to be *invisible*. Foolishly and understandably, I had drawn attention to myself, and as I became more and more aware of my feelings of attraction towards certain men, my fears began to grow—would Jesus love all the little poofters? All the little poofters of the *world*? My life was going to be grim! Isolation and despair! Hey, Dad! Can I go to cadet camp this year? I'm excited by the stories I hear from the other boys who go to camp. They get stripped naked and have boot polish put onto their dick and balls! [*Aside.*] I did all right when I was a kid... [*Sings.*] J*esus loves the little* children... [*Pause.*] We'd sing this at school and then kick the shit out of each other in the playground! It felt perfectly normal this kicking of shit, and a constant shock to me whenever I looked into a mirror only to see an Asian face staring back at me. I didn't feel Asian, whatever that meant! I was *determined* to be as good, if not better, than every other Australian kid on the block. I dumped the rice in the bin and ate Vegemite sandwiches, meat pies and vanilla slices like the rest of them, *but not anymore*! I knew too at a very early age that if they so much as smelt a whiff of poofter, then my chances of survival would be greatly diminished. I learnt very quickly the fine art of camouflage.

COLIN, late 30s

A television news reader is heard.

COLIN:

9 April 1989. Sydney, the moral sewer of the Pacific! Over two hundred concerned citizens attended a pro-decency campaign rally today to oppose any future homosexual/lesbian Mardi Gras parades on the streets of Sydney, or anywhere else in New South Wales. Organised by 'Men Fighting For The Family', a new division of The Festival Of Light Community Standards Organisation, its first objective is to mobilise public opinion and Christian action against any future Mardi Gras, which, according to a spokesman, is 'obscene', 'indecent', 'blasphemous', and 'offensive', 'a festival of filth'. 'It is not a gay Mardi Gras,' said Mrs Elaine Nile, wife of Fred, 'but a death march. Many participants have the AIDS virus and will die.' [*A silence.*] I'm gay. No, *she* didn't say that, *I* say that. I am a homosexual!

For fifteen months I have been infected with the HIV virus. Please do not panic, please do not adjust your television sets! This obviously will be my last broadcast to you, and I want to be *honest*. Please listen. As a homosexual who night after night comes into your living rooms—well, figuratively speaking—sir, either eat the potato dangling on the end of your fork or return it to the plate—it upsets me greatly to have to read the sort of crap that I have just read to you. It insults me *deeply*. It is more offensive to me than the shit on Bondi beach.

Please, before switching me off, I'd like to apologise to Rosemary of Ryde who hopefully by now will understand why I cannot accept her proposal of marriage. Nothing to do with AIDS, Rosy! It has everything to do with the fact that I am in a very happy and loving relationship with a beautiful man! Rosemary, you may dispose of my pictures in the same way that you disposed of your Johnny Mathis records: Burn them!

MICHAEL:

Nine years to trial a drug, it's too fucking long! If you've got a cure, some drug sitting on your shelves, you fuckers! Make my lover well! Give it to us now. How *rich* do you people want to be? [*From out of his pockets he takes banknotes, throwing them at the audience.*] Take it! Take my money! Take it! People are *dying*, for Christ sake. How much more do you want? Isn't this enough? Trials—smiles—the bedroom drawer is like a pharmacy—the *poisons* that you are putting into his body. Look at him! Look at him! 'Smile if you feel nauseous, take two soluble aspirin, lie down for ten hours, sweat and sleep your life away!' [*Silence.*] Just make him well...

COLIN:

[*to* MICHAEL] I'd love a tomato sandwich. I said I'd love a tomato sandwich. It's the only thing that I could keep down at this point! Not that I'm expecting it to suddenly arrive. I mean, I'm not expecting someone else to make it for me. I am merely making a statement *not* a sandwich, if you see what I mean. The whole world is in turmoil! I, meanwhile, am lying *on* my bed not *in* it, as everyone seems to expect. 'What's the prognosis, Colin?'—meaning—'*When* are you going to die?' 'How well you look!'—meaning—'Oh! But you're still here!' Friends, dear friends who mean well but who also know *nothing*. Well-meaning strangers who visit... They do not stay long. Bothered by a troublesome conscience, our muffled and hysterical laughter sends them rushing towards the door!

Eighteen months of deterioration, I'll admit, but I'm *here*. Somehow. Who knows for how long *any of us will be here*? *Death has an eclectic appetite.* [*To the audience.*] Don't leave me! [*Silence.*] If we give you the impression you're not wanted, that's not true. Bring me cold rice pudding topped with cinnamon which is good for my palate, the thrush in my mouth. Bring salacious gossip! Sordid tales! Jeff Stryker videos! Dish the dirt as we have always done and will do so for as long as we *all* shall live. [*Pause.*] Some days I hate my bed. I'm sure that it hates me! I'm still here, my legs do work, I do have the occasional gin and tonic...

I do not give interviews. I'm too fucking tired for ghoulish journalists. My energy is precious! I won't be exhibit 'A' for *anybody*. I'm not going to spend the rest of my life hopping from guest spot to guest spot.

MICHAEL:

[*He is talking on a current affairs television program with* COLIN.]

One of the things that I do love about this country, *my* country, is that nothing remains static, nothing stays the same, but because of that, the hardest part is never knowing for sure who your enemies are. In a political climate that pushes *old*-fashioned, white Anglo-Saxon values, my father was murdered. I can't forgive John Howard for opening yet again that can of worms. *He* cannot wash his hands of the matter. Because of what he did, my family and countless others have been made to feel left out, not wanted, like the enemy. We've been blown apart. After years of contributing to this country, of making this country his home, *my* home, my Dad was beaten to death, and if the bastards who did it are watching this programme, I want to say I'm not afraid of you. The fact that you do your killings in *packs*, silently, invisibly, holds no great threat for me. You are *cowards*. And although you are protected by whoever or whatever, there's no pride to be had from what you've done, no honour, and like all wild dogs, in the end you deserve to be *shot*. 'A Fair Go For ALL', Andrew Peacock? A fair go for whom? For me as an Asian? For me as a homosexual? For my lover, Colin? I doubt whether your 'Fair Go' includes us. I'm not stupid, far from it! That's all.

COLIN:

[*on television*] I'm feeling good tonight. I'm looking good too, aren't I! Surprised? I've had a blood top-up, as good as a face-lift! [*He looks at the cancers on his arms.*] Look at that! Michael tells me that polka dots are in. I wish they were not! The media coverage of this illness has been either hysterical or negligible, and I have been as culpable as any of my colleagues. I *have* read the news they gave me to read! Proffer *not* an opinion! For that I'm sorry, and I apologise. 'A New Decade!' 'Interviews!' 'Editorials: What Do We Hope For in the 1990s?' [*Silence.*] None of the editorials listed a cure for *AIDS*! [*Another silence.*] I've discovered a lot about my body. I've become a bit of an expert on the subject—myself! It's a two-way thing, what *they* know about *me* and what *I* know about *me*. I know *nothing* about them, come to think of it! The bond and the trust between myself and the hospital is a very delicate one because I know that so much of what medical science wants to pump into my body is just experimentation. Either you say, 'Yes, I'm desperate. Let me be your guinea pig. Anything is worth a try', or 'No, thank you, I *won't* be your guinea pig. My quality of *life* is more important.' You have to be prepared to say that, and demand! Ask questions! Demand answers! Lobby! ACT UP! Make a nuisance of yourselves. There's enough of us to make a noise. Are there really two hundred drugs on the shelves still waiting to be tested nine years down the track? What will happen to me if I agree to radiation? Will my balls shrink? What *would* happen to me under a Liberal Coalition government? What is our present government doing about AIDS research? Why isn't more money being made available? Why? Why? Why? Why? Why? Why isn't the *media asking why*? I am *not* going to give in. I'm not dying, *I am living*. I have hope! I've taken control of my life and I'm not alone. We are not alone.

Table for One?

Claire Haywood

CURRENCY PRESS

For play description see page 128.

SCENE 7: NICK, a teacher, 35. A deeply insecure man, he covers this with a charming if slightly mysterious exterior.

NICK:

Who is responsible for this little stunt? [*Pause.*] I see. The old class conspiracy routine. [*He singles someone out.*] You! Yes you! No, don't look at the person behind you. I'm talking to you! You find this amusing do you? Perhaps you were the culprit who taped this... thing to my chair. How old are you? Thirteen? Fourteen? Ever used one of these things? Maybe you'd like to come up here and demonstrate on my ruler how to put one on? I'm sure the rest of the class would be most interested. [*He eyes the class.*] I should of course, report this incident to Mrs Bowers, but I won't. Why is that, do you think, class? Because I like you? Not particularly. Some of you I respect as students but most of you frankly, outside of these four walls, I couldn't care about one way or the other. Because I want you to like me? Not really. I'm employed to educate you not set myself up as God. No, the reason I'm not going to report this juvenile little episode is because maybe it's time we faced a few facts together. In a couple of years time, [*Picking on a student.*] if it's not the case already, that... [*Pointing to his chair.*] ... object of ridicule, that soggy little joke, will be the only thing that stands between you and certain death. Rest assured, it's a jungle out there and once those hormones really start kicking in, you'll have to be pretty sharp to survive. Forget 'trust'. That word will have all but dropped from your vocabulary. It's on the way out even as I speak. Yes class, the new sexual order is well and truly in and what you are looking at here is your life preserver. So. What I'm going to do now is... I'm going to go up to the staff room and I'm going to dry my trousers. And when I return you will have all completed a short essay on 'The Practical Use and Abuse of The Condom'. Then we'll see how imaginative you really are.

SCENE 13: ROBERT, a carpenter, 30, who aspires to be a stand-up comedian. Down to earth, he has developed a quirky sense of humour to cover feelings of intellectual inadequacy. High energy with a positive outlook. It takes a lot to rattle him.

ROBERT:

I've been going through an identity crisis lately. My girlfriend said: 'Of course you are. You turned thirty last month. You haven't lived until you've been through your thirties crisis.' I felt like hitting her except she would have hit me back. She's on at me about everything these days. I can't open my mouth without something sexist coming out. According to her, I'm suffering from an acute case of 'terminal verbal phalocentricity', but look at me for Christ's sake! I'm a dickhead! I mean, do I look confused or what? I tell you, being male and thirty in the nineties is a nightmare. Right? Let's face it. Macho is retro, wimps are self-destructing faster than the rebirth rate, and gay... just isn't everybody's scene. I spend hours in front of the mirror, asking the same question: will the real Robert Reeves please step forward? All I get is this blank face staring back at me. Even my acne scars are fading into insignificance. And you won't get any help out there! Everything out there is aimed to confuse, I swear. The other day, for instance, I'm hanging out my girlfriend's washing and I string up a line of undies with 'His Pants For Her' stamped around the waistband. Have you ever seen those? [*He waits for a response.*] I see. [*In a macho voice.*] I'm no wimp. No way! Not me! Catch me hanging out my chick's washing in a fit, no sirreee! What are ya, some kind of pervert or something? [*In his normal voice.*] 'His Pants For Her'. No kidding. It sent me into a real ego spin-out. Am I being over-sensitive or what? I mean what is the deep and hidden message behind this? What's a bloke supposed to think? 'His Pants For Her'. Frankly, I feel ripped off. I'm standing there at the Hills Hoist surrounded by wet knickers, and all these horrible thoughts leap into my head. What next? Her Pants For Him? And paranoia plus: if She's wearing His pants, who's getting into Hers? Or worse still... Theirs? Next, it'll be Our Pants For Them and then where will we be? All over the bloody shop!!! I MEAN WHATEVER HAPPENED TO PLAIN OLD MY PANTS FOR ME?! THAT'S WHAT I

WANT TO KNOW!!! No wonder I'm so fucked up. Cross dressing was a piece of cake compared to this. At least it was on the outside. You knew where you stood. But this is downright subversive! Am I right?

SCENE 16: NICK

NICK:

There was this teacher, you see, and he shared a house with this woman... a student teacher. One night, it was exam time. The middle of winter. She was sitting on the floor of her bedroom marking some papers. He had often seen her like this. The truth is... he used to position himself in the lounge room where he could see her through the open door. He could watch for hours while she worked. She was a beautiful woman you see, and he liked beautiful things. He liked the way she held her pen; the translucent blue-white of her hands. She had a tiny mole under her bottom lip which she teased with the tip of her tongue when she was deep in thought. This night in question, he was lying in front of the fire and he began to doze off. He fell asleep with the image of Suzanne... that was her name... in his mind. When he woke up, night had fallen. He could still see Suzanne through the open door. She was lying on the floor, on her side over the paper she was marking. She looked pale and beautiful. Like something straight out of a fairytale. He realised then how much he... cared for her and that he had never really expressed how he felt. Now, seeing her lying there like that... he walked in and closed the door behind him. He leaned over to kiss her—

That's when he saw the blood coming from her nose. It was no more than a thin red line as if it had been drawn on with the marker that lay beside her on the floor. He touched her cheek and it was still warm. He shook her. She rolled onto her back. He carried her to the car. If he hadn't been there that night... if he hadn't been watching her... She went straight into surgery. When she came out, her head was shaven, her face was white but she had survived. Two months later, she came back to the house. He watched her grow stronger. Her illness, it seemed, had made her even more serene and beautiful. She talked to him about her pain, and he listened. He was a good listener. She never told him that she loved him. She didn't need to.

He knew that one day he and Suzanne would— [*He stops himself.*] She was the woman of his dreams. Then, one day, she told him she'd fallen in love with someone else and soon after that, she… left him. [*With bitterness building.*] And from that day, he decided, he would never let any woman, ever, betray him like that again. So you see, Jennifer, there's a perfectly reasonable explanation.

The Passion… and its deep connection with lemon delicious pudding

Sue Ingleton   CURRENCY PRESS

For play description see page 131.

ACT 1 SCENE 15: TOM, Silver's father

TOM:

Africa. Such dry heat and dust and humming of earth in this place and the fluid laughter of a language that is another river to me. I must possess the world in some big way.

So many boys, my age but with bodies so different—ebony brown, all surfaces dusted white, painted, patterned, glorified. My golden skin is whitewashed, like Mama's outhouse—Two tall Nuba walk towards me, their great white teeth glistening, their mouths roar laughter—they hold hands these two huge Lothars, hold hands like girls! How disgusting, yet in their stance is pride and brotherhood. I long to be there, I feel it in my heart and in my groin, I will not have the ordinary—I will have the dark skin, the panther, the wild man. This is manhood, this is making the marrow wake up, it runs like quicksilver in my bones—ah I could leap and conquer—I could fight the panther and be victor—I could be God.

> [*A silk top hat appears and another, more fancy ladies' chapeaux.*]

Father…! and mother…! watching in disbelief. The sexuality rises in their nostrils like the smell of over-ripe fruit on a hot day—they turn away in disgust and disappear over the ridge. Thank God…

[*Someone takes his left arm, a warm strong hand holds his arm above the elbow, another youth comes to his right side—*]

... they are gabbling on at me, I don't understand a word they say, but I know what's going to happen—from the marks on their arms—the arrow marks of manhood engraved on the muscle, the nine rings in their ear lobes... Arrows and rings—all these are for me! My body etched, broken open and healed—all this is for me! [*He smiles.*] Let's go!

ACT 1 SCENE 21: TOM

TOM's *dream. Occasional seagull cries.*

TOM:

I am standing in the sand dunes at Point Leo backbeach, my wife, Ellie, and our children are in the car and I tell them to get out, the children that is, because I have found a place that sells ice creams, a little kiosk in the sand dunes with a Peter's cone on the roof. It's painted green and it's very little, like a toy-town shop. But it's real and it's got strawberry ice cream with real strawberries in it and I tell Ellie to drive to the beach over the sand dunes and we'll meet her there and I tell her to drive over the dunes to the beach and I know about the cliff and so does she yet off she goes. I'm beautifully under control, my calm is astounding, the children suspect nothing. Kay's voice is in my head. 'She won't have the guts,' she says—'she won't realise until it's too late.' I smile. There are a lot of people gathering in the dunes. Some of the men I play cards with are there—I wave to them, commanding their attention—they cheer me on—

The children are eating strawberry ice cream cones, it's running down their chubby hands—who will clean that up I wonder? There is a loud cheering from the dunes as the car rolls over the embankment, goes down the wet sand and rolls into the huge surf. I am walking along under the water. I look into the car—it's empty. I look around I walk over the sand, where can she be? I find her lying like a statue, cut in half—there's no blood, just two smooth surfaces that should have been joined together. Well she's gone and now I can start again.

ACT 2 SCENE 22: RAOUL, Silver's ex-husband

RAOUL's *dream.*

RAOUL:

I'm a grown man, trailing behind a shrunken, white haired dwarf—logically this isn't happening. Ah, we have entered a cavern underground. A still, silver lake lies before me, a boat like a great seed pod rests at the shore. The old dwarf stands beside it and motions me in. I hesitate and he gives me one of those looks that I often give the Boy—You mean we're going to have to argue about this? I'm going to have to explain, all over again, the purpose of this?! I step into the craft, praying my foot won't go through the base, I glance back at my guide, he nods and makes the sign that I should sit down. I sit with some trepidation, it rocks slightly, I wait for him to join me, however the little pod swiftly moves off from the shore without him! But, but! [*He turns in frantic panic.*] —he stands on the shore, gazing disinterestedly after me then turns on his heel and disappears back into the darkness. The pod moves with silent swiftness over the silver surface. I dip my hand in and scoop some out—Mercury! Jeezus a lake of mercury! A poisonous lake. The cavern is substantial. [*Gazes upward.*] I wonder where the soft light comes from. I cannot see the roof, the air is thick, not moving. A sound. [*A bell tolls.*] A tiny glowing light, another, two, three, rocking toward me—I see the forms of little barques with tiny lanterns, in formation they move straight toward me. A cold fear creeps upon my flesh. There are ten vessels, no, eleven, the last is huge, black, no lights hang from it. My little pod moves swiftly. I daren't breathe. They pass me by. They do not notice me. In each there stand three maidens in soft white robes, their hair is long, twisted, braided, bound and loosed, their eyes are blackened, their skin is whitened, they hold chalices in their hands. Three in each barque. Invisible to the eye what makes them move, the cortege flows past me, for that surely is what it is as I see the final boat; black satin drapes its sides, no lights, black feathers in its prow and lying on the deck the body of a young man—silver armoured, helm beside him. His glorious face, serene and white, gazes lifeless to the firmament above. Who is this prince, I wonder, whose very presence breaks open my hardened heart and makes me want to cry, cry for the lost courage, the valour, the glory of man?

Mates

Peter Kenna   CURRENCY PRESS

This play studies the intersections of masculinity, mateship and homosexuality, behind the sexual pairing of a drag queen and a famous football star. Sylvia is a richly drawn character presented as engaging, clearsighted and deluded by turns.

SYLVIA, a man in his middle 30s

A cabaret dressing room.

SYLVIA:

[*Dressed in a loose robe and high heeled shoes, he sits at a table and finishes removing his make-up.*]

He came in to see the show about eight weeks ago. We do two a night. One at eleven and another at one o'clock. They were at the first. A whole team of them. Apparently they'd won that day and came in for a dare. They were a rowdy lot, stamping around sending everybody up; we were relieved when they left. But, guess what? He was back again for the second show. By himself. And he waited around afterwards. And we got into conversation. And then I went back to his place with him.

I wasn't dressed up like a girl after the show. And he certainly didn't expect me to behave like one. Exactly the opposite. Well, after that we just went on seeing each other and the first month was terrific. Sometimes he'd come back to my place and we'd laugh and eat and muck about. We never made arrangements to keep it going. Oh no. That way it was like every time was going to be the last and so we made the most of it. But then, about two weeks ago, something happened. He was driving me home and we stopped for a traffic light and someone waved to him from another car. Apparently that was all it needed. He blushed to the roots of his hair and the light changed to green again without him even noticing. He'd been caught with me, you see, and he's never been the same since. He gets later and later picking me up and some nights he'll ring and leave a message for me to take a taxi over there. Now, I'm not a fool.

Usually when that sort of thing starts to happen you can see the writing on the wall. They might as well pick up a violin and start playing 'God save the Queen'. But this time it's not as simple as that. I know he isn't getting tired of me. It's just who he is and what people would say if they found out about us. And maybe... maybe he can't bear needing me as much as he does.

Strictly Ballroom

Baz Luhrmann and Craig Pearce   CURRENCY PRESS

The story tells of the struggle for love and creativity to find expression in a world limited by rule and regulation.

SCENE 96: BARRY FIFE, aged 50. A fleshy, sweaty man. President of the Dance Federation. The most powerful man in Ballroom Dancing.

Kendall's Dance Studio. Main salon. Late afternoon.

BARRY:

He was the most beautiful dancer I'd ever seen. He could have been the greatest champion of them all; but he was like you. Threw it all away. [*He looks at an old black and white photograph on the wall.*] I'm talking about the man who was potentially the greatest ballroom dancer this country's ever seen. I'm talking about your father, Doug Hastings.

You think it's funny? You think it's funny, do you? I worshipped that man, we all did. Doug Hastings was an inspiration to us all. I know to look at him today it's hard to believe, but once, once, ah once...

Doug and Shirley Hastings were the best bloody couple this country had ever seen. Couple number 100. Y'know Scott, your Dad... he had it all, looks, charm, confidence. He had everything. Everything. They were magnificent. They had it all before them. A perfect career and then everything changed. Your Dad became, I dunno, self-obsessed, focused on himself, a selfish dancer. I didn't know what to make of it. He started doing his own thing.

Improvising. Throwing in crazy, wild, crowd-pleasing steps. A bit like yourself, Scott. Not always strictly ballroom. Shirley'd put up with it for as long as she bloody-well could. It was only a matter of time before she eventually cracked. I tried to warn him. But no, he wouldn't listen to any of us, he'd lost touch with reality. He was convinced he and your Mum could win the Pan Pacific Grand Prix dancing his own steps. Of course, they lost.

I was lucky enough to win the title that year. It was horrible. The shock sent Doug crazy. He vowed never to dance again. For a while we didn't think he'd pull through. Slowly, little by little, day by day, he managed to crawl back from the dark pit of despair, and tack together some semblance of a life.

When you were born, Doug found a reason to live. He vowed that one day you'd win the trophy that he could never win. That's why I've been so hard on you, Scott. For Doug to see you so close and, go the same way he went, it would be too much for him to bear. I really think it'd kill him. [*He pauses, fighting back tears.*] Your father's proud Scott. He wouldn't want me to do this, but I'm begging you—dance with Liz and win the Pan Pacifics once, just once for Doug. He's suffered enough, Scott. Don't you think he deserves a little bit of happiness? [*He pauses and wipes the tears from his eyes.*] Ultimately it's up to you of course. You do what you think's best. [*He pats* SCOTT *on the shoulder.*] I know you'll make the right decision.

The Glass Mermaid

Tobsha Learner   CURRENCY PRESS

A powerful story about grieving, suicide and those whose lives are shattered as a result.

ACT 1 SCENE 7: JANKO KAVOIC, 34, a Croatian refugee

The Australian Coast, present day, an isolated beach house south of Surfers Paradise.

JANKO:

When I was soldier we were crossing the Sava River. It is frozen over. We have packs on our backs. Heavy. Our bayonets are tied to us. We are walking. The ice is hard like glass. We are alone, there is nothing, only the cry of crows and this thud, thud. War somewhere else. Suddenly there is sound, cracking. The slab of ice we are walking on, tilts up... We are sliding, our fingers clutching at the surface, no one is screaming, it is too quick, we are sliding into the river, the freezing river. And the ice, she closes up above our heads. As if we had never been there... I see the others floating down, struggling with their packs. Like crazy ballet dancers. I am dying I think. My cousins' faces like ghosts in the green water. I cut myself free. Up up to the surface. My face is pressed against the ice. My skin sticks to it. I push my bayonet through the ice. I hear people shouting. They cut a hole and pull me free... Not war. Nature. Nine men pulled down into the water. I never see my cousins again. Not even the bodies...

For a year afterwards I was like machine, no thought, no emotion. I have become invisible. There have been many woman here. I become what they want, I have been living in my skin. It is safe that way. I am no longer Janko Kavoic...

Wolf

Tobsha Learner   CURRENCY PRESS

For play description see page 135.

ACT 2: DANIEL LUPUS, the Wolf, 24, an art student

1969. The kitchen of a commune in Balmain. DANIEL *enters.*

DANIEL:

I'm at a party, dig? And there's some beautiful bird on the other side of the room. All tits and arse under silk, dig? And I love silk. Now I'm hot. I walk into that room with every muscle screaming here I am! Brown, taut, gleaming! Touch me! Touch me! Touch me! So she's checking me out, she's thinking, who's this guy? Man or

Maoist? Her eyes, hungry eyes cutting across the room. Do I look back at her? Do I go over? No way. I want to juice her up, wanting me so badly her yoni is burning holes in the carpet. So I turn to another bird and start talking, loudly, dig? Like I am reciting, weaving the air, man... Marxism, Apollinaire, Wilhelm Reich. The room's turning, dig? All eyes are on me. Heating me, like the fucking sun. So I begin to move while I talk. Like my words are music. And just when I have all of them like this. [*He draws a net in with his fist.*] Bang! I stop. Total silence. And I mean total. I get up, walk across the room. Past her. Straight past her. And man, I can smell her wanting me. And then I lean against the wall. And every time, that cool chick, that ice queen comes over and says something like, 'Cheryl told me you were a painter, a real painter.' And I say, 'I do okay.' 'You've got a really unusual face.' And she says, 'You're teasing me.' And I say, 'I never tease...' One week later, I've got her on canvas. Two weeks later we've gone through the Karma-Sutra. Three weeks later I'm not answering her calls...

That's winning, that's all I want. That moment of power, of them looking up at you out of control.

ACT 2: DANIEL

1969. The commune. ZOE *is curled up on the floor.* DANIEL *sits beside her.*

DANIEL:

And while the young girl sleeps, hair spread, the Wolf... our Wolf watches her. The eyes fluttering behind the eyelids. The sweet breath. The breasts that demand. The Wolf watches, he is Nubis, he is Cerberus he is silent.

[*There is no response from* ZOE.]

Zoe... Zoe?

[*There is no movement.*]

Okay, so I didn't come home. But like we don't need vows, like we're free to love, Zoe, each other and anybody else. I mean let's get real here. I'm young. I like women and women like me. It's a natural happening. I've got too much to give to give it just to one person. Anyway, if it really makes you feel better, I didn't make it with her. I was going to but when it came down to it, it just wasn't a happening thing. I guess that means something. Like maybe you're special. Anyway what's important is that I'm back now. Seven in the morning and I've just left someone to be here so I can be with you, Zoe. When you wake up. Now baby, that's commitment.

[*He curls up beside her and starts caressing her.*]

Zoe, Zoe?

[*Her body rolls.*]

Bart! Call an ambulance!

[*He begins to give* ZOE *mouth to mouth.*]

Bart! Call an ambulance!

[*He goes back to mouth to mouth desperately.*]

Come on, baby, wake up, come on baby…

[DANIEL *cradles* ZOE's *body.*]

No, she's not dead. She's just sleeping, aren't you? Aren't you baby, sleeping.

ACT 3: BART, Daniel's art dealer

1979. BART *is sitting in a chair with a glass of scotch in his hand.* DEIDRE, *a senior politician and* DANIEL's *wife, walks in wearing a coat and carrying a briefcase.*

BART:

Today has been so quiet, so silent. The phone hasn't rung once. Not even my mother.

It's silly really, it's just that today was going to be our seventh anniversary. Not that we would have made a big deal about it. Probably a walk through the Botanical Gardens then maybe the art gallery. Michael liked doing the galleries. I think that's why he liked me. Some ridiculous idea about status.

It's the intimacy I miss. The habit of him. Little things, stupid things, like the sound of him in the mornings singing, 'I like coffee, I like tea, I like the Jabberwok and it likes me'… He never got the words right. And he always put too much milk in the tea. It's ironic really because I always made out I was with him for the sex. I was never much good at beat stuff, all that steam and floating faces. Michael was the first lover I wanted to wake up with.

Yes, there are always others.

Blood Relations

David Malouf   CURRENCY PRESS

For play description see page 138.

ACT 1 SCENE 7: EDWARD, 26, dark, good looking, with an
air of cultivated toughness and menace

The living room of WILLY'*s house, in a tropical coastal area of
North Western Australia.*

EDWARD:

I don't know how it happened—I was too young—but my father got
into some sort of financial trouble. Luck was against him: he was a
man who never had any luck. He got strange. Even my step-mother
couldn't deal with him. He had this idea he was about to be accused
of something—some kind of fraud—that all the evidence was being
piled up against him. He just sat there. Brooding. Waiting for them
to come. I didn't know how to speak to him, what to say. I was
ashamed. Then one afternoon I came in from football practice, and
when I called out from the kitchen—I'd just poured myself a glass of
milk from the fridge—there was no answer. I went out into the hall.
The TV was on in the lounge room. *Happy Days.* The twins loved
that. There was no one there. I went upstairs, still sipping the milk. I
wasn't really worried. But there was something odd just the same.
This sound. A sort of buzzing. The thing is, it had always been there,
and I'd just become aware of it. I'd been carrying it inside me.

I let it lead me. And with the glass of milk in my hand, still in my
football boots and guernsey, I came to the door of my parents'
bedroom. I'd just taken a sip of milk. I can feel it in my throat right
now. Curdling. Turning to blood. I couldn't believe it! He'd taken
them with him—all four of them—and left me out of it. Why? Was it
my luck: because I was late home from school? Or did he choose
that afternoon because he meant to leave me out: because I'd never
been one of them? Maybe he'd simply forgotten I existed.

All that... blood. It explained something. The way the world is. To
change it something extraordinary would have to happen. I thought it
couldn't be done. Now, I'm not so sure.

I've been sleepwalking. I'm just beginning to wake up.

Milo

Ned Manning   CURRENCY PRESS

For play description see page 138.

ACT 1 SCENE 2: TOBY, school friend of Milo's, a grazier in
outback New South Wales

The kitchen table after dinner. MILO *and* TOBY *are having a beer.*

TOBY:

[*to* MILO] Some shockin' things have been going on out home. You
remember Billy Adams? Well, like the rest of us he's been struggling. Had to borrow more, was encouraged to borrow more, and…
well, the place was going down the mine. You know the story. Interest rates, wool prices, petrol prices, etc etc. Anyway Billy was told
that he'd had the word, that he'd have to sell. I mean, that's a family
like ours. Four generations. A lot to let go. He told the bank that if
they foreclosed, if they tried to force him off he'd… it'd be over his
dead body. Well that sort of thing doesn't worry a figures man, does
it? I mean if the books balance that's all they give a fuck about.

Yeah. Only trouble was, Billy was dead serious. They closed off
the mortgage. I saw him in town. Pissed on rum. He told me all
about it. He just got up, drained his glass and headed off. He was
fucked. You know what he did? He got home, got out the .303 and
blew Mary, the kids and himself away.

I mean, fuck Milo, what do you do? What can you do? This isn't
about rich people, those days are over, we won't be sending our kids to
boarding school and holidaying at Terrigal. We'll be lucky to survive.

ACT 1 SCENE 2: MILO, an idealist, works part-time as a laboratory
technician

A little later.

MILO:

[*to* TOBY] He was a great bloke, old Jock. Taught me heaps. I'll
never forget one day. I was mustering with him. We were moving
this mob, about one thousand all told, towards this paddock we'd

kept specially. We were pretty pleased with ourselves because we reckoned we'd got through. It was gettin' late and there was one of those sunsets beginning which make your hair stand up on end. I was day-dreaming about going to town and getting on the piss. I remember leaning forward to stroke my horse's mane when I noticed all the sheep heading up the hill. Why the fuck would they do that when all the feed was down the creek? I just sat there and watched them. Then it clicked. I screamed out to Jock to watch the gate. I galloped up the hill after the bloody mob. Over rocks, past blackberry bushes. The hill was covered with gullies. There was a big one running all the way down to the creek. Erosion. It must have been ten feet deep and it split the paddock like a canyon would.

I galloped flat out up that hill and sure enough there they were. The fuckin' sheep were diving headlong into the gully and smothering each other to death. By the time I got there they must've been about ten deep. I jumped off my horse and began throwing them out. I was screaming and the tears were flowing down me cheeks.

I was standing in a gully full of suffocating sheep. I could feel them dying under me feet. I yelled and threw and bawled like a baby. The ones I threw up just hit the wall and rolled back down on top of me. It was hopeless.

I looked up and there was the old fella sitting on that big mongrel of a horse, silhouetted against the sky, just looking. He didn't say a word. His shoulders were hunched, his hat was back on his head. He looked at me and shrugged, turned his horse and slowly walked off. I must have saved a few I s'pose. The rest were dispersed by the dogs. I climbed out of the gully and looked down on that sea of death. At least three hundred sheep had committed suicide. I was broken. I caught up to him and we rode home in silence. I never really recovered from that. I vowed the bush would never get on top of me like that.

ACT 1 SCENE 2: TOBY

A little later.

TOBY:

[*to* MILO] I never dreamt… never in a thousand years. I've seen other people go under and I've always thought we could survive. I always knew we could pull through. And I... I just can't accept that we won't.

I was born on the Western Plains. It's my country and don't tell me it isn't. I know all about the history but I'm not talking about that, I'm talking about us. Four generations of our family. How could I leave it? I can't watch Yallaroy go under, it'd be like... like watching yourself drown. It's like my guts are being dragged out of me.

I love that place... riding out on that stupid mongrel of a horse, just me and the dogs... so peaceful and so, I dunno... at times it's even... *(beautiful).* Flat and dry to everyone else but to me it's... All the pasture we've put in, all the clearing, the hours we dragged rocks and shit away, ploughing, twelve hour shifts getting bogged and I feel... proud. Because it's our country, it's Murray country. Wherever I look I see the old man and my grandfather and his father and I think of them clearing all that scrub country. I look at the big scribbly barks and river oaks. I watch the sheep huddling under them and I think of how smart they were to clear so selectively. You're not the first person to talk about conservation, Milo. There's people who've raped this country all right but don't you fucking well forget about the ones who've looked after it either. I never raped no-one, I never kicked any bugger off their land, all I ever done is work me bloody guts out. It breaks my fuckin' heart... and I just can't handle it that it's me... who's fucked up! Yallaroy is, is everything, it's everything that I... I love. I've, I've let the whole bloody shooting match go down the gurgler... Christ Almighty what am I going to do?

ACT 2 SCENE 1: MILO

MILO *is alone, rolling a joint.*

MILO:

What is real? The world is tearing itself apart and what the fuck do you think you can do about it? Cry for the poor? Exorcise a little guilt by sending a donation to Freedom from Hunger? Big deal. You don't have any impact and you're fooling yourself if you think you do. Foreign Affairs just deals in diplomatic solutions. Temporary ones at that. It's human nature that has to change. It's us and our jealousies and our capacity to justify whatever we do. 'Ethnic cleansing', Pol Pot, Ceaucescu, the Holocaust, the CIA. On and on into the deep abyss of man's capacity to indulge himself in barbarity and butchery. What do Governments and their advisers do? Compromise. Divide the spoils. Ahh fuck it...

[DI *enters half dressed.*]

[DI: What would you know about anything, Milo?]

MILO: I know...

[DI: Nothing.]

[*She exits.*]

MILO: Nothing? I know nothing... is that it? We'll see about that.

Steal Away Home

Phil Motherwell   CURRENCY PRESS

For play description see page 140.

JACK, a country and western singer in his late 20s

JACK *has returned from working in a carnival. He has travelled much and has no family that he knows about.*

JACK:

Stealing was fun... No one lasts forever, though, and one fine day my brilliant run came to an end. I'd only come undone over one, but the way I went in linked me to another one, and bingo! It was like a chain reaction... The plea my mouthpiece is making to the bench opens with a heavy string section... 'My client was orphaned while still a baby...' Every woman in the place reaches for her hanky as he cranks out the story I've passed on to him—same one they told me... Well, the magistrate is just about on his last legs and he doesn't seem to be up to all this, a hundred not out, slow as a wet week and so close to being senile that it doesn't make any difference. 'What about this Aboriginal blood?' My mouthpiece leaps to his feet. 'Your worship seems to be on the wrong tram.' The old geezer has got me fixed in a withering stare, his eyes clouded over with hate, no word of restraint can reach him. 'Nothing confusing about this, by golly, nothing at all.' He plucks my adoption papers from the ruins of the brief... "This fair-skinned child is to be taken from his Aboriginal mother and placed..."' Best country in the world. And there's no stopping him; he's off and running, never dreaming that I've never been told anything about my mother, not even her race. 'If you'd stayed on your own side of the river, over in Collingwood where you belong, and robbed your own kind, I would have taken a very different attitude towards you... But you've robbed friends of mine, people in my street, some of them more than once. You've robbed county court judges. You've come over to our side of the river and plundered the homes of the very people...'

And at the end of the day I came home with a stern warning, a bond, and an apology. Still no wiser about my mother—all I knew now was that she was black. But that seemed to be enough for some people...

Well you know how word gets around about this sort of thing. Next thing Mary isn't allowed to see me. Her father won't let her leave the house at night. I climb up to her window most nights and spend some time with her. She was so angry at first, giving as good as she got. They couldn't bully her, so they bought her. Cost them a trip to Hawaii... That was the last straw...

So watch out for me! Here I am standing in the shadows! Laying in wait in your garden, creeping through your rooms... I fondle your jewellery, every nerve alive... I breathe the romance of the night air... Tread the rich carpet of wet grass... Freestanding mansions on either side of me shining like Christmas trees in the night.

JACK:

Studley Park Road runs sharply down from the hills of the eastern suburbs and over the river to Collingwood. Friday night and drunken cars float past riding their brakes... The sleeping suburb so black you can hardly see your hand in front of your face. I know my way around this house though... I've been here quite a few times before, always on a Friday night, and I've got his whole pay packet every time. Seven or eight hundred in an unopened envelope sitting on the mantelpiece. This fellow is unbelievable, isn't he? I've got him for his wages again...!

Slow steady breath heaving quietly behind me in the dark bedroom, his wife is harder to hear, quicker, almost like a little gasp. One leg stretching down from the window to the trellis. Gain a foothold, cling to the wall... Then this taxi turns into the drive—the headlights sweep across and find me pinned to the wall like a moth fresh from the kill bottle. These people's son has arrived home from a party and he's chasing after me down the lane while the taxi driver radios the police... 'Stop thief!'...

And I'm off, vaulting from the driveway into the lane—I've reached the gardens at the other end before boy wonder has scaled the paling fence. Another block and I'm still stretching my lead and just about to lose the jerk. Then a couple of jocks join the chase, joggers out for a run. They've heard the alarm and they want a piece of my hide. They're after me, all of us stampeding over the footbridge behind the Anchorage in a headlong rush of charging shadows—they're just about breathing down my neck... On through the back streets of Abbotsford, running blind over Hoddle Street— *kerthump* and one of the jocks gets cleaned up by a Kombi—*whop* right behind me and it's bounced him back into the arms of his mates...

On through the Housing Commission estate—up the back steps of the flats and I'm in luck, the stairwell door is open. Home free! It's snibbed shut behind me and I'm leaning back against the feeble frame of ply, heart leaping in my chest, lungs burning like they've been left out in the sun... voices outside, heavy feet stamping on the stairs and kicking at the door.

Really up against it now, that last door opened to the stars. Slammed it shut behind me, but there's nothing to wedge it shut with. Sprinting the length of the building, leaping over the edge. No way back from here. Nowhere to go from here... [*He spins around as though confronting an intruder.*] Stand back or I jump!

Atlanta

Joanna Murray-Smith
CURRENCY PRESS

For play description see page 141.

ALEX, thoughtful, anxious, quiet. Alex is a journalist and Atlanta's lover. He is plagued by anxiety about meaning, responsibility, truth.

ALEX *is alone.*

ALEX:

After perfectly sweet, pleasant evenings with friends, dinner parties, we'd come back to my place, gossip in the car, how inedible the food was, how fat so and so was... and we'd make toast and drink coffee and watch *News Overnight* and talk about the news anchor's hair-style... and then out of nothing, out of that, all that sweetness and dullness, she'd just weep. Really weep, stare out of the window into the night and cry as if she were about to lose her very soul... I would hold her and stroke her and ask her over and over. I'd say: 'Tell me. Tell me what's wrong. Tell me.' And she would say she didn't know... A diabolical state to be in... sure... But let me just say that it is a much worse thing to witness. At least if you are grieving, you are consumed by it. But if you're just there on the edge, watching, you are hopeless... helpless... She suffers in her weird dark way, inside her, in a way that I can never suffer.

Sure, I feel pain or happiness... Happiness... When Atlanta, watching the sea, looks up suddenly and smiles at me. A classic smile. Unthoughtabout. [*Pause.*] But what she feels—no. I don't come close. And yet the idea of leaving her—for what? For a woman like me? Someone who doesn't get all that worked up? A woman who takes the ordinariness of life in her stride? God! Can you do that once you've known the other? Can you begin a life that's normal and pleasant and inane? No tears and no hysterics and no passion. No long discussions, no detailed analysis of what every option, choice, word means. Just a take it or leave it life. Just a world full of little things. [*Pause.*] Maybe, after all, a life like that would be good for me. Life without Atlanta. Or will I wake up one morning without her and wonder what it's all about. This thing. This getting up and going out into the day thing. [*Pause.*] Maybe a simple life is actually more horrifying than a life which knows, in some way, what horror is.

Così

Louis Nowra   CURRENCY PRESS

Lewis, a young, first-time director, is hired to direct a variety show as part of a therapeutic program at a state-run psychiatric institution. Whilst he's not exactly equipped for the job he's willing to give it a go—Lewis is drifting and needs some direction in his own life. He becomes involved with the lives of his actors as their operatic extravaganza lurches forward and anti-Vietnam protests take place in the streets. It is 1970.

SCENE 26: DOUG, 20s, a wiry, intense pyromaniac

Inside the hall. Day.

DOUG:

[*to* LEWIS] Mum had five cats. We had been having a few... differences, Mum and me, so one night I rounded them up, put them in a cage, doused them with petrol and put a match to them. [LEWIS *thinks that* DOUG *is joking.*] Yeah, funny, eh? Well, boy O, boy, what a racket! Then I let them out. They were running around the backyard burning and howling—there's no such thing as grace under pressure for a burning cat. Mum comes outside to see what's happening. Totally freaked out, she did. I figured I'd wait a couple of hours until the cats were dead and Mum was feeling a bit sorry for herself and I'd knock on the front door and say, 'Hi, Mum, I've come to talk about our unresolved conflicts', but O no, one of those fucking cats ran into the house. In a couple of minutes the whole house was alight and there was no bloody front door to knock on. [*A beat.*] If it wasn't for that damn cat, I wouldn't be in here.

Crow

Louis Nowra   CURRENCY PRESS

For play description see page 151.

ACT 1 SCENE 4: VINCE, Crow's son, Boofhead's brother

Backyard of the hotel. Day.

VINCE:

[*to his mother and brother*] You'd love it. The tent and all. See, they pay their money, thinking, 'I don't need to go three rounds, I can punch this Abo out in one.' They get excited seeing me. This boom boom of the bass drum calling the audience in, BANG! BANG!, the spruiker outside the tent— [*Imitating a spruiker.*] 'Come in, see if you can go three rounds with the Ebony Prince—see if you can knock him down.' They strip, looking like white grubs. They put on some gloves, thinking they're world champions. They come swinging, like some piece of corrugated iron flapping in a cyclone. All around me there is this sound—this roar and if you listen real careful you can hear what the crowd's shouting, 'Kill the Abo!' The first times I wanted to kill the bastard. Christ, his defences open. Easy, easy as pie to take him in one punch.

Doesn't make a contest, doesn't make the tent show money. Boss doesn't like it. So you play with him. Make 'em think they're good. They swing away, hardly landing a punch and everyone's fooled, thinking I'm being beaten by some yahoo. Round one, he goes back into his corner. Cocky. His friend's slapping him on the back. 'Give it to the boong next round.' I jab at him in round two. Just on the shoulders, hitting his arm muscles. [*He demonstrates.*] Just there.

His arms begin to feel like lead. He begins to understand, though his mates don't, that I am playing with him. I can take him out any time. In his eyes you see—he's got The Fear. Back on his stool at the end of round two, his mates are wiping him down, urging him on, 'Go on, Ern, punch that black bastard out.' The bell rings for round three and he comes towards me trying to look tough, but his gloves feel as heavy as medicine balls and he's afraid of what I am going to do to him, but he can't run because his mates would laugh at him. For the first time he's got The Fear of a blackfella. He swings and to the spectators they look like they're connecting. I jab him back, for every time he takes a swing at me. My punches look piss weak—but he'll have the bruises for weeks. He wants to fall down and get it over with, but his mates urge him on. He's like those cattle down at the abattoirs who, just before the whack behind their ears, know they're going to cop it and are stunned at what's about to happen. I throw a punch. It seems wild and a last gasp, a lucky punch, but it hits him where I want him to be hit. It's like a sledge hammer into his stomach. He gasps, like a tyre being punctured and I smell the terror and the booze pouring out of him. The crowd go quiet seeing this white grub wriggling on the canvas. See, they think it was just a blackfella's lucky punch. They're all clamouring to have a go at me. I make the Boss a fortune.

ACT 2 SCENE 3: VINCE

The mangrove swamps. Morning. VINCE, *dirty and exhausted, enters, leading* RUTH *by a rope he has tied around her neck and in the other hand he carries a bayonet. She, too, is dirty and exhausted.*

VINCE:

I could punch the living daylights out of you. [*He goes to hit her.*] I'm just a tent boxer, Ruthie. Just a tent boxer. When I left, I thought I could do it. You know, do a bit of tent boxing—be seen by some fella who'd think I was championship material. And this fella in Rockhampton did. A month in the tent show and I'm on my way—so long fellas! Cock of the hoop, cock of the walk. Did three professional fights. Each time, I've got him. Got him like a kangaroo in the spotlight. And I start in for the kill, but I get angry and wild, wanting to finish him off—I leave my guard open—I lose the fight, then the next three. Same thing—a rush of blood. I should have won them all. My manager gives up on me. I do the grog, I do the gambling and pretty soon I'm back in the tent show again, tail between my legs. I dream of getting back into pro, doing it right. But each night another town, another drink, another game of cards. Like, I can't stop myself. All the time I'm thinking of you—

The truth, Ruthie. The truth. I'd think of you, how good looking you are but I couldn't write. Didn't have the right words. Then one month I saved, saved up heaps. It wasn't like pockets of gold but it was enough, you know. I was in Cairns and thought to myself if I stick with the troupe I'm gonna spend it, so I think I'll hitchhike back to Darwin, back to you. First ride I didn't get far and I was stranded in some town miles from anywhere. I wait for a lift, I drink a bit, try out my luck with cards. Couple of days later, I get another lift. Another town. I do the same thing. I don't know why. I don't want to, but I do. All the time I want to come home to you. It goes on and on. I ask one driver to drop me off in between towns. He thinks I'm loony but I think, 'There'll be no temptation out there', and I walk through the red dust, through the rain and I feel low. I hitchhike my way to the next town and I gamble more and my stake gets smaller and smaller. I can't even explain to myself, Ruthie: I love you, I want to come home with money and I lose it, like I got some demon inside me saying, 'Spend it, Vince, spend it', and I do. All of it. 'Til, finally, I hock me gloves. That's all I got left and I hock 'em. Fifty miles outside of Darwin I got nothing. Nothing. Can't even tell you I'm making it as a pro boxer. I sit down on the side of the road and I think to myself, don't go to Darwin, turn around and go back—she won't want you. Then I think, make this your last gamble, Vince. First car or truck that stops, wherever it's going, I'm gonna take it. Sort of like gambling with God or fate, I guess. A cattle truck stops and it's going to Darwin. I think to myself: this is fate. It wants me to go to Darwin and to you. Now I think, Ruthie, that the driver was the devil.

The Temple

Louis Nowra   CURRENCY PRESS

A former truckie and slaughterhouse owner, Laurie Blake turns entrepreneur, building his 'Bridges of Dreams' and letting the bank worry about the billion dollar debt. A womaniser, art collector and friend to Prime Ministers, the 'Takeover King of Australia' rampages his way through the eighties when the whole country seemed out of control.

ACT 1 SCENE 5: LAURIE BLAKE

LAURIE:

Butchers are always happy. Have you noticed that? Women are happy when they visit a butcher. They imagine him undressing her. Because he knows flesh so well. The muscles, the soft underbelly, and he can be so tender to the insides. She knows, can feel the hand that has put a knife between the ribs, but has also felt it, tenderly like this. Butchers are the only men who know how easily flesh bruises. And he places her on the chopping block and she hears herself landing there, like a flat slap, like the slap of a piece of soft, tender, steak slice. Because they know what it is to slaughter, they know the body better than anyone. Now, I'm going to fuck you like a butcher.

ACT 2 SCENE 4: LAURIE

LAURIE:

[*to* BARRY ST JOHN] People ask me why I do something. I answer, 'Why should I not do it?' Yeh, why do I do things, Baz?

[*He grabs a knife and slashes the Monet painting.*]

Like that. Because I like to play for keeps. You're terminated, Baz. You'll never get out of this financial black hole.

[*He whips* BAZ's *sunglasses off him.*]

Let's see the whites of your eyes. Without your sunnies, Baz, your eyes are a dead give away. I have seen that look, many, many times. It's the look of fear. You see it in an animal's eyes when it's about to be slaughtered. They enter the chute, a bit nervous. But confident, but as they advance down the chute into the killing rooms, they smell blood. They look around and see men with these things in their hand. And although they are not terrified yet, they are afraid. Their eyes grow large and twitch. Hands grab them, sure, certain hands. Hands that have done this a thousand times. The animals are locked into a position they struggle against but cannot escape from. You place the stun gun behind the back of their ear and the feeling of the metal, the sense of being trapped—at that split second, they know. They are going to die. Before the whack, there is such a look of terror and fear in their eyes that you never forget it. You're looking into the soul of an animal and seeing the greatest terror a man can see in another beast.

The Hope of the World

Errol O'Neill   UNPUBLISHED

Brisbane in the mid 1980s. A thousand blue collar public sector workers strike over the use of contract labour and are sacked by the government of Johannes Bjelke-Petersen, now at the peak of his power. For Red, the present troubles are an echo of past events which occurred in the very same streets, under the same administration.

ACT 1 SCENE 11: RED MORRISON is a nationally renowned journalist who returns to his home town, Brisbane, during this industrial dispute. He is trying to give up the drink and put meaning back into his life.

JIM *and* CLARE'*s house. It is late at night.* RED *is talking to* CLARE, *his lover when they were students fifteen years ago.* CLARE *is a social worker, involved in the dispute as a volunteer counsellor to the sacked workers' families. (Note: Mount Coot-tha is pronounced as: Mount Cootha)*

RED:

There are some honest cops who don't like what's going on. But not many people out there give a shit. I know you treat the Special Branch as a joke... But they weren't always funny. [*Pause.*] They came up to my room at college, one night. They said, 'Reginald Patrick Morrison. You're under arrest. Would you please accompany us to the City CIB?' [*Pause.*] We went for a drive to Mount Coot-tha. They handcuffed me in the back seat, and pulled my pants down, and stuck a gun into my genitals. Then one of 'em put a gun to my head. He said there was only one bullet in the chamber. The bloke on my left opened his fist and showed me the other five... He pulled the trigger. Four times. Then he said—I will never forget these words—'Reggie, you're a lucky little bastard so far. You've got one more chance. If you don't co-operate with us, we'll blow your fucking brains out! We'll bury you here in the bush, and no one'll ever find you.' [*Pause.*] They wanted me to confess to assaulting that cop at the Quang demo. I was scared shitless, but I just felt like taking them on. I said, 'Shove it up your arse!'... I heard the trigger click, and I fainted. Next thing I knew, I woke up with this massive pain in my stomach. Then I realised I was on the ground beside the car with these four cops kicking the shit out of me. I looked up, and honestly, these guys were frothing at the mouth. They got back in the car and I could hear them laughing. They were pissed! I can still smell the alcohol on their breath... I couldn't move. I could feel the blood and the snot pouring out of my mouth and nose. I was thinking: what is this? A Third World country? A South American dictatorship? They drove off and ran over my arm... [*Pause.*] I'm lying there in the dark, looking at the stars, thinking: Vietnam, South Africa, Queensland. The basis of authority is not democratic suffrage, it's physical violence... Then I felt my arm hurting... By the time you got back from holidays, the bruises had healed. [*Pause.*] But some part of me, some innocence, had been killed, and I had no knowledge of how to cope with it. No personal ability to right the wrongs. No way to overturn the system... [*Pause.*] Come to Sydney with me... Let's start again where we left off.

Dead Heart

Nick Parsons   CURRENCY PRESS

A small Aboriginal community to the west of Alice Springs is thrown into turmoil after the death of a young man in the police lock-up. The play dramatically portrays some of the many complex issues facing both black and white Australians in the 1990s, as a nation attempts to come to terms with its past and to address the problems of the present.

ACT 2: SENIOR CONSTABLE RAY LORKIN, white, 30–40

The community advisor's living room. Night.

RAY:

Thing is, I'm after some advice. About Tony. I've been doing a bit of thinking in my quiet, plodding way. I mean, I've never seen a death... ignored like this before. It bothered me. And then... the body was very clean. I mean, he went out drinking, he was sitting in the dirt all night... you know. Next morning he doesn't have a bit of dirt on him. What d'you think of that?

[*Silence.*]

Well, I thought it was a bit weird. Then Sarah told me another weird thing: his feet are bruised. It's in her report. When you die the blood collects at the lowest part of the body. It makes a bruise. You don't always see it on a dark skin, but she said it was pretty clear. Now if he was lying down... and had a heart attack... why did the blood go to his feet? But then... something came along which helped a bit: now, we know that... Tony was having an affair... with Kate. The point is: I just found out their last... their last meeting happened at a spot where there's men's business going on. You know that?

[*Silence.*]

That sort of brought it into focus. So I've put these facts together into a theory. And I'd like your opinion. Tony was killed for fucking his girlfriend on a sacred site. What do you think?

[*Silence.*]

Let me spell it out a bit. He went out drinking with his mates, he drove home. Maybe someone drove him, I dunno. He was killed, the body was left in the car. The blood settled... to his feet. They washed him... in a ceremony while they sung his spirit out. And he was put in his bedroll so that Kate would find him in the morning... and work out where she stands. And there's no mourning for him because... well, because he broke a big sacred law.

There's a way of killing a man by... [*Crooking his elbow.*] blocking both arteries in the neck. Maybe someone in the back seat. If you do it right there's a reflex stoppage of the heart.

I think the old men commissioned a young bloke from around here. Strong physically, and really strong in his culture. Someone he knew. Course, most of the young blokes around here: they're out... chasing girls or sniffing petrol. They don't have that secret law. But there's one... that I can think of... who might.

But how can I prove it? I don't think that'll be too hard. I just need to find someone who... who saw it happen. Or heard about it.

You know: the washing, then carry the body around... I mean all the way to Les and Kate's, for God sake. I thought: just about everybody must've known. Aboriginal people. You, for instance.

I'm curious to know, Dave... how you knew there wasn't a mark on the body... before he was examined.

[*Silence.*]

I put it to you this way: I'm giving you a chance. Like you gave me. You tell me if that little bastard is the one or I'll go to any of about a dozen people out there. Any one of whom will tell me if I want 'em to. And when they do I'll have you for concealing and you'll be fucked. Might even do time. Or have I got it wrong? Do you want to hang round here the rest of your life? [*Picking up a brochure.*] ATSIC for you, wasn't it? Ladder up the public service? You better work out your priorities, boy.

ACT 2: SENIOR SERGEANT WARREN OAKS, white, mid 40s

The lock-up, day. BILLY, *the police aide, sits huddled on the concrete floor, calling out.*

OAKS:

[*to* RAY] What the fuck is he doing in the lock-up? The man is not a dog, Constable.

[*He steps close to* RAY.]

Listen, you dirty little tyrant, you don't make the rules out here. This is not your private fiefdom. You think it is, don't you? You think you know better than the poor plodding coppers back at head office, following all those pedantic little rules and regulations that big men like you really can't be bothered with. Let me tell you, the rule book is there for a purpose. It keeps us all out of trouble, and when you chuck it on the shit heap in the end you always wind up under it. And believe me, that's where you're going. A mate of mine tells me Internal Affairs is looking at you right now and you have no chance of staying here. In fact, on current form I'd say you don't have much chance of staying in the Force. Understand? That story—That... interview... on television made you look like a nut case. A vicious little thug who likes bumping off the odd boong. The local papers are berserk; *I*... have been fielding questions from *The Sydney Morning Bloody Herald*, for God sake. I'm sure by the weekend we'll be a mini series.

They're going to throw you to the lions, mate. And I think it's no more than you deserve.

Now. Release that man. I have to do an interview with your Mr Reynolds, try and clean up this mess. Fortunately I am on good terms with Mr Reynolds. You can have your office back.

ACT 2: RAY

Desert waterhole. Morning.

RAY:

[*levelling a shotgun at* DAVID] Don't fuck around! If I blew your fuckin' head off who would know? Eh? So listen to me: I'm warning you. Alright? [*Indicating the waterhole.*] You couldn't find this water by yourself: he must've brought you. I knew that: it's why I'm here. So where is he?

    [*Silence.*]

You're trying me, Dave. You're really fuckin' trying me. God, he's a clever little cunt. He set a trail he knew I'd get out and follow. When I got back to the car he'd let the tyres down, put sand in the tank... Completely fucked it. He's clever. But he's got more than he can chew this time. [*Laughs.*] You're a fuckin' white man, Dave. A fuckin' white man. I got more blackfella in me than you'll ever have. So I'm gunna ask you once more, and you better fuckin' tell me: where is he?

[DAVID: It was like... a man, a spirit...]

RAY: [*interrupting*] No! No! No! Don't give me that bullshit. That spooky Aboriginal bullshit. I don't want to hear it; I don't want to know. Christ. Time was the man was dead and that was it. A man was just a man. Now they follow you round. If he's dead he should be in the *ground*; in the cold fucking ground; he should be... growing into something else, not... crawling out and trailing you with his long rope hangin' off him. That's not... the way it's done. I won't stand for it.

I've *worked* for people. I've tried to make... They gotta *learn* to be whitefellas! [*Tapping his head.*] Up here. That's what the world is. You know that, Dave; you—you *seen* it. Tribal way is finished; it doesn't have a chance, and Poppy is not gunna drag this on and on and on till every last young fella's drunk himself to death or... strung himself up because he doesn't know what he is any more. And some poor fuckwit walks out the station and sees that... sees that... that thing... hangin' there and... and carries it round for the rest of his life. I'm telling you: Poppy is going down for what he's done. I've got something on him and he's going down.

[*Pause.*]

I try and think of him... like he was, you know? Like on the footy field or something. But I can't see his face any more; it's all got... sucked out somehow. All I can see is a... black tongue hangin' out. Swollen up. Nothing else will come, you know? That's all that's left. Of him. In my head. A black... tongue.

Strangers in the Night

Abe Pogos   CURRENCY PRESS

Daniel, a young Australian writer, researches in New York's red light district. Chance encounters and a growing fascination draw him ever deeper along the mean streets into the stark realities of the city that never sleeps. On his descent into hell, he discovers the darkness that lurks in the hearts of all men; and in his own.

ACT 1 SCENE 1: GERRY

Night. GERRY*'s house.* GERRY *has returned home with a man he believes to be a television star.*

GERRY:

Does your wife know you pick up boys? [*Pause.*] Look, I don't mean to hassle you. I know it's difficult—Very difficult. To live your life in... in pieces. To portray a perfect family man to the world when the bit that really matters, that drives you, your life force is always in the shadows. Look, I understand. My parents don't know what I do nights. The people I work with would be mortified. At least I live alone. But you're married. You pretend when you work, you pretend when you come home. [*Pause.*] It must be hell to live this half life, this… lie. When I come home there's no lie. I go to clubs and I'm an open book. I can be myself most of the time… but you? Does your wife know? Are you honest with her? Are you you when you're with her? You're not here. Not at the moment. Right now you're in disguise. And you continue the lie. I mean, when are you ever you? Truly, whole, completely you. Did you tell me your real name tonight? What is your real name? Do you use it? Will you ever use it? When you die do they engrave it on your headstone and you're finally you? Or will that be a lie too? [*Pause.*] What I'm saying is… I think it must be very hard.

Feet of Clay

Betty Roland   CURRENCY PRESS

A fastidious young sculptor, Phillip Strong, has been commissioned to sculpt a classical figure for an imporant art gallery. He has succeeded brilliantly, but in the course of his work has become obsessed with the idea of physically possessing the eroticised marble figure. He has invested the statue with what he believes to be the attributes of the perfect woman. With the statue finished Phillip faces the prospect of losing her and finds himself unable to bear the thought of letting other people see her.

PHILLIP, a young sculptor

Late afternoon in the studio of PHILLIP STRONG. *The figure of a woman carved in marble can be seen in the dim light.*

PHILLIP:

Have you ever heard the story of Pygmalion and Galatea? Pygmalion was a king and he fell in love with the statue of a woman. It's only a legend, but the story goes that he loved her so desperately that the gods took pity on him and turned her into flesh and blood. Well, the same sort of thing has happened to me.

Listen. They left the choice of a subject to me. The only stipulation was, a classic figure in white marble… and this story took my fancy. You remember how I was those first few months? I couldn't tear myself away from it. It seemed like magic. I couldn't go wrong. I never seemed to get tired. All the lovely lines and curves were growing under my fingers as though there was something outside myself that helped me. It was sheer inspiration. The kind of thing that comes once in a lifetime. *I* made that thing... every inch of the perfect body... lovely limbs, rounded curves, long slim lines... no one can understand what it is like to touch them. That figure became more than a mere piece of work to me. She was *my* ideal woman... *my* hidden wish... taking shape before my eyes. That's why I sent away the model. I wanted to be by myself. I used to lie there by the hour, in a kind of dream, thinking of something fresh to give her. A dimple, a curve. I felt I was creating a woman as I would have *the* woman. And I've done it. *She is marvellous.* There's nothing in the world for me but that woman... and she's made of stone. It's driving me mad!

A Touch of Silk

Betty Roland   CURRENCY PRESS

Set in a drought striken farming community in the 1920s, pressures build on Jim and his French bride Jeanne, whom he met during his service in World War I. The play traces the issues of acceptance, culture, loyalty and love. A travelling salesman sparks Jim's jealousy and rage and brings the play to a tragic climax.

ACT 2 SCENE 2: JIM DAVIDSON

JEANNE*'s farmhouse kitchen, eleven o'clock at night. His mother sits heavily in a chair, fanning herself with a handkerchief.* JIM *stands in the middle of the room.*

JIM:

Fool! I'm not being a fool, I'm just coming to my senses. We've made her life a hell between the lot of us, do you know that? All the time I've been looking for her tonight I've been remembering... things we've said to her... the poor little kid.

She's been ill, and we've expected her to go on working just the same. She's been lonely... homesick... and we've called her discontented. Hell! Do you wonder? When I look at this place... *this* place... and think of what I brought her from, I wonder she stuck it out six months. And just because she still loves pretty things... I said the things to her, that I said. If anything happens to Jeanne... I'm through!

You had her damned from the first minute you got my letter saying I had married a French girl. That was enough for you. No matter what she did, it was the wrong thing in your eyes. All her little mistakes, that anyone else would have smiled at, you talked about and worked on until you made them into crimes... and you made me think the same.

What about this afternoon? What did you have to say about Osborne coming here so often? Doesn't he go to other places as well as this? What did you want to pick on Jeanne for, any more than on Mrs Ryan or Mrs Thompson? Except that no man on earth would look at those old hags! I never believed it of Jeanne and nothing on God's earth would ever make me believe wrong of her, but I repeated the rotten things you'd said to me... and now she's gone.

There's nowhere else we can look. We've got to wait for daylight.

The Garden of Granddaughters

Stephen Sewell
CURRENCY PRESS

For play description see page 161.

ACT 2 SCENE 10: MAX, a world renowned Australian conductor

The lounge room at night. LISA *follows* MAX *into the room.*

MAX:

This civilisation! Our civilisation! That lets you and me challenge the world, celebrate it, defy it; this civilisation, Lisa, fought for over the centuries; that declared the Rights of Man, that outlawed slavery, that recognised women as part of the human race and charity and compassion as virtues worth cultivating! Is that what you want to throw away now? What the last generation wants to do with the pain and sacrifice of their forebears!

This is civilisation as it should be: wild, chaotic, argumentative; if what you're hankering after is the simple life with straight-forward principles, go to Teheran or Baghdad, that's where you'll find things at an elementary level of pristine purity— [*Moving closer to her.*] Because that's what we are, Lisa, that's what human beings are: mad, rabid, brawlers and the only way you can shut 'em up is by sticking them against the wall and shooting them.

The human spirit keeps growing, and the chain of being keeps extending, and that's the most important thing: that chain that links the past and the future, that connects our mothers and fathers with our children and grandchildren: the continuity of life, Lisa: that terrible, unfathomable will to hope that's kept people going through the darkest horrors: *that's* what makes life worthwhile that our parents live in our children and that we live in a world made better by their struggles, that we can make better still by our own—Isn't that the challenge we all face? To pick up that chain and forge the next strong link? To risk hope and in the face of all reason, say, 'Yes, life is worth living, worth continuing, worth fighting for?'— Isn't that the obligation life demands of us? To hold it sacred and to celebrate it in everything we do?

It's a privilege not to have been in Dachau, Treblinka, Buchenwald! It's a privilege not to live in the Sudan or be an Arab on the West Bank! It's a privilege to have clothes to wear and food to eat and children who'll grow up in front of you without being frightened they'll be hacked to death by some rampaging band of lunatics with another prescription for the perfection of the world! It's a privilege to drink clean water and breathe clean air and feel the sun on your skin on a winter's day! This is privilege! What we have is privileged! What did you want me to do? Tip you all in the dust so we could all, everyone, be equal in our misery?! When everything I had when I arrived in this country was in a bag no bigger than that sponge-bag I carry around with me now? Was I supposed to give that away as well for some remarkable principle?! Seeing the stars is a privilege, feeling the earth beneath your feet is a privilege! Being alive at all is a privilege and thank God we've been granted it.

The Family

Jill Shearer   CURRENCY PRESS

For play description see page 165.

ACT 2 SCENE 2: FRANK, a Police Sergeant

The Stevenson's bedroom. BARBARA, FRANK'*s wife, is in the bed.* FRANK *is sitting on it. He gets up and walks to the window.*

FRANK:

Dave. Deputy. Must've held his mouth right all those years... eh? Ahh, he deserves it... Some of the stuff he's come up with. It's an instinct. He always had it. Something more than nuts and bolts. Something you're born with. [*Pause.*] Huh, we used to talk about the first time we were offered money. Me? I ever tell you? My first month in Traffic. Night time. Me and this Sergeant had just pulled this bloke over for speeding. All over the road he was. We'd had to go after him, cut him off. That's when I reckon the Serg spotted who it was. 'Your charge, Constable,' he says, not budging, him who'd always been first in at the kill. So I walked up and opened the door of the car and this old bloke, full as a fowl, some tart sitting next to him... gets... nearly falls out. Thought I knew his face. Wouldn't give his name, his address. Then it happened, he takes out his wallet, peels off a couple of hundred and says. 'Give's a break, mate. I didn't hit anyone.' And here's the funny part. You wouldn't believe it but as he waves the money over his shoulder... up in the blackness... I saw it. It came directly into my vision. A shooting star.

Sounds like a yarn doesn't it, but I swear to God it happened. This thing... [*Gesturing.*] whoosh! Like a sign to a kid who'd hardly left school, never been further outside the place than my uncle's farm. This Marist kid, still with his cross 'round his neck, still full of hell and damnation, who'd served as altar boy half his life. So I charged the bugger. [*Pause.*] He was a pollie, wouldn't you know it, got off, walked down those court steps and laughed at me. Someone said the judge was a mate, someone else said the Commissioner was. Whatever... the result was the same. Well, I'm still a Sergeant, aren't I?

The Sum of Us

David Stevens   CURRENCY PRESS

Jeff is a pretty regular guy. A plumber in Sydney, he shares a house with his widowed father, Harry, who likes a few beers and is actively looking for a permanent mate. Jeff is gay and Harry accepts and encourages his son's lifestyle with an enthusiasm that borders on meddlesome. Tolerance rather than intolerance, is the focus in this film about gay people. The film is set in Harry and Jeff's house in Balmain, an inner-city suburb on Sydney Harbour, as well as the Botanical Gardens, pubs and clubs and various other locations around town.

SCENE 1: JEFF MITCHELL, Harry's son, a plumber

JEFF:

The first time Dad took me to Gran and Aunt Mary's for my holiday, I was maybe... I don't know—eight or nine. And I remember playing footy with Gran and my cousins in the front yard. You know those days, when everything's perfect? It was one of the greatest afternoons of my life... You see, Gran would form us all into one team and she'd be the other... It amazes me to think of the hours she'd spend playing with us and she never seemed tired... And later in the afternoons she'd play Ludo or Snakes n' Ladders or tiddly-winks. I used to love those games with Gran. She used to keep an old Monopoly set hidden under the stairs because Mary wouldn't let her play it... Real strict Salvation Army, Mary was... I mean Gran too, but you know, not as bad as Mary. But this one time, Mary went out... for a while and the minute she was out the door Gran got out the old Monopoly board, her eyes all glinting. 'Not a word to Mary', she said. It was the best game of Monopoly I've ever played. My Gran and me were doing something really naughty—really wrong. [*Laughing.*] Fire and brimstone stuff, you know... Well some people might think those days with Gran and Mary had a bad influence on me...

I was there once, some of my cousins were staying too. So I had to sleep in the spare bed in Gran's room, you know... I remember... I could see it so clearly: waking up that first morning, looking across to Gran's big old double bed... and there were Gran and Mary, tucked up in bed, wrapped up in each other's arms. Gran was snoring, I remember. I lay there looking at them for such a long time. Just looked natural, somehow, you know? Like the most natural thing I'd ever seen. Like love.

SCENE 47: JEFF

The living room. JEFF *and* HARRY *are putting up Christmas decorations.*

JEFF:

It's not that flamin' easy. Doesn't just happen to order. The choice is a bit more limited for one thing. Maybe some places like San Francisco, all the blokes wear their dicks on their sleeves, they reckon.

I don't want to live like that, Dad. I don't want to live in a world that just begins and ends with being gay. I like having all sorts of people around kids and old folks, every sort of person there is. I don't want to live in a world without women. I like women. Me and the girls in the office get on great. They know and they don't care. We laugh about it. Fancy the same blokes sometimes. Even fancied a couple of the girls. Done it with a few of them just to make sure I wasn't missing out on anything.

> [HARRY *suddenly pokes his head out from behind the Christmas trees.*]

See what I mean about getting your hopes up? I like doing it with blokes, Dad. I don't think that's ever going to change because I don't want it to. I don't want to be limited by other people's ideas of who I am. Yours or anyone else's.

You've been great, mate. Best Dad in the world, I reckon. Fairest, that's a certain fact. I don't often say it, but it's Christmas, so thanks mate, for everything. You give me the first class shits at times, and I suppose I do you, but I don't think there's many got a father like you.

SCENE 56: JEFF

Hospital ward. HARRY *is in bed.* JEFF *enters.*

JEFF:

Hi, mate. They said you'd be with us soon. What'd you go and do a silly, bloody thing like that for? You've had a bit of a stroke, Dad. Well, it was more'n a bit of one, actually. Did they tell you what it was going to be like? You'll be all right mate. I'll look after you, no sweat. Things'll be just the same as always, Dad, I promise.

Can I get you anything? Need to go for a wee or something? Silly eh? Suppose they look after that sort of thing here. But still, you never know.

> [JEFF *notices* HARRY*'s hand moving. He puts his hand on* HARRY*'s right hand.*]

Why do you keep moving your hand? Can you hear me?

> [*Pause.*]

Once for 'yes'.

> [*Pause.*]

Twice for 'no'.

> [*Two fingers of* HARRY*'s hand touch* JEFF*'s hand twice.* JEFF *leans down and cries on* HARRY*'s hand.*]

Oh, Dad.

SCENE 69: HARRY MITCHELL, Captain of a Sydney Harbour ferry

HARRY:

My mother was eighty, she was getting infirm and Mary was a bit younger, but neither of them could look after each other any more... and we all made the decision to split them up. My brother took Mum, and Mary went to a home. It was for their own good. How many times did we tell ourselves that?

We drove Mum away and she didn't say a word. She didn't speak for days, she just sat in her new bedroom with her suitcase full of memories. She died in her sleep one night, not long after that. And I never had the chance or the guts to ask her the one thing I wanted to know. I always wanted to know what they said to each other that last night, lying there in that great old brass bed, knowing it was for the last time, knowing that they were never going to see each other again, knowing they were being taken away to different places to die. I can't imagine... what they would have said. How do you say 'thank you' for forty years of love? What words could you possibly find? By then, they were both as deaf as posts, so did they lie there shouting their love and their goodbyes to each other...? Did they find comfort in the idea that they might meet again soon, in the next world?

So, I don't know what I would have said to Jeffrey if I'd known the stroke was going to happen. I know I would have said something. Only now I'll never know what it was.

State of Shock

Tony Strachan CURRENCY PRESS

For play description see page 169.

ACT 2 SCENE 1: LAWYER, in his 30s

Stuart Prison, Townsville. Day. The LAWYER *enters* EDDIE'*s cell. He holds up a bulging string bag.*

LAWYER:

Oranges.

[*He drops them on the floor.*]

They tell me you've given up salt, sugar and tobacco.

[*Pause.*]

The bad news is, the Government won't give us any funds for your case. In fact they're annoyed we want to do it. The good news is, we've decided to push ahead anyway. We've already sent one of our lawyers to talk to reserve councils. And the Aboriginal Legal Service has agreed to collect information on past cases going back twenty years. We've even persuaded two students here in Townsville to spend their spare time in the library researching for the case. And me? Thanks to you, I've flown out of here twice already with a briefcase bulging with information, eh mate? My boss is blown away by all the help you've been giving. Ecstatic he is.

[*Pause.*]

You've had your thinking time, Eddie. Now it's time to talk. Talk, Eddie.

[*Pause.*]

Fuck, eh?

[*Pause.*]

You're up on first degree, mate. They're out to get you, to put you in a box like this for life. Understand? But the Public Defender's Office is going to spend months working on your case to show everyone in this country the full story of reserve life, about Yambala and about the troubles and feelings inside you. We think that reserves are wrong for Aboriginal people and that you wouldn't have killed if your life had been better…

[*He waits for an answer.*]

Or maybe you would have anyway, eh? Maybe you're a mad fucking boong who can't think, can't talk and ought to spend the rest of his life in a cage…

[EDDIE: I killed my woman. I must die.]

LAWYER: You die and you'll help no one. If you live you can help your people.

[*Pause.*]

I've sent a letter to your grandmother. Maybe she'll know how to get through to you.

[EDDIE: She given up on me.]

[*The* LAWYER *prepares to leave.*]

LAWYER: Today you've spoken. I'm happy about that. Really happy.

[*He exits.*]

ACT 2 SCENE 2: BERNIE O'CONNOR, a public servant, mid 50s

The reserve at night. O'CONNOR *has invited* EDDIE'*s grandmother,* MRS JENNY BOB, *into the visitors' house.*

O'CONNOR:

You people have never been able to do your own business... and I don't think you ever will. I've been around this State long enough to know that.

You just can't cope with the whitefella's way. When I was a young bloke I visited a mission with my father, Dad, and you know what? Listen to this: all the blacks around this mission had been tamed, all except this blackfella called Potato. Potato lived in the bush and kept to himself; wouldn't come near the station. No one could catch him, not the missionaries, the police or the local government officers. And do you know why they couldn't, Jenny Bob? Do you know why? Because he kept himself covered from head to foot in his own shit. That's head to foot. No one'd touch the bastard. Fact... This Land Rights Committee, Jenny Bob, they're just like that fella Potato.

You better vote for me or I'll have the lot of you crawling for your crust. And if I hear you've been stirring up anti-National Party trouble here, I'll move your whole family off Yambala and I'll make sure they never go back. Never. Understand?

You're out of your depth in this game, old woman. You've been a thorn in my side for years with your non-stop nagging about our shortcomings, when you can't even keep your own house in order. Look at your family: a daughter who's a bludging hypochondriac, a useless son-in-law whose only skill is croc shooting and bending his elbow, and two alcoholic murderers for grandsons. Who have I left out? I'm sure they're just the tip of the iceberg.

Third World Blues

David Williamson
CURRENCY PRESS

Graham, a conscript just back from the Vietnam War, is awaiting a reunion with his wife, Keren, when her lover, Neville, appears instead. Their confrontation is interrupted by the arrival of Neville's pregnant wife, Elizabeth, and then by Keren herself.

ACT 2: GRAHAM, mid 20s

The action takes place in the living room of KEREN'*s inner Melbourne terrace house in 1972.*

GRAHAM:

[*to* KEREN] First thing after you wake up at dawn you clean your weapons. And I didn't. Not thoroughly enough. We hit a clearing. Too big to skirt. Johnny was out there in front and I was covering him. Which was a big honour for me because it meant I was finally accepted. Covering means just that. He advances and you stay put behind cover scanning everything ahead of him down the barrel of your M16. Suddenly I saw movement. A weapon's swinging around to cut Johnny down. I squeezed the trigger and nothing happened. M16's jammed. The weapon turns out to be a machine gun and Johnny hits the ground screaming for covering fire. I tried to get the M16 firing again, but my hands are shaking and I drop the bolt I'm trying to clean. Then their rockets start exploding in the trees around us and Johnny's still screaming for cover but by this time I'm in a total red haze. I'm gone. Johnny gets up and runs for cover but a rocket slams into his back and his arm comes cartwheeling towards me.

We've run into a crack North Vietnamese battalion and there's only thirty of us. The machine gun starts on me and a second machine gun has opened up to the left and is pinning the rest of blokes at the edge of the clearing. And they've all seen me let Johnny get killed. I'm totally paralysed with terror and shame. The tree I'm behind is disintegrating and basically I'm dead. And after what I've done none of our blokes are going to lift a finger to save me.

My worst dreams aren't about Johnny, they're about this part. Dread and cold fear. There's nothing quite like the horror of being certain you're about to die and knowing there's absolutely nothing you can do about it. Dread and cold fear. Then just as the ammunition was about to run out—and that's when you're *really* dead—a mob of Yank cowboys arrive in helicopters and start shooting the shit out of Charlie—and we're not dead. Or some of us aren't.

I get the M16 fumbling dream two or three times a week, but I cop the 'about to die' number three or four times a night. Every night. And as if that wasn't enough, even when I'm wide awake I keep seeing those jug ears of Johnny coming back towards me, and I feel that I had one crucial test in life and I failed.